Presented by

THE STAR
INDIANAPOLIS
THE NEWS

LARRY BIRD
An Indiana Legend

SPORTS PUBLISHING INC.
Champaign, IL 61820
www.SportsPublishingInc.com

Acknowledgments

There are literally hundreds of people at the *Indianapolis Star* and *Indianapolis News* whose hard work and dedication have made this book possible. The efforts of the many reporters, columnists, editors, executives, and photographers were all essential in bringing the extraordinary career of Larry Bird to the pages of the newspaper. A few of those who were instrumental in assisting us in this project were Frank Caperton, Lyle Mannweiler, Charlie Nye, Nancy Winkley and Sandra Fitzgerald. From the *Star/News* sports pages, we specifically want to acknowledge the contributions of Mark Montieth, Conrad Brunner, Bill Benner, Robin Miller, Phil Richards, Paul Sancya, Mike Fender, Rich Miller, and Kelly Wilkinson.

Space limitations preclude us from thanking all the other writers and photographers whose work appears in this book. However, wherever available, we have preserved the writers' bylines and the photographers' credits to ensure proper attribution for their work.

SPORTS PUBLISHING INC.

©1999, Indianapolis Newspapers, Inc. All rights reserved.

Coordinating Editor: Lyle J. Mannweiler
Photo Editor: Charlie Nye
Developmental Editors: Joseph J. Bannon, Jr. and
Joanna L. Wright
Director of Production: Susan M. McKinney
Interior Design and Layout: Susan M. McKinney and
Michelle R. Dressen
Dustjacket Design: Julie L. Denzer

Unless otherwise indicated, all photos are from the archives of the Indianapolis Star and Indianapolis News. Individual photographer credits are indicated for each Star/News photograph. In the event that proper credit has not been given, necessary changes will appear in future editions.

ISBN 1-58261-008-8
Library of Congress Catalog Card Number: 98-89116

Printed in the United States.

Sports Publishing Inc.
www.SportsPublishingInc.com

CONTENTS

THE ESSENCE OF A LEGEND

BY PHIL RICHARDS

As a youth in French Lick, Larry Bird had neither gas money nor need of it. His family had no car. His father, Joe Bird, seldom made more than $120 a week working in a shoe factory in Paoli, or at Kimball Piano and Organ Co. in French Lick, or at construction sites all over the area. His mother, Georgia, worked two jobs, mostly as a waitress, and made even less. The Birds were one of the poorer families in Orange County, the state's poorest.

Bob Heaton, a Terre Haute insurance agent who played basketball with Bird at Indiana State University, recalls a card game at the house on South 11th Street they shared during Bird's senior year. They played nickel-dime poker and blackjack. Bird got $2 down. He stood and excused himself. He had no more money to lose.

Jill Leone recalls an irresistible endorsement opportunity she arranged for Bird early in his 13-year National Basketball Association career with the Boston Celtics. The deal called for a television commercial that would require about a four-hour shoot at Boston Garden. The day was open; the Celtics didn't have a game until the next evening. The remuneration would be $350,000.

"I was very excited. I called Larry to tell him," said Leone, an agent who has handled Bird's endorsements for more than 20 years. "He said no. I almost fell off my chair. I asked him why and I remember very clearly what he said: 'If I miss my afternoon nap, I won't be rested enough to play my best for the fans.'

"Money never has been his motivating factor. Excellence is his motivating factor."

Bird is back in the NBA, as the rookie head coach of the Indiana Pacers, with an open-ended contract that will pay him about $4 million this year. That is approximately $1 million more than the Miami Heat pay Pat Riley, their president and head coach and the man Bird considers the best in the business. Of course Bird has declined to do the traditional coach's radio and television shows, a choice Leone said will cost him "six figures." This is a man whose priorities are as clear as they are inflexible.

"Money means nothing," said Bird, 40. "I didn't get back into this for money. I want to spend as much time as I can concentrating on my duties as coach."

Bird is back in the NBA because he couldn't not be. Playing is competing, and coaching, he said, is the next best thing to playing. When Pacers president Donnie Walsh asked Bird to be his coach last April, he made an offer Bird couldn't refuse. Summers in French Lick and winters in Naples, Florida were good. There was golf and leisure and a little corporate work. But it was boring. He craved competition.

In fact, sometimes competing has not been enough. Sometimes Bird has had to do more. K.C. Jones coached the Celtics from 1983 to 1988, a span that brought them two championships. He recalls many such instances. He recounted one.

Boston was at Seattle. The score was tied and there were only a few seconds to play when the Celtics took a timeout and decided, of course, to go with their first and best option. At the conclusion of the timeout, Bird strolled onto the floor. He sidled up to SuperSonics forward Xavier McDaniel, who was guarding him.

"He says, 'X, I'm getting the ball and I'm going to take two dribbles over here, then step back and stick it,'" recalled Jones.

The ball went to Bird. He took two dribbles. He stepped back. He shot. With the ball still in the air and his hand still extended in follow-through, he turned and trotted off the court. When the ball went through the basket, he wasn't even watching.

Bird challenged McDaniel and the SuperSonics, sure. Even more, he challenged himself.

"I remember he came into my office one time—this is the first day of training camp—and said, 'I'm not going to have a beer until after the season is over,'" said Mr. Celtic, Red Auerbach, Boston's longtime coach, president and patriarch. "Now it's not that Larry was a big beer drinker, but it was just something to give himself a challenge. He didn't have a beer the whole season. He looks for challenges."

The Pacers qualify as such. After eight consecutive visits to the playoffs, they tumbled to 39-43 last season, when their injuries were innumerable and insurmountable and, said team captain Reggie Miller, their commitment wavered. Bird knows. He not only watched them, he studied them.

It was an intermediary who made the phone call last March, an agent but not Bird's agent, who asked Walsh if he might be interested in Bird as his next coach. Walsh knew that his current coach, Larry Brown, was leaving. He wasn't certain he was interested in Bird, but he was intrigued. The parties met in the Simon & Associates offices during the NCAA Final Four in Indianapolis.

"I walked in interested but just in a casual, guarded way," Walsh said. "I walked out thinking this is the only guy I would want to coach this team."

Throughout a session that lasted nearly three hours, Bird spoke with the feel of a player and the authority and perspective of a coach. He told Walsh how Pacers personnel could best be used, how they could run and improve. He told him how they could get center Rik Smits a shot on any possession, a maneuver the team not only wasn't using but one it hadn't considered.

He told him that if the Pacers had beaten New York in the sixth game of the 1994 Eastern Conference finals at Market Square Arena, they would have won the title. The matchups in the championship series with Houston, he said, would have been so favorable they would have dictated the outcome. Instead, Indiana lost Game 6, went back to New York and lost Game 7.

"New York was just tougher. Mentally. Physically. That's why they won," said Bird, who recalled how the Celtics bullied the Los Angeles Lakers to win the championship in 1984, then got knocked around by the same team in the Finals in 1985.

"We played (the Lakers) in '84 and we were physical with them. We wanted to get them irritated. We came back and we thought we were going to do the same thing and they were tougher than we were. A coach does that stuff. You stay on 'em. You never let them take shortcuts and you stay right on 'em."

Who better to stay on 'em than Bird, thought Walsh. Who was tougher? Who was smarter, harder working, more disciplined, more competitive or better prepared? Who better to instill and develop these characteristics in a team?

Dave Gavitt is president of the NCAA Foundation and chairman of the board of trustees of the Basketball Hall of Fame. He served as Celtics chief executive officer from 1990 through 1994.

He recalls walking into the Boston locker room before a game one evening accompanied by *Boston Globe* sports columnist Bob Ryan. As is common in NBA locker rooms during the pregame period, a videotape of the Celtics' last encounter with the evening's opponent was playing.

"Larry's the only one really watching this," Ryan said.

"And I'll guarantee you something else," responded Gavitt, "he's the only one not watching himself."

Bird always made certain he was prepared. When he broke

his ankle during his sophomore year at Springs Valley High School, he shot free throws while leaning on crutches. No wonder he led the NBA in free throw percentage four times. No wonder he won the league's 3-point shooting contest each of its first three years.

When the Celtics lost to the Lakers in the 1985 Finals, Bird dedicated the offseason to improving the proficiency of his left hand. It didn't matter that he had won the second of three consecutive NBA Most Valuable Player awards that season.

Georgia Bird, who died last year, was a woman of dedication and conviction. So was Bird's grandmother, Lizzie Kerns. Bird was instilled with the same qualities by the women who reared him.

He scored 21,791 points, collected 8,974 rebounds and 5,695 assists and set a Celtics' record with 1,556 steals before retiring because of back problems after the 1991-92 season. He was a 12-time All-Star who won three championship rings, but he remained a Hoosier. Every offseason, he went home to French Lick, there to further refine his game.

Rick Carlisle, a Celtic teammate and now one of Bird's assistant coaches, visited several times. Every morning they were up at 5:30, on bicycles by 5:45.

Quinn Buckner, who became one of Bird's best friends while playing for the Celtics from 1982 through 1985, was another summertime guest. He recalls Bird shooting for hours and refusing to quit until he made 10 consecutive free throws without touching the rim.

None of it surprised Buckner. The morning after the Celtics beat the Lakers to win the 1984 championship, Buckner phoned Bird. He was out running, explained Bird's wife, Dinah.

"I asked him about it," said Buckner, who will serve as television analyst on about 30 Pacers games this season. "He said, 'If you're going to win another one, you've got to start getting ready now.'"

Morning after morning last summer, Walsh arrived at work to find Bird already there. Larry Brown didn't even have an office in the Pacers' East Market Street complex.

You want tough? Bird endured a shattered knuckle on his right index finger, dislocated and tore all the ligaments in his right pinkie finger, popped both Achilles' tendons on the same move, took cortisone injections in his right elbow, broke his nose, suffered a fractured cheekbone, had operations to remove bone spurs from both heels and twice had back surgery. He just played on.

Joe Bird taught his son to be tough and when Joe took his own life with a shotgun in 1975, Larry was. He didn't cry.

One after another, Bird's friends will tell you that one of his strongest assets is his ability to read and handle people. He is at once tough and sensitive, demanding and understanding, passionate and compassionate. Throughout his career, he has been friend and champion of the 12th man, players like Eric Fernsten and Greg Kite with the Celtics.

Bird has been "a breath of fresh air" in the Pacers' office, said one team employee. He already knows many by name and he greets people with a warm word or a needle.

"That's how it was with the Celtics," Gavitt said. "People from the security guard at the back door to the guy who mopped the floor between periods, 'Spider.' They all loved Larry because he always had time for them. He knew all their names, lots of little people who were volunteer workers at the games. He would be at funerals and christenings."

Buckner has a theory on all that. It goes back to 1974, when Bird was a member of the Indiana team for the Indiana-Kentucky All-Star series, the first time he achieved widespread recognition. Bird was assigned to the second team, which contributed to Indiana's victory at Louisville and played well in the first half as the two-game sweep was completed in Indianapolis. But in the second half of that game, Indiana coach Kirby Overman forgot about Bird until the final minutes. When he tried to send Bird into the game, he refused. He felt he had worked as hard as anyone. He felt wronged.

"I sincerely believe that had a prolonged effect on him," Buckner said. "He got overlooked. He knows what that feels like and he has a soft spot in his heart for people everybody else takes for granted."

Bird has been effusive in his praise of Pacers captain Reggie Miller, whose unwavering practice effort has set the tone throughout training camp. He will measure his team members in the same manner he measured his teammates, on the basis of effort, not talent. He doesn't expect anyone to play like he did. He expects everyone to work like he did.

"If they don't want to compete in this league, they shouldn't be in it," said Bird. "This is a competitive league, every night. I never liked to go home and say, 'Magic Johnson played better than me. He beat us tonight.'

"Some of these guys, if you don't watch them they'll take little shortcuts every day at the same time, especially when you push them a little bit. It irritates me, but I haven't said anything about it. I'll just run them harder."

Former Utah coach Frank Layden recalls a Jazz visit to Boston Garden. At one point, Bird set up in the corner, just off the end of the Utah bench. Layden came up behind him. "You know what?" he prodded Bird. "I'm going to pull down your shorts and embarrass you in front of the whole place."

The ball went to Bird in the corner. He looked over his shoulder at Layden and sneered, "Oh yeah? Take this." Bird's 3-pointer hit nothing but net.

When you daily make 10 consecutive free throws without hitting the rim, you know you're not going to miss with the game on the line. When you shoot 3-pointers hour after hour

under French Lick's midsummer sun, you know they are going in when it matters. That's why, just prior to the NBA's 3-point contest, you ask the other contestants if they've figured out who's going to finish second.

Call it constructive arrogance. Miller sees it. And he loves it.

"He and his coaching staff, they exude arrogance," Miller said. "You look at the Bulls and the teams that have been successful over the last six or seven years. You've got to have that arrogance, that sense of confidence. He has that. That's just how his personality was when he was on the floor. He knew he was going to win. I think that's starting to parlay on this team."

Bird is keenly aware of the failed superstar syndrome. Magic Johnson may have been one of the half dozen best players in NBA history, but he went 5-11 as a coach in 1994 before quitting in disgust. Wilt Chamberlain went 37-47, Bob Cousy went 141-209, Dave DeBusschere 79-143. Wes Unseld was 202-345.

Bird says things like "vee-hicle" and "them guys" and "he's ran hard" and "if I had my rathers." Gavitt calls that kind of delivery "camouflage," but there's no disguising Bird's keen intellect. He has an ability to grasp nuances, to discern and set aside peripheral issues and go directly to the heart of a matter.

He selected Carlisle and Dick Harter as assistant coaches and he leans heavily upon them. Harter, who has served under Chuck Daly, Jack Ramsay and Pat Riley, is a defensive genius. Carlisle's areas of expertise are player development and opponent preparation.

Bird lets them coach. He is learning every day, but his technical knowledge and his substitution patterns and when he calls timeouts always will remain secondary in importance to his ability to read and motivate people.

Said Harter: "What you've done in practice and how hard your players have prepared and what their mindset is affects the outcome of games much more than those kinds of decisions."

That mindset seems good. Miller said this training camp was the toughest and the most enjoyable, the most demanding and the most rewarding of his 10 as a professional. Small forward Chris Mullin, a 12-year veteran, echoed him. When Bird demands two hours of headlong hard work, he isn't bashful about practicing four hours to get it.

"He has the ability to work them really hard, then say something that makes everybody smile," Carlisle said.

Just about everyone who knows Bird expects him to succeed as a coach, but history is the only infallible judge. No one knows for certain, not even Walsh.

"He is honest and he is smart and when he tells you something he doesn't change his mind two days later. The players are going to relate to him because of that," Walsh said.

"There's risk, yeah, there's risk. I'd rather bet on Larry with no experience than three quarters of the guys in this league with experience." ■

MEET THE ALL-STARS

BIRD "GROWS" INTO STARDOM

June 17, 1974

BY BILL BENNER

Four inches measured up to a mile of difference in the basketball career of Springs Valley's Larry Bird.

Just a "good" 6-3 ballplayer after his junior year, Bird came back after the summer as an "excellent" 6-7 athlete, and the additional size enabled the quiet youngster to land a scholarship at Indiana and a berth on the Indiana All-Star team.

The latter came as somewhat of a surprise since Larry had been passed over on most all-state selection committees. But he quickly proved his value against the Russian Nationals in April when he had an outstanding game.

Now 6-7 and weighing close to 190 pounds, Bird averaged 30.6 points and 20.6 rebounds for the Valley this past season and took with him nearly every school record, many of which were held by his older brother Mark. He has single-game highs of 55 points and 38 rebounds.

An excellent ballhandler for his size, Larry says he learned most of that skill when he was shorter, then retained it as he grew.

He's also a tremendously strong rebounder and one of the hardest workers in Coach Kirby Overman's All-Star camp.

Larry expects to have a strong contingent of Springs Valley support behind him when Indiana hosts Kentucky at Hinkle Fieldhouse on June 29.

"My uncle sold 300 tickets to the game himself," Larry says. "And that was after a lot of people had already bought their tickets."

Bird plans to major in business at I.U., which he picked from over 250 colleges seeking his services.

"He's got the mark of a great athlete," says his coach at Springs Valley, Gary Holland. "The whole team was molded around him. Every kid in the school looked up to him...they all wanted to be like Larry Bird."

BIRD'S THE GUY AT "VALLEY HIGH"

March 8, 1979

BY BILL PITTMAN

Springs Valley senior Larry Bird poses as a member of the 1974 Indiana High School All-Star Basketball Team.

The Springs Valley Blackhawks meet Princeton in the regionals of the state high school basketball tourney this weekend, but they are not getting the usual big attention because the name on almost everyone's mind is Larry Bird.

In Springs Valley, which encompasses French Lick and West Baden, the 6-foot-9 All-American center for Indiana State University is Superman, Mr. Wonderful and Captain Ice all rolled into one. Posters and billboards proclaim his feats and a street was named for him during last week's celebration of Larry Bird Week.

Larry Bird Boulevard signs have been erected along the street that runs past Bird's alma mater, Springs Valley High School.

It is enough to turn a young man's head.

His friends don't think it will. They remember him as a nice, polite, fairly shy, dedicated young man with a good head on his shoulders. No one seems to begrudge him his fame, or his possible fortune.

"I expect Larry appreciates all the fuss, but I don't think he cares as long as he can play basketball," Jeff Mills said.

Mills, who owns the Shell filling station in West Baden, has known Bird a long time. He used to hang around the station a lot with Mills' brother Kevin, and his buddy Jay "Beezer" Carnes. Kevin also is at ISU, and Carnes works in the valley.

"They were just normal kids who hung around together and played basketball," Mills said.

Talk about basketball and girls?

"They talked about basketball. I don't think girls

figured into Larry's life," Mills said.

Georgia Bird, the mother of six children—Mike, Mark, Linda, Larry, Jeff and Eddie—was widowed a few years ago, and as she said, she has to make a living. She works at the Medco Center, a nursing home, on the east edge of French Lick.

Since Larry's college basketball exploits brought him under the national eye, she has been harassed by news people from near and far.

Indiana State is 29-0 for the 1978-79 season and ranked first in the nation. This Sunday the Sycamores enter the Midwest Regionals of the NCAA tournament.

"As soon as we win the NCAA, I'll let everybody take my picture," she said, declining such an opportunity for the moment.

She did talk about her famous son over the telephone.

"I think he can handle all this well now," she said of the spotlight on Bird. "He can adjust to anything."

Mrs. Bird said her son doesn't discuss his future with her.

"People call me and want to do this and that, but it is not my decision to make. He is very smart and he will be all right," she said.

"He listened to other people and went to I.U. when I didn't want him to. But he didn't want to go to school at all. It took a lot of pressure. You better believe that the boys pressured him and I pressured him. I told him to go anywhere but to go to school.

"He wanted to go to the University of Kentucky. I really wanted him to go to ISU all the time.

"Now he wants to teach basketball in the seventh and eighth grades. He will make a tough coach. He has always been a perfectionist, except in school, but now a B-plus average isn't good enough for him.

"He has been a great influence on the younger boys and Jeff has started to bear down in school because of him," she said.

At Springs Valley High School, Coach Gary Holland is preparing for the regional tourney. But he seems happy to take time to talk about Bird.

Holland coached Larry in his senior year, the year he scored 30.6 points a game with a high of 55 and had 516 rebounds. Holland minimizes his role in getting Bird to ISU.

"People say his grades were poor, but he had a C average. He had no trouble getting in as a predictor.

A picture of Springs Valley High School's most famous athlete, Larry Bird, hangs in the school hallway. (Mike Fender)

But he had no desire to go to school. Education means a lot to his mother, though," Holland said.

"He was a perfectionist in basketball. I have a picture somewhere of him twirling a basketball on the forefinger of each hand. Nobody else around here could do that," Holland said.

"He really matured in his senior year and took on a lot of responsibility. He began to get his name in the paper a lot, and he'd come to me and ask, 'Why can't we get Beezer's name in the paper some, too?'

"I never saw a kid who played basketball so much. He didn't have a car or much money, so he spent his time at basketball. He was so good it could have hurt us. The other kids would pass the ball to him and then stand and watch," he said.

"Kentucky looked at him and they were nice to us. He thought that was where he wanted to go, and he enjoyed his visit there. They called and said they decided

(Indianapolis Star/News Photo)

Larry should look elsewhere.

"He was very disappointed and then he didn't know what to do. He had been 17 in December of his senior year, so you see he was really quite young. He decided

HOMECOMING FOR BIRD

April 6, 1979

IT WILL BE HOME SWEET HOME April 29 for All-American Larry Bird, Indiana State University basketball star.

A big homecoming celebration is planned for the basketball wizard.

Jerry Denbo, an English teacher and a coach at Bird's alma mater, Springs Valley High School, is chairman of the homecoming celebration. Tickets to the 7 p.m. banquet at the French Lick Sheraton Hotel are priced at $20 each and are available through the Springs Valley National Bank in West Baden.

Denbo said the banquet guest list also includes Gov. Otis Bowen and Sens. Birch Bayh, D-Indiana and Richard Lugar, R-Indiana.

There will be a reception for Bird following the prime rib dinner, giving guests an opportunity to meet the ISU star who led the Sycamores to the final game of the NCAA championship.

Meantime, the French Lick Town Board is having more Larry Bird Boulevard signs made to replace those taken by souvenir hunters.

The signs began disappearing shortly after they were erected on what was formerly Monon Street, which runs in front of the Springs Valley High School gymnasium. Town officials said the new signs will be welded to the poles to fool future sign-fanciers.

Although her son's name has become a household word in Indiana, Georgia Bird's lifestyle has changed little and she doesn't expect it to. She doubts fame and fortune will cause much change in her son, either.

on I.U. but it was so big and the atmosphere was so different he became homesick and missed his family. So, he came home," Holland said.

"With so many brothers and a sister, Larry grew up unselfish but pretty independent. He would share anything with anybody, you can tell by the way he plays how he was brought up. He can take an average player and make him look like a star," Holland said.

Coach Holland said the younger Birds also play basketball and are trying to emulate their older brother, and you can see the pride shine in their eyes at the mention of Larry's name. Jeff, 15, is a freshman at Springs Valley, and while he appreciates his older brother's accomplishments and is proud of him, he is also trying to be his own person. Young Eddie, however, has copied the Big Bird's moves.

Downtown, the shop windows are shared somewhat unequally by Bird and the Blackhawks. At the Alco Dime Store is a huge display of Bird memorabilia, gathered over about 9 years, by Patsy Nelson. Randy Baker, manager of the store, tells the story of how her car caught fire and she saved her Bird collection but let money burn up in the glove compartment.

Another Bird booster is Jim Ballard, publisher of the *Springs Valley Herald*. Ballard said, pragmatically, that while the national exposure in newspapers, magazines and television may not help business in the valley all that much, it sure can't hurt.

"We are all pleased because we are proud of Larry. He is a mighty fine young man. Some people have made a

lot out of his working on the city trash truck the summer before he went to ISU. I don't think he cares a whole lot about that kind of publicity, but it shows he's not too good to do the work.

"The only thing is, some signs have been stolen off Larry Bird Boulevard for souvenirs. I guess we'll have to paint his name on the sidewalks," Ballard said.

They may just wind up putting his name on the gymnasium of the new $5.5 million elementary school. Why not? ■

Bird shined in an Indiana High School All-Star game against Kentucky. (Jerry Clark)

ALL-STAR ANGUISH STILL VIVID FOR BIRD

Pacers coach has viewed such exhibitions with disdain ever since he felt slighted in 1974 contest.

February 8, 1998

BY MARK MONTIETH

Larry Bird's feelings on all-star games are clear, and his emotions run deep. He didn't care for them as a player and he has even less interest in coaching one, as he'll grudgingly do in today's NBA All-Star game at Madison Square Garden.

Bird has his reasons. He sees them as meaningless, show-off exhibitions that don't fan the fires of a competitor. He believes their freelance nature puts them in the hands of the point guards and makes them exercises in futility for forwards and centers. All the hype that surrounds them runs counter to his private nature. And, perhaps most of all, they present too much opportunity for hurt feelings.

Bird has felt that way since Saturday evening, June 29, 1974, when the Indiana High School All-Stars met Kentucky in the second game of the annual two-game series. Bird, a relatively unknown player from Springs Valley High School, was left on the bench for most of the second half of a 110-95 Indiana victory and then refused coach Kirby Overman's offer to go into the game for the final few meaningless minutes.

The incident has been distorted by countless tellings and re-tellings. Today, even the principal characters relate slightly different versions of what happened that night at the former Butler Fieldhouse, now Hinkle. But there's no question it had a lasting impact on Bird.

"Being from a small town, if you make the team, that's supposed to be good enough," the Indiana Pacers' rookie coach recalled. "But if you feel you can play, and you get out there and practice with them and you know you're one of the better players on the team and you don't get to play, it hurts. That set the tone for all the all-star games I played in."

Overman, the "villain" of the story as it is commonly told, was 34 years old at the time of the all-star series and had just finished his coaching career at New Albany High School, where his team won the state championship in 1973. He's coached at three colleges and four high schools since then, including his current job in Sebring, Florida, but the story has followed him wherever he's gone.

He's the coach who left Larry Bird on the bench.

"Nobody knew how good he was going to be," said Overman, whose name was spelled "Olberman" in Bird's biography, *Drive.* "I wouldn't do it any different today knowing he's all-world and everything else. He wouldn't either if he was in my situation.

"Three or four people have written books about Larry, and the stories have gone from the sublime to the ridiculous. Some of the stories that are told are out-and-out lies. There are times I've been angry about it, because I want the truth to be known."

Bird was viewed as a standout small-town player coming out of Springs Valley, but nobody was predicting the legendary career that would follow. He was only third-team All-State and was a somewhat surprising selection to the All-Star team. Steve Collier and Roy Taylor were co-Mr. Basketballs that year, and other players such as Walter Jordan, Wayne Walls and Jim Krivacs were better known. Bird's best claim to credibility was the scholarship he accepted to attend Indiana University.

Around his hometown of French Lick, he was a source of tremendous pride, and many in the town were eager to express their loyalty to him.

Bird's High School Statistics

	G	FG-FGA	FT-FTA	PTS	AVG	R	A
Soph	2	3-4	2-3	8	4.0	8	5
Junior	22	137-279	79-105	353	16.0	217	136
Senior	25	305-606	154-205	764	30.6	516	107
Totals	49	445-889	235-313	1125	22.9	741	248

"My uncle sold 300 tickets himself," Bird told a reporter several days before the All-Star game at Hinkle. "And that was after a lot of people had already bought their tickets."

Bird played as well as anyone throughout the practices and games leading up to the team's final showing. It had first gathered in April to play a touring Russian team at Hinkle and won 92-60. Bird came off the bench to score 12 points, hitting 6 of 8 shots, and grab nine rebounds.

The squad gathered again in June. It defeated Circle Leasing, a standout AAU team made up of former Indiana collegiate players, 110-104 in an exhibition tune-up. Bird scored 22 points off the bench, hitting 9 of 15 shots, and grabbed nine rebounds. Bird started and played well again in another exhibition game in French Lick. Then, in the first game against the Kentucky All-Stars, he came off the bench to score 12 points and grab seven rebounds in a 92-81 victory.

Bird already was frustrated heading into the final game at Hinkle because he thought he had played well enough to earn a starting position. The frustration mounted during the game.

He came off the bench late in the first half and scored six quick points to spark a comeback that resulted in a 47-42 halftime lead. He started the second half and helped get the team off to a good start but was pulled from the game after a few minutes as Overman tried to distribute playing time. Bird seethed as Indiana's lead continued to grow and the clock ticked down.

Most versions of the story claim Overman simply forgot about Bird.

Don Bates, the All-Star game's director, recalls reminding Overman late in the game that Bird hadn't played in a while, and says Overman cursed, jumped up and asked Bird to report.

"I think Kirby just spaced out in the heat of battle," Bates said.

Overman, however, said he asked Bird to go into the game on two separate occasions after pulling him early in the second half but was turned down both times.

Regardless, Bird was crushed.

In a story headlined "Sweep Not Without Gripes," the *Indianapolis News* reported that Bird wiped tears from his eyes in the locker room and was inconsolable.

"I don't like the coach," he said when asked what was wrong.

"I don't blame Larry," Overman was quoted as saying in the story. "It's this way in an all-star game. When you've got a lot of talent, you try playing as many as you can."

There would be other all-star slights for Bird. After his college career at Indiana State, he and Magic Johnson were teammates on a team led by Kentucky coach Joe B. Hall. Hall played his Kentucky players most of the game and left Bird, Johnson and another future NBA star, Sidney Moncrief, on the bench much of the game.

"We had a better team on the bench than what was on the floor," Bird recalled. "I felt I was wasting my time. I've just always had a bad feel for all-star games."

Today, Bird will find himself on the other side of the all-star dilemma, parceling out minutes for the 12 members of the Eastern Conference team in a game that will be televised in 190 countries and reported by 1,817 journalists. You can be certain he'll do his best to be an equal opportunity employer.

"I intend to play everyone the same amount of minutes," he said.

Meanwhile, in Sebring, Florida, Overman will be watching with a sense of irony—and a sense that, perhaps, he provided an unwitting assist to Bird's career. ■

2

1976-1979

ON THE MAP

6-7 Larry Bird Leaves Indiana

9/17/74—Larry Bird, a freshman basketball recruit at Indiana University, has left the campus and apparently will not be returning.

Coach Bob Knight reported that an uncle of Bird's said the 6-7 forward from Springs Valley thought the university was too big and the class work will be more than he wanted to do.

*9/20/74—**Larry Bird, the 6-foot-7 Indiana All-Star** forward who accepted a basketball scholarship to Indiana University and then withdrew, has enrolled at two-year Northwood in his home area.*

Jim McElhiney, academic dean of the 200-student school, says Bird will be eligible to play basketball for coach Larry Bledsoe this winter.

"That was the one thing we both were interested in and we did a great deal of checking before he made his decision and the college allowed him to enroll," McElhiney said. "There is no question about his eligibility."

Bird was a high school star at nearby Springs Valley. ■

Indiana University basketball coach Bobby Knight ponders what could have been if Bird had remained on campus. (Indianapolis Star/News Photo)

BIRD FLYING HIGH AT INDIANA STATE

Sycamores stand tall at 6-1

December 15, 1976

BY MAX STULTZ

Considering that a college basketball floor stretches only 94 feet end to end, it doesn't take a pair of binoculars to see that Indiana University's loss is Indiana State's gain.

And the one who got away from the Hoosiers is a big 'un—6-9$\frac{1}{2}$ and 215 pounds worth of Larry Bird, a former prep All-Star by way of Springs Valley.

The lanky blond, who first tried I.U., then Northwood Institute briefly before settling in at Terre Haute, isn't the only reason the Sycamores are galloping at a 6-1 pace. But he's made the second half of Bob King's dual role of athletic director-cage mentor more of a pleasure than a chore.

People who can score 20 points standing on their heads have a way of doing that. And while Bird hasn't yet tried a shot from 10 feet below the ring, neither has he been limited to as few as 20 markers.

St. Ambrose College out of Davenport (Iowa) came closest, employing a box zone with chaser to hold him to a season low of 22. Still, Bird fell short of his average with a 25-point output in last Saturday's 80-69 triumph over Ball State at Muncie.

The average stands at 27.7 with a high of 33 against Robert Morris in the first round of the Hulman Classic. Bird also fired 31 in the Sycamores' Chicago State opener and popped 32 in last Thursday's 94-69 romp over Augustana, South Dakota.

He was good for 24 in the Classic championship conquest of Denver, and punctured Purdue's defenses for 27 while the Boilermakers were posting an 82-68 victory.

Nobody ever will accuse the young man of being afraid to fire. But an average of 21 shots for 34 minutes playing time per game doesn't border on trigger happiness—not when anything from 25 feet is within range and more than half the shots are connecting.

With State marking time until Central Michigan appears in Hulman Center Saturday, he is hitting .533 on 80 of 150—

a satisfying figure to all but the player who has his sights set in the 60-65 percent range.

Equally efficient from the stripe, Bird is a .790 converter with 34 hits in 43 tosses.

He also does a few other things well, such as rebounding—a 14.5 average—and delivering assists, 43, which is only seven less than the combined total of guards Danny King (27) and Jim Smith (23).

If Bird has a fault, it probably is reflected in the "turnovers" column where his 39 errors also represent a team high. On the other hand, only people who do nothing avoid making mistakes. Against Purdue and Ball State, most involved "traveling" while starting a drive for the hoop.

Bird, whose 20th birthday occurred on the night I-State lost at Purdue, would be a valuable asset even with average scoring ability, according to Coach King who declares his real strength "is rebounding and passing....he has great hands and a good sense of where the ball is going."

Prior to the season's start, King already was on record with the declaration: "At this stage of his development, Larry is as fine a player as I have ever coached ...I think he's going to be super."

King, head man at the University of New Mexico 10 years before switching allegiance to Indiana State, was placing Bird in the same class with Mel Daniels, Ira Harge and Willie Long—familiar names in these parts.

Indiana State doesn't get into serious Missouri Valley Conference competition until next season, and won't meet the first of three league foes this year until hosting West Texas State Monday night.

But Bird already has impressed a few folks outside Vigo County—the MVC named him "Player of the Week" for the first one in December.

BIRD TO PROS?

No answers yet

March 26, 1977

BY JIMMIE ANGELOPOLOUS

Twenty-year old Larry Bird is one of college basketball's hottest pro basketball prospects. But will Indiana State's richly-endowed sophomore turn pro next season? You won't find complete answers today—only partial ones. Next season? That's something else.

But you can find this quiet, 6-foot-9, 210-pound kid with the quick-silver touch and the golden future in pro basketball. Talk with him? That's something else.

Larry was home the night after ISU dropped an 83-82 NIT first round thriller at Houston March 9. "Is it possible to talk with Larry?" came the query over the phone. It was possible.

"Larry's tired now," said his mother, Georgia. "We brought him back with us from Terre Haute. We just got back. Their plane was delayed."

Larry rested amid family and friends in serene little French Lick that nestles in scenic Southern Indiana away from the limelight of high-powered collegiate basketball. And the glare of publicity spotlighting his talents as the nation's No. 3 collegiate scorer with a 32-point average.

There's poignancy in Bird's life. But Larry's mother is pleasant and forthright. She may hold the key to Larry's future.

Ask if Larry will go pro, his mother responds, "I hope not. Money isn't everything. We've not had any real problems. He has two more years to go. I'd like for him to stay. That's what I hope. He's real satisfied with school."

Says Spring Valley coach Gary Holland: "I talked with Larry after our sectional game here and he said, 'I've got two more years of school and I want to continue.' But he sorta cut me off quickly and didn't say anything more about it. I hear some pro scouts really like him."

Larry could go the hardship route. If he does, he'd be almost open game for NBA teams. If he stays in school another year, this might give the Indiana Pacers an excellent chance at a first-round draft choice which they gave up this year.

Mrs. Bird hasn't had things easy. Pleasantly, she relates: "I only missed two (ISU) home games this year. I was hoping to go to New York. I've never been to New York. I haven't been any place.

"For three years, I've worked about 16 hours a day. I'm a short order cook in 'Slick's' Restaurant. I've had some arthritis in my back. But I don't have any trouble.

"When Larry was born he weighed 11 pounds, 12 ounces and he was 23 inches long. Larry's the third boy. Their (the boys')

Indiana State superstar Larry Bird signs autographs for young fans. (William Palmer)

ages are 24, 23, 22, 20 and 13."

At Springs Valley, Larry sprouted from a spindly 6-3, 155 pounds in his junior year. "I used to list him as 6-7, 180 pounds in his senior year," explains Holland. "His biggest improvement came between his junior and senior years. He does so many good things without the ball you can't write about."

Said Mrs. Bird: "We thought Larry would average about 19 or 20 points in college and get a few rebounds (Larry averaged about 13 boards). And he'd always give 101 percent but he's done better."

So much better writers and scouts, like bloodhounds, keep sniffing for meaty answers.

Would Larry return a call the next day after sleeping?

"I'll tell him," his mother replied. "But I'm not sure what he'll do."

Neither is Coach King. ■

ISU Bird To Fly Away—Someday

BY RAY COMPTON

5/21/77—SOMEDAY A SUGAR DADDY of the National Basketball Association will cross the Wabash River, pop open his briefcase and slap down a professional contract in front of one of the local basketball laborers.

The dotted line will guarantee big money. Bigger money than the fatherless beholder had dreamed about. The future will promise stops in New York, Los Angeles, and Chicago. All far removed from French Lick, the tiny hamlet in southern Indiana where he dribbled as a tot.

Someday Larry Bird will sign that contract. Someday Larry Bird will become an instant millionaire. Someday Larry Bird will call a sprawling city his home.

Someday.

"I want to try professional ball someday," admits Bird.

And professional basketball wants to try Bird. The slender 6-foot-9 blond bomber blasted his way into college basketball's frontier with a 32.8 average last season, his first year of collegiate competition after two years of waiting to gain his eligibility at Indiana State.

The Bird watchers included NBA scouts, coaches and general managers. The accolades thundered in. One general manager likened Bird to UCLA's Marques Johnson, this year's selection as college basketball's player-of-the-year. Most scouts agreed Bird was a sure-bet to make it in the pros as a forward who could run, pass, shoot and rebound.

Someday.

According to the NBA statutes, that someday for Bird and the NBA could be this year — as early as June 10 when the NBA holds its college player draft. To qualify, all Bird would have to do is appeal for hardship status and his name would be on the draft list. That would mean big money ..... forfeiture of his last two years of college play.

But Bird says no to money, no to bright lights and no to the professional lords. At least, this spring he's saying no.

"Some people want me to take the money now," says Bird, who helped Bob King's Sycamores manufacture a school-record 25-3 record last winter. "They talk about how much money I can get. Sure we (his family) never did have much money, but we have always been able to get by. If my mother needed the money real bad, then I'd go professional. But we are doing all right without the money."

Bird has other reasons for neglecting the pros this year. It is called loyalty.

Through his accomplishments on the hardwood, the 20-year-old junior-to-be has become Terre Haute's No. 1 citizen. Tickets to Indiana State's 10,000-seat Hulman Center became precious items in Larry's first season. Indiana State gained national recognition, edging into the national polls and rating an invite to the National Invitation Tournament.

And off the court, Bird assumes an ambassador role for the school, speaking at grade schools and other functions about his college.

Yet despite these services, Larry Bird feels he still owes Bob King and his coaching staff something.

"Coach King has been like a dad to me," said Bird, whose college life was aborted in 1974 after a few days at Indiana University. "Whatever Coach King would want me to do, I'd do it. If it wasn't for people like Coach King and Coach (Bill) Hodges (King's assistant), I probably wouldn't even be in college.

"I didn't like college while I was at Indiana and didn't

want to go to school anymore. But Coach Hodges talked to me and got me interested in playing ball and going to school. At the time I wasn't interested in playing in the pros, but now I am when the time comes."

That time could be next year ("it is something I'd have to think about," he admits). Despite his auspicious first year with the Sycamores (32.8 ppg, 373 rebounds, 80 steals and 29 blocked shots in 28 games) Bird knows another year of polishing his skills would boost his selling points. Or would another year —perhaps with not as impressive ratings in ISU's first adventure in the Missouri Valley—damage his goods?

"I think I can have just as good a year next year," says Bird, who ravished ISU's record books last year, "although our schedule in going to be tougher. And my role could be different next year. This year I figured I had to score more so the team could do well. Next year we may have several guys who can score."

Another place Larry hoped to share the load is the publicity area. Despite his shyness and sometimes avoidance of the pencil press, Bird was the target of the news media from the moment he launched his college career with a 31-point, 18-rebound production.

The fact that his teammates were often ignored bothered Bird. "Harry Morgan (a 6-7 junior forward) is a great player and could score a lot if we needed him to," he said.

"After the season I don't mind talking to sports writers, but after games I would feel down if we lost or didn't play well," Larry said. "And I felt embarrassed about them always doing stories on me instead of the team. The team deserved the publicity."

But so did Larry Bird...and so probably will Larry Bird next year, when he continues his drive to march Indiana State into the basketball spotlight.

Overlooking the pressing interest by NBA scouts, Larry Bird chose to remain at Indiana State. (Lyle Mannweiler)

How Good Can He Be?

BY JOHN BANSCH

11/1/77—THAT'S THE QUESTION everyone will be asking about Indiana State basketball star Larry Bird this winter. Here are some facts to throw into any discussion about the 6-9 Bird, who just might be the best player in the nation.

The Sycamore averaged 38.3 points per game in his 15 outings a year ago. He had eight games of 40 to 47 points down the stretch. He is only the 12th major college sophomore to average 30 points or more over a season. Among the others are Indiana's George McGinnis, Notre Dame's Adrian Dantley and Cincinnati's Oscar Robertson who prepped in Indianapolis.

Another interesting fact is Bird ranks as the No. 2 returning rebounder in Division I, averaging 13.3 last season. No player has ever won both the scoring and rebounding titles. Bird has a clear shot at both.

(Indianapolis Star/News Photo)

(Lyle Mannweiler)

BIRD LOOKING TO FUTURE

December 15, 1978

BY ZACH DUNKIN

Since Larry Bird nixed the opportunity to turn professional last year, most of the talk about his pro career has subsided.

His coach, Bill Hodges, says Bird is only concerned with playing for Indiana State right now.

"He's not worried about playing pro basketball," said Hodges, "just about playing for us and winning a championship.

Hodges further explained Bird's intentions.

"I think what he wants out of pro basketball is security," he stated. "He wants to be able to do what he wants and that is coach basketball. When he gets through with the pros he wants to coach basketball.

"I'm not talking about coaching pro basketball. He wants to go down to Southern Indiana and get a good coaching job and enjoy himself. The only way that he can do that and never have to worry about being fired is to make a lot of money and save it."

That's security.

ANOTHER SIDE TO THIS BIRD

February 12, 1979

BY WAYNE FUSON

There are two sides to Larry Bird, Indiana State's All-American basketball player.

Most people think of him as a great scorer, which he is, and a great rebounder, which he is, and a super passer, which he certainly is. Bird is the nation's leading scorer with a 29.1 average and the nation's third leading rebounder with 15 a game.

Bird, a product of little French Lick, also is pictured by many as an introverted kid who does nothing but think basketball. Larry, some thought, had holes in his head because he didn't take the big pro money last year when he was drafted in the first round by the Boston Celtics of the National Basketball Association.

Larry, who does indeed come from spartan stock in southern Indiana, told Bill Hodges, his coach at ISU, that above all he wanted a degree. Therefore, he concluded, he'd pass up the NBA gold to finish his senior year at Terre Haute. Those who think he is majoring in basketball ought to check with the faculty at ISU. Not only does he go to class, but he's carrying a B average (majoring in physical education) and, by golly, will graduate in June.

Bird has avoided some reporters because he claims he has been misquoted. As a result, he has been pictured as something of an ogre.

But the kid isn't.

The other night after he had scored 37 points in a game, he was racing off the floor at Terre Haute's Hulman Center. A photographer blocked the path to the locker room. Larry gave the photog a fake and in the process knocked a 9-year-old fan down.

Larry stopped, swooped the youngster up into his arms and carried him into the locker room. He asked Hodges, who insists that nobody be allowed in the Sycamore locker room until after he has had his postgame talk with the team, if he could make an exception for the youngster.

Hodges agreed. Larry sat the boy down on a bench in front of his locker, got a program and he and all members of the unbeaten Sycamore team signed it for the lad. You can be sure that was one happy boy when he left that inner sanctum.

In this day of big money in sport, few can understand a young man like Bird, who isn't impressed really with all the offers made to him. Sure, he'll play pro ball with the Celtics after he finishes at Indiana State. And sure, the big money will come.

Meantime, Larry is willing to wait. He has only one thing on his mind at the present time—that is getting Indiana State into the NCAA tournament, which seems almost a sure bet at this time.

Then it'll be time for the pros.

The pressure of a winning streak like Indiana State's has to be tremendous, but the Sycamores seem to be weathering the storm fairly well.

Carl Nicks, who had been quoted as saying that he felt some jealousy because of all of the attention given Bird, was tremendously upset by the report. "Nicks is the most giving and unselfish person anywhere," says Hodges, the Zionsville boy who moved into the head coaching job at Indiana State when Bob King had to give it up because of illness.

"That report that he was jealous of Bird almost killed him," said Hodges of Nicks. "I can't believe they said that of me," Nicks said of the *Sports Illustrated* article.

Then there is Brad Miley, the unsung hero of the Indiana State team from Rushville. He is one of the nicest kids you'd ever meet. During a tense moment recently, he went up to Hodges and said, "Coach, I just want to tell you that no matter what they offer me, I am going to stay another year with you."

Miley is only a junior, of course. He accomplished what he tried to do and broke the tension.

Bird Shows 'Em He's "A Tough Individual"

March 12, 1979

BY RAY COMPTON

Fighting Gobblers, Billy Packer, a national television audience, sports writers from the four corners of the nation and 15,110 eye witnesses in Allen Fieldhouse learned something yesterday that Indiana State trainer Bob Behnke knew all the time.

Larry Bird is one tough individual.

"He's a rare bird (no pun intended)," Behnke said. "He has a kind of toughness in him that no other athlete has had in my 18 years of work. He plays with problems that would cause the average player to just sit and watch the game."

Yesterday, Bird played his first game after suffering a triple hairline fracture of his left thumb in the championship game of the Missouri Valley tournament March 3.

And what did he do? The 6-foot-9 Sycamore All-American scored 22 points, snared 13 rebounds and dished out seven assists in Indiana State's 86-69 conquest of Virginia Tech in the second round of the NCAA basketball tournament.

The victory hurls the 30-0 Sycamores into the Midwest Regional at Cincinnati Thursday when they will oppose Big Eight champion Oklahoma (21-9).

There was intense concern in the Indiana State camp over the weekend about how Bird would perform with the fractured thumb. Because of NCAA restrictions, he could wear only a rubber pad over the swollen thumb.

"We won't know how he will play until tomorrow afternoon," Indiana State coach Bill Hodges said in a Saturday press conference.

Hodges had refused to allow Bird to be administered Novocaine or any other painkilling drug. "We aren't going to take a chance with Larry's future to win a basketball game," Hodges said.

Nothing was needed, Behnke said.

"You're not going to find a lot of people who would go out and play the way Larry did," said Behnke after the Tech victory. "He did his Larry Bird thing. He just ignored his injuries."

This Recipe Is For Bird

BY THOMAS R. KEATING

3/8/79—WHEN YOU'RE ON TOP, everyone wants to help.

A large number of Indiana State University basketball fans have expressed concern this week about all-American Larry Bird's broken left thumb.

All that sympathy is nice, but as the undefeated Sycamores prepare for Sunday's opening round game in the NCAA tourney, they now have a concrete offer of remedial assistance from an unexpected source.

Late Wednesday morning, comedian and political activist Dick Gregory phoned the ISU athletic department long distance to offer a special herb recipe he guaranteed would allow Bird to play without noticing any pain in his thumb.

Gregory explained that he was serious about the recipe. He added that he used the herb when he was 44 and made his well-publicized run from Los Angeles to New York City. By adding the herb to his diet, he claimed he made the trip pain-free despite a broken toe.

The comedian also said he had given the recipe to Muhammad Ali after the heavyweight champion suffered a broken jaw in a fight against Ken Norton.

Gregory said he was calling because he had read about Bird's injury in a newspaper and because he had been on the track team at Southern Illinois University with Indiana State gymnastics coach Roger Counsil.

There was no word from Indiana State officials as to whether Gregory's offer was accepted. They may be afraid to ask what exactly he meant by "feeling no pain."

Despite his notoriety for being a high scorer, Bird also was a powerful rebounder. (Lyle Mannweiler)

Bird, who also has worn a football girdle pad frequently this year to protect his backside from falls after taking charging calls, will again have to have the thumb wrapped this week. A fracture normally takes six weeks to heal, though there is hope that if Indiana State qualifies for the Final Four in Salt Lake City on March 24 and 26, he would be sufficiently recovered.

"It's healing well," Behnke said.

The one part of Bird's game that Hodges feared would be impaired because of the injury was his rebounding. "He's a two-handed rebounder," Hodges said. "He grabs the ball with both hands, so he has to use his left hand."

Bird did not grab his first rebound until almost seven minutes had passed yesterday. And later in the first half, there was a brief scare on the Sycamore bench when Bird winced with pain after collecting another rebound.

"It's sore," Behnke said.

But Bird refused to let his wounded thumb detract from his game. After Hodges had announced in a pregame meeting the Sycamore offense would be altered so Bird would receive passes on his right side, Bird asked that the patterns go unchanged.

And shortly before tipoff, he informed guard Steve Reed that the injury would not hinder him.

"In practice I usually threw to his other side," Reed said. "But he said not to worry about it."

Bird remained speechless to the press over the weekend and did not comment on the injury.

"Unless Larry decides to, he won't be talking to the press," Hodges said.

But there were plenty of folks from Terre Haute babbling in Lawrence yesterday. More than 3,000 Sycamore fans made the trek as they and a huge and vocal throng from Arkansas (which also sold more than 3,000

Bird cuts down the net after ISU gained a spot in the NCAA playoffs. The ISU standout suffered a triple hairline fracture of his left thumb in the game. (Charles A. Berry)

tickets) filled the Kansas fieldhouse to near capacity.

Indiana State was closed Friday so students, faculty members and other associates could make the trip to Lawrence. On Saturday, 10 buses made the nine-hour trip to Kansas City. Some passengers waited in line 12 hours to purchase a bus ticket.

Indiana State will be allotted just 750 tickets for the Midwest Regional. ■

Award Makes Bird Talkative

March 14, 1979

BY WAYNE FUSON

Indiana State's All-American Larry Bird, who has received all kinds of criticism because he doesn't talk much with reporters, was in a talkative mood the other day in Chicago when he received the Associated Press player-of-the-year award.

He talked about the award—"I wouldn't be here if it weren't for my teammates."

He said he was thinking not only about himself but his teammates when he decided to not talk with reporters. "Playing college basketball is supposed to be fun, but if I had had to spend an hour or so every day talking to reporters, I wouldn't have had time for much else.

"If I let Carl Nicks and others talk to the press, it helps them. Now they get the publicity they deserve. I can handle the press. I can talk. But when they say something bad and put me down, it hurts my family.

"I know a lot of players out there that are great and I'm happy to be the one picked," Bird said at a news conference at which his coach, Bill Hodges, was named college basketball coach of the year.

"It means a lot to me and my family," said Bird. "If it were not for my teammates, I would not be here. I want to thank them for everything they've done."

Someone asked him how he felt about being referred to as pro basketball's "great white hope."

"I'm not a racist but there aren't many whites left because there are so many good, great black players. I hope I can hold myself up with them. I know they're waiting for me."

He was drafted last year by the Boston Celtics and has until 24 hours before the June 24 National Basketball Association draft to sign with the Celtics or he goes back into the poll and probably will be the No. 1 pick.

"I can't comment on that now," he said. "Right now I have only one thing on my mind (the NCAA tournament). I'm pleased I stayed at Indiana State. I think I can come to terms with Boston. If not, and Chicago drafts me, I wouldn't mind and I'd love to play with Artis Gilmore.

"Yes, I think the Boston team is suited to my talents," said Bird. "I don't only score. I can sacrifice myself and get the ball to Dave Cowens and Bob McAdoo."

Bird and Hodges, 36, the first rookie coach to be so honored, flew to Chicago in a private plane along with Dr. Richard Landini, president of Indiana State.

Bird was asked about his famous left thumb when he alighted from the plane. (The thumb was fractured in the Missouri Valley playoff final, but Larry played well in ISU's victory over Virginia Tech in the first round of the NCAA. He got 24 points and 13 rebounds.)

"It still hurts," said Larry. "Every time I get the thing hit, it hurts for five minutes or so." He got it bumped before the game with Virginia Tech even began. "Some guy bumped it when we were shaking hands on the floor," said Larry.

What about this week's Midwest Regional tournament at Cincinnati (ISU will go for its 31st straight victory against Big Eight champion Oklahoma tomorrow night in Riverfront Coliseum).

"I'll play," said Larry. "Maybe it'll be better by then. The only thing I wear on it during a game is tape. It does bother me, sure. It affects my long shots and it bothers my passing some because I like to throw the ball with two hands. But at a time like this you have to play with pain. Maybe I'll be an example to other players if I go ahead and play. Maybe they'll realize that you can play with pain."

Bird was impressed by the trophy he received. It was given in memory of the late Adolph Rupp, coach of the University of Kentucky for so many years. Larry, from Southern Indiana, was a great fan of the Baron. By the way, Adolph Rupp Jr., who runs his late father's cattle farm and is a military school teacher as well, arrived in Chicago just in time to hand Larry the trophy.

Hodges, who took over the ISU coaching job only last fall when Bob King, also the athletic director, stepped down because of illness, won the coach-of-the-year award by a mile in the voting of sports writers and broadcasters. "I accept this trophy not only for myself, but for Bob King," Said Hodges. "I owe all of this to him.

Ray Meyer, the veteran DePaul mentor whose team also is still alive in the NCAA, paid tribute to Hodges as a great young coach. "This is just his first award. I have been impressed by Indiana State's discipline. And, don't get the idea that Hodges has a one-man team, because he doesn't."

MSU Bird-Dogs Sycamores

March 27, 1979
Salt Lake City

BY MAX STULTZ

Favored Michigan State dealt the Indiana State Sycamores a crushing defeat in the game the Hoosiers wanted to win most of all Monday night, a 75-64 setback with the NCAA title at stake.

Sparked by its 1-2 punch of Earvin (Magic) Johnson and Greg Kelser, the two of them getting a big boost from guard Terry Donnelly, the Spartans ascended the throne room of collegiate basketball in handy fashion.

Indiana State, rated No. 1 in the country but a six-point underdog at the tipoff in Utah's Special Events Center, came to the last hurdle unbeaten in 33 outings. But the Sycamores, whose brilliant all-American Larry Bird was limited to 19 points, fell out of contention in the first half and never posed a really serious threat anytime in the last 20 minutes.

It was supposed to be a two-on-one dual with Johnson and Kelser against Bird, but Donnelly, a 6-2 junior guard, slipped in through a side door to help lay the haymaker on Indiana State.

Averaging only six points per game, Donnelly broke loose for 15—all but two in the second half—after Johnson and Kelser carried the 26-6 Spartans to a 37-28 lead at the break. Kelser, the only starting senior for the Big Ten tri-champions, and Donnelly, who was getting loose in the corners, carried the No. 3-ranked Spartans to a 44-28 bulge before Indiana State broke the ice after nearly three minutes of play.

Guard Carl Nicks, second high for the Sycamores with 17, snapped the spell with a jumper making it 44-30. But Donnelly ripped the nets for three

more without a miss, the last one presenting Michigan State with its fourth 16-point lead of the ball game and the Missouri Valley Conference champions never moved closer than six points.

That brief surge consisted of three points by Bird and another by Nicks which closed the gap to 52-46 before Magic took charge with a free throw and drive-in basket. Michigan State bolstered its margin to 11 points at 61-50 with about five minutes to go. Johnson picked up a rare four-point play on a drive to the hoop.

Sycamore guard Bob Heaton was charged with an "in the air personal" which allowed Johnson two free

In the matchup of the century, Bird met MSU's Magic Johnson in a battle for the NCAA title. (Photo courtesy of Michigan State University Sports Information).

Every time Bird touched the ball he was swarmed by MSU players. (Photo Courtesy of Michigan State University Sports Information)

fielders, got the only Sycamore markers in the span with a jumper from the key.

Later in the half it was more of the same after Nicks' one-hander sliced the margin to 30-23. MSU ran off five more in a row, Kelser feeding Johnson underneath, then driving an alley-oop flip from the brilliant sophomore through the cords the next time down the floor and finally hitting one of two free throws when fouled by Alex Gilbert.

Bird, who fired 21 times for his seven fielders and missed 3 of 8 free opportunities, finished the first-half scoring with a point from the line on the rear half of a one-and-one.

And poor free throwing was greatly responsible for the difference if not the title as ISU outgoaled the Spartans 27-26. But they made only 10 of 22 from the line, Gilbert failing four times and Nicks making only 3 of 6.

More points were involved than meets the eye, however, as the Sycamores blew the one-and-one three times and Gilbert once missed both opportunities after drawing a shooting foul.

Indiana State, which had hit at a .503 clip on its 33-game victory streak, slipped badly against the defensive-minded Spartans, skidding to .422 with their 27 fielders coming on 64 attempts.

Michigan State, which came in with a .524 field mark, improved considerably with 26 of 43 ripping the strings, a blistering .605 pace.

The Spartans enjoyed a healthy advantage at the line, canning 23 of 33 including 15 in the final 20 minutes, one of them a technical charged to Bird.

The call came after Steve Reed connected from outside and Bird slapped the ball away from Johnson as he prepared to toss it in bounds. That put Michigan State up 69-60 with 49 seconds to go and State turned the play into two more free throws when Donnelly was fouled along the sidelines by Bird.

Bird, who was double and triple teamed and had trouble even getting the ball inside, was credited with just two assists while Johnson settled for five.

Johnson and Bird also were the most error-prone, each being charged with six turnovers as Michigan State made 16 mistakes to 10 for the Sycamores. Indiana State

throws rather than one and he sank both.

It was the second such call against the Sycamores. Mike Brkovich hit on a drive-in in the opening six minutes and guard Steve Reed was charged the flagrant violation of which Brkovich sank the second of two attempts.

Brkovich's play was in the middle of a nine-point spree which saw the Spartans begin to show signs that they were going to take command. Erasing an 8-7 Indiana State lead, the Sycamores' last of the game at 9-8 on Donnelly's first basket, the winners pushed their advantage to 16-8 before Bird tallied the second of his seven baskets on an out-of-bounds play.

Bird, Nicks and Heaton moved the Sycamores up to 23-17 but they again suffered a dry spell, getting outscored 7-2 as Michigan State slowly pulled away to a comfortable 30-19 lead. Nicks, who also popped seven

Coach Bill Hodges said, "We just had a bad shooting night, both from the field and the free throw line. When you come down to the final night, you have to have a great game to win, and this wasn't one for us.

"I'll tell you, though," he declared, "We had a great year and we're proud of that.

"Of course, we are disappointed. Our team goal was to win the NCAA."

Hodges, the first rookie to bring a team to the final four undefeated said, "Rebounding was an obvious problem. We weren't getting too many second shots the first half. Michigan State played extremely well and it is hard to come from behind all night."

Bird, though being held below 20 points for only the second time all season, still moved into fifth place among NCAA scorers. ■

Larry Bird guards MSU star Greg Kelser in the NCAA title game. Michigan State ultimately beat the Sycamores, 75-64. (Photo Courtesy of Michigan State University Sports Information)

MICHIGAN STATE (75)   INDIANA STATE (64)

	Min.	FG	FT	R	A	PF	TP		Min.	FG	FT	R	A	PF	TP
Brkovich	39	1-2	3-7	4	1	1	5	Miley	24	0-0	0-1	3	0	1	0
Kelser	32	7-13	5-6	8	9	4	19	Gilbert	20	2-3	0-4	4	0	4	4
Charles	31	3-3	1-2	7	0	5	7	Bird	40	7-21	5-8	13	2	3	19
Donnelly	39	5-5	5-6	4	0	2	15	Nicks	36	7-14	3-6	2	4	5	12
Johnson	35	8-15	8-10	7	5	3	24	Reed	36	4-9	0-0	0	9	4	8
Vincent	19	2-5	1-2	2	0	4	5	Heaton	22	4-14	2-2	6	2	2	10
Gonzalez	3	0-0	0-0	0	0	0	0	Staley	17	2-2	0-1	3	0	2	4
Longaker	2	0-0	0-0	0	0	0	0	Nemcek	2	1-1	0-0	0	1	3	2
Totals	—	26-43	23-33	34x	15	19	75	Totals	—	27-64	10-22	31x	18	24	64

x—includes 2 team rebounds   x—includes 2 team rebounds

Halftime Score: Michigan State 37, Indiana State 28
Turnovers — Indiana State 10 (Bird 6), Michigan State 16
(Johnson 6, Brkovich 5)
Steals — Indiana State 6 (Bird 5), Michigan State 6 (Kelser 2)

Bird To Sign Pro Pact Soon

March 27, 1979

Any day now Indiana State will retire Larry Bird's famous No. 33 uniform.

And, any day now the kid from French Lick, Indiana who became everybody's All-American this year when the Sycamores won 33 straight games, will become a millionaire.

Bird is expected to sign momentarily with the Boston Celtics for $1 million a year for three years. Earlier, there was some chance that he might go to Boston immediately, but that seems impossible now because of his broken thumb.

Unfortunately, Bird was a little off range last night and Michigan State, the Big Ten tri-champion, defeated the Sycamores, 75-64, in the NCAA title game.

"Larry had a great career for us," said Bill Hodges, the rookie ISU coach, at a press conference after the game. "He asked to be excused from this press conference, saying that he has given his just dues and just wanted to relax. That might not make some people happy, but he has done a lot of talking on the floor and is a good person."

Bird, physically and emotionally drained, did issue a statement through Indiana State sports information director Ed McKee.

"Michigan State is an excellent team. They play very tough defense and had a real good zone," the 6-foot-9 whiz said. "Unfortunately, the ball wouldn't drop for us and we missed too many free throws.

"I hate to lose, just like all the other guys on our team, but I guess we did all right. We won 33 games. We gave it the best we had had—we just didn't hit the shots.

"It's been a long season, but I'd like to play Michigan State again. It certainly could be a different story."

Bird and his Sycamore teammates were to be feted today in a huge celebration at Terre Haute. ■

(Indianapolis Star/News Photo)

Further Word About Bird

March 30, 1979

BY DAVID MANNWEILER

So much has been written about Larry Bird, the reigning wunderkind of college basketball, there can't be much that is unknown.

Wanna bet?

Trivia fans looking for ammunition for bar bets should consider:

1. Last summer, playing golf, Bird made a hole in one on a 128-yard hole.

2. Bird was an outfielder on the Terre Haute Platolene 500-Carpetland All-Star slow-pitch softball team. He hit 12 home runs in 20 games last year and batted in 48 runs.

3. There will be a drawing tomorrow to give away the road uniform Bird wore in the 1976-77 season. The uniform has been displayed in a glass case in a Sears, Roebuck & Co. store window in Terre Haute.

4. Kurt Thomas, the best gymnast in the United States, works out in the Indiana State gym next to a high school physical education class taught by student teacher Larry Bird. Thomas says Bird is better at gymnastics than Thomas is at basketball.

5. Denny Crum, the University of Louisville coach, tried to recruit Bird when he was a high school senior. Bird said he wasn't interested. Crum insisted. He challenged Bird to a game of "horse." If Crum won, Bird had to visit U. of L. Bird walked out 40 feet from the hoop and made five straight shots. He never made the visit.

That is the kind of trivia Ed McKee, the 33-year-old sports publicist for ISU, has had to dredge up as the nation turned its eyes on Bird, the ISU team and Terre Haute. McKee, his secretary and his parttime student assistant Craig McKee (no relation) have been besieged by fact-hungry journalists.

"I can't tell you how many thousands of calls we've had," McKee said. "It hasn't let up, not as much as people might think now the season is over. I just got off the phone with a college in Erie, Pennsylvania, that wants Leroy Staley to play in the Cage Classic One, an all-star game.

"A *St. Louis Post-Dispatch* photographer is over at the gym for a Sunday picture feature on Kurt Thomas. Bird will play in the Pizza Hut all-star game Saturday. Wide World of Sports will carry the NCAA gymnastics finals this weekend, with Kurt. (Coach) Bill Hodges goes to Las Vegas today. All that means our phones are still ringing."

McKee's life turned extra frantic after ISU broke into the Top 10 ratings. "When we were 20-0 and still not ranked first, it made for controversy. People always wanted our reflections on not being No. 1. We got as much mileage out of not being No. 1 as we did being No. 1."

Every aspect of superstar Larry Bird was scrutinized. "A woman from the National Solid Waste Association called to confirm that Larry had worked on a garbage truck. I told her he worked for the French Lick Parks Department. Collecting garbage was one portion of his job. He also drove a tractor to cut the grass on the highway median and painted park benches. She wanted to know if he was a driver or a can pitcher on the garbage truck.

COAL PEOPLE COVER

"Larry also is on the cover of *Coal People* magazine this month. The guy who does the play-by-play for the University of Charleston is an ad salesman for the magazine. He did a brief pregame interview with Larry and talked to him about being from French Lick, and how that is in coal country. So here's a 2-page story with five pictures and a color cover of a basketball player who may or may not have any relations who used to work in the coal business."

McKee, a 6-9 workhorse who was picked by the Indiana Pacers in the first ABA draft but failed to make it in the pros, played for the Goodyear Wingfoots basketball team two seasons and worked three years in the Goodyear public relations office before moving to his ISU job in 1971. When he took the job, he had never seen a college gymnastics meet, knew very little about football (his college played soccer) and he had seen one college wrestling meet.

"The last six weeks, I felt like I had a growth coming out of my ear from the telephone. It's very difficult to continue with the day-to-day activities. But we happened to be the news item of the nation, with the top player in the country and the top coach," McKee said.

"I heard on the radio that nearly one-quarter of the nation's populace watched our game with Michigan State. It was the most-watched game ever. That's amazing when you think that Indiana State, which had never been on national TV until February 25 and has now been on five times within a month, can do that.

"I think our coaches would concur that Indiana State and Terre Haute are now on the map. It's up to us, to the university and the other athletes to continue that excellence."

> "I think our coaches would concur that Indiana State and Terre Haute are now on the map. It's up to us, to the university and the other athletes to continue that excellence."

Saying Thanks To ISU No. 33

April 28, 1979

BY WAYNE FUSON

Terre Haute staged a 3½-hour love-in for Larry Bird last night. More than 1,000 Indiana State fans put on their "best bib and tucker" and paid $50 each to salute the best and most famous basketball player ever to wear an ISU uniform.

The party was billed as a "Larry Bird Appreciation Dinner" and that's just what it was. Everybody from Gov. Otis Bowen to Bob Heaton, Bird's roommate, saluted the nation's premier college basketball player.

Those who attended the dinner of beef steak and cold duck chipped in more than $22,000 to establish a scholarship at Indiana State in honor of Bird, who came to ISU from French Lick. The stipulation on the scholarship is that it first must be awarded to a basketball player from Larry's high school, Springs Valley. If no player from Springs Valley qualifies, then any player from Orange County would be eligible. After those geographical qualifications are exhausted, then any player from any county adjacent to Orange would be eligible.

Gov. Bowen sent his greeting in absentia and made Bird and his teammates "honorary governors" of Indiana. Bird, who was the only player not in formal attire, allowed that it was only fair that Bowen missed his fete. "I didn't go to his in Indianapolis this week either," said Larry. (Gov. Bowen had a luncheon at the Convention Center Thursday honoring all the Indiana college teams which participated in postseason tournaments.)

Bob King, ISU athletic director and basketball coach until this year when he was forced to turn over the reins to Bill Hodges because of illness, announced that Bird's famous No. 33 uniform was being retired, a first in the history of ISU athletics.

Richard Landini, the ISU president who looks a little like Walter Matthau and talks a lot like the late Everett Dirksen, accepted Bird's jersey. "I'll always cherish the memories of Larry Bird," said Landini, who jokingly added, "I think I'll wear this jersey tonight and pretend I'm Larry Bird. Tomorrow I'll present it to the university to be retired."

"We didn't really realize how great Larry would be when we recruited him," said King.

King also paid tribute to Hodges, who as a rookie won national coach of the year honors for leading the Sycamores to a 33-game winning streak and to the finals of the NCAA tournament.

Hodges returned the compliment. "The two greatest things a man can give another are knowledge and a chance. Bob King gave me both. We won't really ever

Number 33, Larry Bird, is known as the greatest athlete to wear an Indiana State basketball uniform. (Lyle Mannweiler,)

miss Larry because he gave us something that no one can ever take away—a winning tradition."

Highlight of the party was a presentation by ISU's audio visual department depicting the great moments in Bird's career. It was done on a specially built 110-foot long screen and was absolutely spectacular. The show was presented every hour on the hour today for ISU fans at Hulman Center. By the way, Larry didn't miss a single shot during the entire presentation. And the fans cheered every one.

Bob Woolf, the Boston lawyer who is trying to get Bird a $6 million contract for six years with the Boston Celtics, was among the guests. When asked how the negotiating was going with Red Auerbach, the Celtic general manager, Woolf said: "terrible."

Later he expressed some confidence that an agreement would be reached with the NBA club, maybe one that would make Bird the highest paid rookie in the history of the NBA.

Al McGuire, the city slicker former coach of Marquette who now does commentary for NBC television when he isn't turning down offers to coach again, put on his "down home" face and regaled the audience with personal stories about many of the basketball greats he has come in contact with.

McGuire had a word of warning for Bird, however. "You'll be all right, Larry," he said, "but it won't be easy." McGuire said he allowed as how Bird would score only 15-20 points a game during his rookie year in the NBA. (He averaged 30 a game in college.)

It was Bird's night, but the rest of the team came in for their plaudits, too. Kurt Frudenthal of United Press International presented a trophy to the Sycamore seniors emblematic of their national poll championship as determined by that wire service. Finally, it was Bird's turn to talk. The shy kid from Southern Indiana who shied away from talking to reporters most of the season seemed relaxed at the microphone. He thanked his mother and his grandmother, his teammates and those who have guided and assisted him along the way from Springs Valley to the undisputed No. 1 basketball player in the country.

Bird, in his own folksy way, got the biggest laugh of the night when he said, "I appreciate all this, but I'm still the same hick from French Lick."

Or something like that. ∎

(Rick Wood)

Sycamores of '79 gather in memory of a special year

August 13, 1989
Terre Haute, Ind.

BY DAVID BENNER

EVEN A JADED VETERAN of the hand-shaking, autograph-giving, picture-taking banquet circuit could see this was different.

"I do so many of these things, you can't get caught up in them," said Larry Bird, "But this one's special."

Yes, you could say that.

Saturday night in Hulman Center, the Indiana State University basketball team of 1979 gathered for a reunion that brought back a lot of memories from a special season of basketball.

That's why 530 people showed up for dinner and another 500 came into Hulman Center for the program that followed: to relive a season that's still hard to believe.

Flashback to 1979 for a minute. The Sycamores, led, of course, by Mr. Bird, won the Missouri Valley Conference championship and went 33-0 before losing to Michigan State in the NCAA championship game. The Spartans, ironically, celebrated their 10-year reunion this weekend as well.

But Saturday night in Terre Haute, what was going on in East Lansing didn't matter. Bird, now the multi-million dollar NBA star of the Boston Celtics was on hand. So, too, were 10 other players from that team, along with Coach Bill Hodges, who now coaches Georgia College, Athletic Director Bob King, now retired in New Mexico, assistants Terry Thimlar and Danny King and former sports information director Ed McKee.

It all made for a nostalgic night, one the participants reveled in.

"This may only happen once," admitted Bird. "I may never see these guys again."

"I wouldn't have missed this for the world," said Carl Nicks, who now plays professionally in France. "But I have a bittersweet attitude about this. I'm afraid after this is over, I won't see these guys for another 10 years and I don't like that at all."

But for a night Bird and Nicks reminisced with the old gang.

There was Leroy Staley, who lives in Terre Haute and is an activities director at the U.S. penitentiary; Brad Miley, also living in Terre Haute while working as an insurance representative; Bob Ritter, a songwriter who lives in Nashville, Tennessee; Rich Nemcek, an air traffic controller in Chicago; Scott Turner, an analyst for Ford in Bedford, Indiana; Eric Curry, who lives and works in Terre Haute; and Tom Crowder, an engineer who lives in Danville, Illinois.

The only ones missing were assistant coach Mel Daniels, who was ill; Rod McNelly, who works for a water purification company in Indianapolis; and Steve Reed, who is in the process of moving his family from Atlanta to Denver.

But all were remembered and honored for what they brought to Indiana State University, Terre Haute, the state of Indiana and, probably, the whole country 10 years ago.

"It was wonderful, truly wonderful and I'll never, ever forget it," said Hodges during the program. "Thanks for what we had, what we'll always have and we'll be back."

Hodges, former ISU President Dr. Richard Landini, King and Heaton all took turns speaking during the program, emceed by Terre Haute attorney Craig McKee who was the assistant sports information director in 1979.

Also featured was a replay of the 1979 Sycamore highlight film, which helped carry the prevalent theme, one of nostalgia, which everyone in attendance definitely felt.

"I told my daughter, it's like being happy and depressed at the same time," said Hodges. "It's neat seeing the guys because we had something so wonderful that slipped away and you couldn't do anything to hold onto it.

"It's kind of like putting together a jigsaw puzzle or painting a Rembrandt. Once you're done, you can't redo it. This team was kind of like driving a car with cruise control, you just guide it.

"They were so good at what they did."

Former ISU coach Bill Hodges (Indianapolis Star/News photo)

With Bird leading the way, the Indiana State team of 1979 won the Missouri Valley Conference Championship and went 33-0 before losing to Michigan State University in the NCAA title game. (Indianapolis Star/News Photo)

Players reunite to recall ISU's best team

August 14, 1989

BY CONRAD BRUNNER

WHERE ARE THEY TEN YEARS LATER?

THE PLAYERS

Name, Residence	Occupation
Larry Bird, Boston	NBA player
Carl Nicks, France	active player
Alex Gilbert, Alton, IL	prison guard
Bob Heaton, Terre Haute	insurance representative
Leroy Staley, Terre Haute	recreational specialist, U.S. Pen.
Brad Miley, Terre Haute	beverage distributor
Steve Reed, Denver	hospital administrator
Rich Nemcek, Chicago	air traffic controller
Scott Turner, Bloomington, IL	senior analyst
Tom Crowder, Danville, IL	engineer
Bob Ritter, Nashville, TN	songwriter
Eric Curry, Terre Haute	munitions worker
Rod McNelly, Cicero, IN	sales representative

THE COACHES

Bill Hodges, Milledgeville, GA	head coach, Georgia College
Bob King, Belen, NM	retired
Mel Daniels, Indianapolis	NBA scout
Terry Thimlar, Fort Myers, FL	head coach, Cypress Lake High
Danny King, French Lick	construction

Bird had place to spread wings after eventually landing at ISU

November 1, 1992

BY ROBIN MILLER

Indiana University was too big and Northwood Institute was too small, but Indiana State turned out to be a perfect place for Larry Bird to educate America on the finer points of basketball.

From 1976 through 1979, Bird was magna cum laude between the baselines as he taught fundamentals and hard work while his Sycamores gave this country a memorable lesson in success.

Bird was The Word as he helped shoot ISU into national prominence and rocket college basketball into the next decade with a newfound appreciation and audience.

A shy kid who was overwhelmed by the size of IU's campus wound up dazzling a nation with his smart, savvy play as he revived college basketball interest from Terre Haute to Portland to Bangor.

In three seasons, he averaged 30 points, 13 rebounds and 4.6 assists as ISU rolled up 81 victories and fell one shy of a perfect season and NCAA championship his senior year.

He then graduated to the big time and continued his teachings, but his school days launched the legend.

LANDING AT INDIANA STATE

Even though he was an Indiana All-Star at Springs Valley High School and recruited by several schools, Bird didn't spend much time on recruiting trips. A Florida school came closest, sending him an airplane ticket, but Larry never made the flight.

Instead, he decided to go to Bob Knight's polished program. He could stay in southern Indiana and that was important.

But he never even made it to Knight's first practice. After less than a month, Bird bolted Bloomington because it was too big.

"You had to walk a mile just to get to class and then you couldn't hear anything because everyone was talk-ing," he once recalled. "The school was just too big . . . I never felt at home."

From IU, Bird headed for Northwood Institute, a tiny junior college located in West Baden, Indiana—not far from French Lick. He lasted two months.

"Larry was very unsettled, he had trouble attending class and was very undisciplined," was what Northwood coach Jack Johnson told *Sports Illustrated.*

"It wasn't big enough and the players weren't very good," was Bird's explanation.

Bird was playing amateur ball and working for the city department in French Lick when ISU assistant coach Bill Hodges began talking about the possibility of Bird coming to Terre Haute.

"The hardest thing wasn't convincing Larry to play at Indiana State but to come back to college at all," said Hodges.

"Bill (Hodges) had more to do with Larry's decision than anyone else," said Bob King, then Indiana State's head coach.

With their prized catch being redshirted in 1975-76, the Sycamores managed a 13-12 record and the coaching staff could only salivate while Bird scrimmaged.

"Larry practiced almost every day and he would take four reserves, scrimmage the varsity and beat them," said Ed McKee, ISU's sports information director during Bird's career. "I don't think anybody realized he was going to make us as good as he did but it was obvious he was special."

King recalled, "I'd heard good things about him but never saw him play until the summer of his redshirt year. He didn't have any speed and he was a very average jumper but there wasn't any doubt. He had such great peripheral vision, he could pass with either hand and he could shoot.

"He was very above average for a college player at that time and we couldn't wait for the next season."

Larry Bird received the Eastman Award as outstanding college player in 1979. (James McGrath, New York Daily News)

February 13, 1979

1. Indiana State (43)
2. UCLA (19)
3. Notre Dame
4. North Carolina
5. Duke
6. Louisiana State
7. Syracuse
8. Michigan State
9. Louisville
10. Marquette

11. Arkansas
12. Texas
13. Purdue
14. Iowa
15. Temple
16. Georgetown
17. Ohio State
18. Detroit
19. Vanderbilt
20. Alabama

Indiana State's unbeaten, newly crowned Missouri Valley Conference champions could afford to breathe freely tonight at Southern Illinois, except the eyes of the nation's pollsters are on the Sycamores who just this week established a school first in being named coast-to-coast No. 1 by the Associated Press.

STRONG SOPHOMORE SEASON

Bird's ISU debut turned out to be a preview of great things to come as he went for 31 points, 18 rebounds and 10 points in the Sycamores' 81-60 win over Chicago State.

Beating Chicago State, St. Ambrose, Robert Morris and Denver—all at home—wasn't exactly reason to think the program had turned around. But following a loss at Purdue, ISU ran off 12 wins in a row before dropping a 70-64 decision at Illinois State.

Attendance shot up like ISU's record as the Hulman Center was suddenly the place to be.

Bird & Co. closed out the regular season with nine consecutive triumphs, including an 80-65 eye-opener at Hinkle Fieldhouse in which Bird bashed Butler with 47 points and 19 rebounds.

"That kid looks like something special to me," declared Tony Hinkle after watching No. 33 at work.

Ranked 16th in the national polls, ISU's first postseason game as a Division I school would be in the National Invitation Tournament at Houston. The Sycamores lost in the closing seconds 83-82, but won some respect as Bird outshone Otis Birdsong by notching 44 points and 14 boards in defeat.

"We didn't come here to lose and we gave it our best shot, but we'll be back," vowed Bird, who wound up averaging 32.8 points, 13.3 rebounds and 4.4 assists in ISU's 25-3 run.

ANOTHER YEAR OF GROWTH

With Harry Morgan, Richard Johnson, DeCarsta Webster, Leroy Staley, Brad Miley and Steve Reed in the cast for Bird's junior year, ISU appeared deeper and stronger.

Enthusiasm abounded for 1977-78 but experts still had trouble taking seriously a schedule that boasted the likes of Westmont and Baptist.

Sycamore skeptics were silenced in the second game of Bird's junior year when ISU pummeled Purdue 91-63 and the star had a rare off night in the accuracy department even though he finished with 26 points.

ISU won its first 13 games before losing at Southern Illinois and going into a five-game skid.

"I hope we're not taking our press clippings too serious," King said during the Sycamores' slump.

A 41-point effort from Bird against Tulsa got ISU going again and it won eight of 10 coming home to finish 22-8 but again was snubbed by the NCAA Tournament selection committee.

So the Sycamores hosted their NIT opener with Illinois State and they squeezed out a 73-71 decision behind Bird's 27 points and 10 rebounds.

Next stop was Piscataway, N.J., and Rutgers prevailed on its home court 57-56. They wound up 23-9 and Bird's numbers were 30-11-4 as he was a first teamer on UPI's All-American squad.

STAGE SET AS A SENIOR

Bird's senior season took a turn for better long before it tipped off. Bob Heaton, a smooth swingman who transfered from the University of Denver, and Carl Nicks, a quick guard who was back at ISU after a year at a junior college, were both in the game plan.

King had been forced to step aside due to health problems and Hodges, with a loud vote of confidence from Bird, was named head coach.

After opening with a rout of Lawrence, ISU traveled to Mackey Arena and put a 10-point haymaker on Purdue. Follow-up victories at Evansville and Illinois State made it pretty obvious this was a serious crusade.

On January 3, 1979, the Sycamores opened Missouri Valley Conference play and a pair of experienced eyes watched with delight. Red Auerbach and Celtics coach Tommy Heinsohn saw Larry go for 27 points and 19 boards in a 101-89 win. But Bird's feeds drew the rave reviews.

"He's the best passing big man I've ever seen," gushed Auerbach, who had drafted Bird the previous April.

"His vision and smarts are what impress me," added Heinsohn.

Nicks' outside threat and Heaton's inside moves helped spread the Sycamores' wealth and it took an act of desperation February 1 by the latter to keep their record unblemished.

Trailing New Mexico State 83-81 with 3 seconds

Bird, Robertson honored

7/23/97—THE MISSOURI VALLEY CONFERENCE has announced the seven conference basketball greats it will induct as the inaugural class of its hall of fame.

They are Larry Bird of Indiana State, Oscar Robertson of Cincinnati, Hersey Hawkins of Bradley, the late Coach Hank Iba of Oklahoma State (formerly Oklahoma A&M), St. Louis University's Ed Macauley, Wichita State's Dave Stallworth and Louisville's Wes Unseld.

remaining, Heaton banked in a 50-footer at the buzzer and ISU prevailed in overtime.

As the winter wore on, the great debate was whether ISU deserved to be rated No. 1. The Associated Press rankings, determined by sportswriters, recognized State as the best team but United Press International, the coaches' poll, kept the Sycamores No. 2 as late as mid-February.

"I question the fairness of UPI's system," said Hodges. "We got 10 more first-place votes than anyone else and yet we're still ranked second. I think politics must enter in somewhere."

Billy Packer, NBC's basketball analyst, also was of the impression ISU got more respect in the polls than it deserved.

But on February 24, in front of a national television audience, ISU put its best feet forward and trampled Wichita State 109-84. Bird broke loose for 49 points and 19 rebounds, while Nicks nailed 25 points and Packer grudgingly admitted he may have underestimated ISU's talents.

READY FOR THE TOURNEY

The Sycamores were made the top seed in the NCAA's Midwest Regional but Bird had suffered a triple hairline fracture of his left thumb March 3. He would face Virginia Tech wearing a rubber pad over his swollen thumb and he proved to be a pain—totaling 22 points, 13 rebounds and seven assists in ISU's 86-69 rout.

"I didn't know how he would rebound but after a couple of minutes I knew everything was going to be all right," said Hodges.

Next up was Oklahoma and ISU stomped the Sooners 93-72, winning the boards 50-22, shooting 58 percent and playing tough defense. Bird, 11 of 19 for 29 points, got great support from Nicks (20), Gilbert (12), Heaton (9) and Staley (9).

"They beat us in every phase and defended us very well," said Oklahoma coach Dave Bliss.

ISU's opponent in the Midwest Regional championship at Cincinnati on March 17 was highly-regarded Arkansas with Sidney Moncrief. It turned out to be one of the most memorable games ever staged.

And it was decided by Heaton's 8-foot, left-handed hook shot at the buzzer, which propelled the Sycamores to a 73-71 win and into the Final Four at Salt Lake City.

"We wanted to get the ball to Larry but I ended up with it so I looped it up there, it bounced around and dropped in," explained Heaton, who was mobbed by teammates and fans alike.

Bird had 31 points and 10 rebounds and Hodges

had this perspective: "That was the most exciting game I've ever been around."

THE FINAL FOUR

None of four teams that converged on Salt Lake City—DePaul, Pennsylvania, Michigan State and the Sycamores—had ever won an NCAA championship and only the Ivy Leaguers appeared out of their element.

That proved to be true as MSU stomped Penn 101-67, but ISU's date with destiny required much more of an effort.

Behind freshman sensation Mark Aguirre and Gary Garland, DePaul all but sidelined the top-ranked Sycamores before falling 76-74.

The Blue Demons were leading 74-73 in the closing seconds before Heaton got open underneath, took a feed from Nicks and scored what proved to be the winning bucket with :49 remaining.

Aguirre, who finished with 19 points and played all 40 minutes with DePaul's other four starters, went for the winner but misfired. Staley claimed the rebound and ISU its 33rd consecutive triumph.

Bird was marvelous—bagging 35 points, including 12 fielders a row, and adding 16 rebounds as ISU shot .625 from the floor.

"I made 11 errors, too," said Bird, whose injured thumb obviously bothered him. "All that matters is that we won and we're in the finals."

The hoped-for matchup was set: the Magic of MSU against Bird and His Court.

But the Spartans had too much firepower and Cinderella was turned away 75-64. Magic Johnson and Greg Kelser powered MSU to an 11-point halftime lead and Terry Donnelly made sure ISU didn't come back during the final 20 minutes as he added an unexpected 15 points.

Bird, double- and tripled-teamed all night, only shot 7 of 21 for his 19 points but simply didn't have enough help. ISU only shot 27 of 64 and also missed 12 free throws.

"The coach gave us a job to do on Larry and we did it," said Johnson, who finished with 24 points in the first of his many showdowns with Bird.

The kid who captured the imagination of the country had come within one game of capturing a prize nobody thought possible three years earlier.

"I hate to lose, just like all the other guys on our team," said Bird. "Michigan State is an excellent team and played tough defense . . . and we missed too many shots.

"But we gave it our best and won 33 games . . . I guess we did all right." ■

Larry Bird led the ISU Sycamores to an undefeated regular season his senior year, falling just one game short of the NCAA title. (Indianapolis Star/News Photo)

Bird's Indiana State Statistics

Year	G	FG	FT	Reb	Ast	Pts
1976-77	28	.544	.840	373	123	32.8
1977-78	32	.524	.793	369	125	30.0
1978-79	34	.532	.831	505	187	28.6
Totals	94	.533	.822	1247	435	30.3

3

1979-1992

CELTIC GLORY

NBA Draft Top 10 Picks

June 9, 1978

1. Portland Trail Blazers—Mychal Thompson, C (Minnesota)
2. Kansas City Kings—Phil Ford, G (North Carolina)
3. Indiana Pacers—Rick Robey, F (Kentucky)
4. New York Knicks—Mike Richardson, G (Montana)
5. Golden State Warriors—Purvis Short, F (Jackson State)
6. **BOSTON CELTICS—LARRY BIRD, F (INDIANA STATE)**
7. Portland Trail Blazers—Ron Brewer, G (Arkansas)
8. Boston Celtics—Freeman Williams, G (Portland State)
9. Chicago Bulls—Reggie Theus, G (Nevada)
10. Atlanta Hawks—Butch Lee, G (Marquette)

Pacers Shuffle Roster Before Bird Debut

October 20, 1979

BY DICK MITTMAN

With the first appearance of Larry Bird in Market Square Arena only hours away, the Indiana Pacers today signed 6-foot-5 guard Joe Hassett after waiving Brad Davis, a 6-3 guard in his third pro season.

Pacer fans, however, will have to please excuse the raucous cheering and waving of green Celtic banners tonight by a group in the upper reaches of MSA.

"There'll be me and his two youngest brothers, uncles, cousins, around 30 of us," said Mrs. Georgia Bird, Larry's mother, by phone from her French Lick home.

"I bought the tickets early. I didn't take the $8.50 ones. I got the $6.50 ones."

Mrs. Bird, who has been forced to quit work due to illness, is still pinching herself over her middle son's basketball success.

"Well, I still don't believe it, not that I have had any doubts. He was great in high school and great in college. It's amazing.

"I talked to him yesterday (Thursday). Everyone is expecting him to go out and get 30 every night. He is a little disappointed he's not getting as many minutes as he would like. He'd like to play all the time and this could be a problem because he doesn't like to sit. He loves to play."

Larry followed brothers Mike (28) and Mark (25) and sister Linda (24) and then came brothers Jeff (15) and Eddie (12).

"Mike and Mark were both good. But in a small town you go more by name than talent. Mike was a student manager his junior year and played football as a senior. Mark was the leading scorer (in basketball) and then played at Oakland City. Linda would have been a great high school basketball player because of her height. She played volleyball and now is a great softball player in Chicago."

Mrs. Bird admits Larry's success has caused some problems for the younger boys, both of whom play football.

"I have to be careful not to compare them with Larry," she related. "Everyone around does it. A teacher, because of the money problem, lashed out at Jeff about a $90 jacket. He said that was Larry's money, not ours.

"It's like Larry said, money isn't everything. Larry hasn't bought any new clothes. He's a very tight person with money. He's going to see what we need.

He definitely has taken care of mom and the boys."

Asked if she had any particular favorite memory about Larry, she gave the typical motherly answer. It had nothing to do with basketball.

"I'll tell you, he loved to keep the house clean," she replied. "He always wanted his clothes, everything clean. He always helped out. The other boys worked while they were in high school, but he didn't."

Sports writers complained during his years at Indiana State about his refusal to talk. Mrs. Bird says she's experiencing the same thing.

"He was more outgoing when he was younger," she said. "Now he hardly tells me anything.

"I've never figured him out. For such a shy person, it has been hard. I think all of this was thrown on him and he wasn't ready. He was not as grown up as his body showed." ■

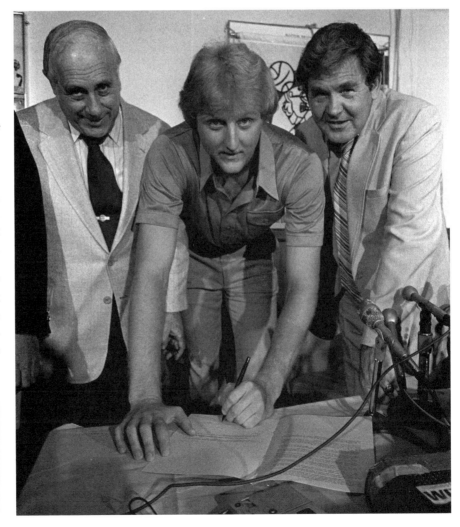

Larry Bird became the richest rookie in sports history at $3.25 million for five years after signing a contract with the Boston Celtics. (AP/Wide World Photos)

Bird Simply Shocking In First Season In NBA

November 29, 1979

BY DAVE OVERPECK

Nobody plays $650,000 worth of basketball in a year, right? Wrong. The Boston Celtics are paying Larry Bird that much this year and for four more. He figures to be worth every dime of it—at least as much for the rest of the National Basketball Association as for the Celtics.

And he's more than paying his way for the Celtics.

A year ago, Boston had 4,500 season ticket holders—and 1,000 of them cancelled after the Celts finished 29-53 last year. This year there are 6,000 season ticket holders—including 500 who made their purchase after the start of the season.

For their first nine games, the Celts had nine sellouts. The average attendance has been 13,850, an increase of 3,896 over last year. Since the average ticket price at Boston Garden is in the $7.50 range, revenue is up in the neighborhood of $250,000 — with more than 75 per cent of the schedule to go.

So if the trend continues, the Celtics will more than recover Bird's salary in increased gate trade.

Of course, Bird isn't the only reason for Boston's resurgence at the gate. But he is a big part of it, because he is a big reason why the Celtics are winning.

So is M.L. Carr, who has filled the void as the Celtics' legendary sixth man. And Bill Fitch unquestionably provides a needed fresh breath as head coach. Dave Cowens and Tiny Archibald are playing like All-Pros again.

So there really is no way of measuring how much Bird, by himself, has increased Boston attendance.

But you can take measurements when the Celtics hit the road. You can compare how many fans turn out for Boston versus the average attendance.

So far the Celts have played 10 times on the road in nine cities. Each Celtic game has drawn more than the host club's average. Four have been sellouts—including October 20 in Market Square Arena, where Bird and Boston pay their second call Saturday night.

The average for the 10 road games has been 14,688, versus 9,755 overall. That doesn't help the Celts' exchequer a bit—there is no gate sharing in the NBA.

The biggest winner has been Cleveland where 15,443 showed up for the Celtics and the 11-game average is 6,366.

The figures for the other games:

City	Ave.	Celts
Indianapolis	10,555	16,973*
San Antonio	11,664	12,893
Houston	9,410	11,635
Atlanta	9,749	15,451*
New Jersey	5,491	7,012
Washington	10,996	17,635
Philadelphia	11,687	18,276*
New York	11,876	19,951*
* —Sellouts.		

Again, the argument can be advanced that it is a super team that is drawing in the fans, not a super player.

And it can be answered by comparing the drawing power of the Celtics and the Philadelphia 76ers, the NBA's best-drawing road show for the last three seasons. Thus far the Celts and 76ers have played seven

Bird (right), and Celtics teammate Rick Roby arrive at the airport on their way to play the Indiana Pacers at ISU in Terre Haute. (Bob Doeppers)

cities; only once has Philly outdrawn Boston. That was at Washington when a sellout 19,035 turned out for opening night.

So it's hard to argue with Cowens when he says, "He (Bird) is good for the team and the league. I'm sure his presence is why we're drawing."

And there remains to be measured the impact Bird will have on the NBA's Nielsen ratings. It's no secret that weekly CBS telecasts have taken a dive out there in TV land the last couple years. And it's no secret that the prospect of losing all those TV dollars is causing acid indigestion in a league where half or more of the clubs would have to shut the door without that ancillary income.

Both the NBA and CBS are counting upon Bird (and Los Angeles' Magic Johnson) to give those ratings a shot in the arm. So far the network has carried just one game (Johnson and the Lakers against San Diego opening night) and won't get into its regular weekly presentations until after the first of the year.

Not until then will it be known if Bird can do for TV ratings what he has done for the box office.

Meanwhile, the pride of French Lick and Indiana State is pleased with his performance to date and is drawing rave reviews from his peers.

Both satisfaction and adulation are merited. Bird leads the Celtics in scoring (19.1), rebounding (10.0) and steals (1.9) and is second in assists (4.5).

"I'm doing okay as a rookie," Bird told the Associated Press this week, "although I don't consider myself a rookie. Even if I miss shots, that's okay. I know I'll do better next time.

"I came into the league with a good attitude. I'm confident. I always was. I worked hard to get here and worked hard all my life to play pro ball, to show the world and the fans I can do it. In the first practice, I knew I was good. I got my confidence in training camp."

About the only problem Bird has encountered has come from the fans, not the play of the pro game.

"I think basketball is the easy part," he said. "But the public feels you gotta do so much. The smart alecks think you should sign autographs all day. The thing that hassles me is I can't go into public places. People hound me for autographs when I eat. In college you were left alone, but here..."

The praise from others sounds like a replay of his college days.

"He shoots, he rebounds, he passes, but the thing I like most about him is the way he goes about his business without complaining," says Red Auerbach. "He's the first to arrive at practice and the last to leave. But

In his first year as a Celtic, rookie Larry Bird drew sellout crowds to Boston Garden. (Jeff Atteberry)

even I didn't think he'd be this good this soon."

Says Fitch, "He's the best rookie I've ever seen. Larry likes the game. That's what makes it so much fun. Even our practices are fun."

Assistant Coach K.C. Jones: "I like his bearing, the way he does his passing. A lot of players pass cautiously, too cautiously, but he's aggressive. Oh, yes, he's aggressive. Bird will get floor burns. You don't see superstars getting floor burns; a superstar figures that's not his role. But Bird has the right attitude. That's the difference."

Cowens: "He's a mix of Rick Barry and Dave DeBusschere. He moves well, he's got good hands, he shoots well from outside, he's smart and he rebounds well."

Perhaps the highest praise comes from outside the Celtics camp, though. Says New York Knicks Coach Red Holzman, "He sees everything you're supposed to see out there and makes every pass you're supposed to make. I'm not saying that out of all the years, he's the greatest player, but nobody ever came into this league and played with poise like that.

"Nobody ever understood like he does." ▪

Bird's 2nd Chance Is A Winner

February 4, 1980

BY DICK MITTMAN

Larry Bird, the blond basketball legend from French Lick, Indiana, slammed his fist into his palm in disgust. He had missed the shot that would have won the first professional All-Star Game he had appeared in.

Because he was a rookie, he might not get a chance in the overtime. National Basketball Association coaches tend to lean toward proven veterans when the game can be won or lost in an extra five minutes of play.

But East coach Billy Cunningham stuck with the Boston Celtic rookie and it paid off yesterday in a 144-136 victory by the East over the West in the 30th annual NBA All-Star Game in Washington's Capital Centre.

With the score tied at 134, Bird got the ball in the left corner. He raised up and drilled a 20-footer that gave the East a two-point lead only to have his rookie counterpart from last year's NCAA Finals, Earvin "Magic" Johnson, tie the score with a driving jump shot.

Down the court came the East and over into the corner went Bird. The pass was to him as the West's Jack Sikma collapsed on menacing Moses Malone, who for the past few minutes had been dominating Kareem Abdul-Jabbar. Bird hesitated, checked his feet to see he was behind the three-point line and then rocketed the ball goalward.

The ball swished through the nets as gently as Pampers are on a baby's bottom. That was the game right there. But before the final buzzer sounded he completed his brilliant play that earned him five Most Valuable Player votes with an unbelievable tip pass on a rebound to George Gervin for the last of the "Ice Man's" 34 points (he was the MVP).

"I was glad he (Cunningham) gave me the opportunity to shoot and hit a couple of shots," said last year's college player of the year from Indiana State. "After I missed that shot I wanted to play."

Bird was the last of the 11 East players to enter the game, getting Cunningham's initial call at 10:21 of the second period. He came onto the floor to a chorus of cheers and a minute later Dancing Harry was on the sidelines doing his thing.

Larry gave one demonstration of his considerable ability when he executed a slick pass on the fast break to Gervin and slammed the ball home when "Ice" missed.

But from that point on until the closing minute of regulation time he wasn't a factor in the game. In fact, once he stepped back to fire a three and plopped his green Celtics sneakers into out-of-bounds territory.

But Cunningham had faith in him. With the score tied in the final minute, the coach of the Philadelphia 76ers inserted Bird not for his shooting but for his passing. He immediately made a nice bounce pass to Malone for the go-ahead bucket that lasted only until Phoenix's Paul Westphal could get down the floor and pump up a jumper.

"I put Larry in because he is a better passer than Elvin (Hayes) in that situation," explained Cunningham. "I knew Larry would show good judgment and he did show his poise by hitting Moses.

"He's just a great basketball player and there's not much more you can say about Larry Bird." ■

All-Star Rookies

BY DICK MITTMAN

January 29, 1980—Rookies in the All-Star Game are rare so it is really unusual that two, Earvin "Magic" Johnson and Larry Bird, have made it this year. Johnson becomes the first rookie starter (for the Western Conference) since Elvin "Big E" Hayes in 1969.

Johnson and Bird have been hyped by television ever since their teams, Michigan State and Indiana State, headed for the NCAA showdown last year. But the two newcomers made the All-Star teams on their credentials and not on a television buildup. Both are starters and have their teams heading toward a possible showdown for the NBA championship next May.

In recent seasons the only rookies to make the team were Walter Davis and Alvan Adams of Phoenix.

Bird, incidentally, has not forgotten his friends at Indiana State. He recently sent athletic director Bob King a gross of golf balls. King had the "audacity" several years ago to announce he had a player, Bird, who was better than Indiana's Kent Benson.

"And he is, isn't he?" King said with a grin the other day.

Bird Looks For A Better Year

October 1, 1980

BY DICK MITTMAN

Larry Bird is looking to have a "better year."

That information should send shudders down the spines of 22 National Basketball Association coaches. Combining scoring average, rebounds, and assists, the self-styled "hick from French Lick" recorded the third best rookie record since Kareem Abdul-Jabbar entered the league a decade before him.

But even more important, he helped turn a 29-53 team and the second worst record in the NBA into a 61-21 mark and the best record. That's a turn-around of 32 games.

Bird averaged 21.3 points, grabbed 852 rebounds and passed for 370 other baskets. Those are the concrete things he did that are written down in the statistics. What can't be measured are the intangible contributions such as enthusiasm that revitalized the sagging Celtics.

"You always look forward to coming back and doing better than you did the year before," said Bird Monday night before the Celtics played the Indiana Pacers in an exhibition game at Market Square Arena.

"I learned a lot that hopefully I can put to use this year. Going around the league, I learned a lot of stuff, you know, as far as playing against players, going and staying on the road for a couple of weeks and getting home and playing at home.

"I learned the whole system. Now if I can go out and maintain a good position on the club, play hard, then, hopefully, with the stuff I did learn I can have a better year."

Bird was suffering with a cold Monday, but still played 40 minutes. Coach Bill Fitch would like to let him sit out a game, but will have him in the lineup tonight in Evansville when the Celtics meet the Chicago Bulls and again Friday night when they play the New York Knicks in Bird's old home arena, the Hulman Center in Terre Haute.

The blond Indiana State graduate said the loss to the Philadelphia 76ers in the Eastern Division playoffs gives the team and him continued incentive to improve.

"I was no more tired than anybody else in the league," he said. "If you play 82 regular season games and all the exhibition games and all the travel, sure you're going to be a little bit tired.

"That's when it gets down to the nitty-gritty when you have to go out and play hard to win what you're going after. We felt we had a great club last year, but it wasn't good enough to beat Philadelphia in the series so maybe this year we've got the backup front line (with the addition of Kevin McHale and Robert Parish) to do it with.

"All we've got to do now is play hard and hope we get in the same position we were in last year," he added.

However, at the moment the Celtics are fighting a problem at guard. Nate "Tiny" Archibald continues to hold out and no other Boston back court player is able to assume his point guard role. Fitch says he is in the market, and started practice yesterday with the idea Archibald would not be a part of the team.

"Hopefully, we can get Tiny back," said Bird. "If he doesn't come back, we've got to go with what we've got. We've got some great players on this club and it's just going to take a little bit longer to put together.

"The guys already know the roles on this team, so we just have to go out and produce and win some games."

Bird spent most of the summer relaxing at his French Lick home, visiting with friends. Although he was anxious to get back playing, he said he just didn't feel in the mood to play for the NBA team against the U.S. Olympic team at MSA last June.

"Anytime you're out of shape you really don't feel you can go out there and prove anything," he explained of his absence.

"I had nothing to prove against those guys. If I was in college I'd love to play against the pro guys, but I really didn't have nothing to prove to go out there out of shape and, you know, make myself look bad."

Larry Bird celebrates his first NBA championship in 1981 with the legendary Red Auerbach. The Celtics defeated Houston 4-2 in the Championship Series. (Frank O'Brien, Boston Globe Photo)

Larry Bird comes home, so do fans as former ISU star draws faithful

December 2, 1981

BY DAVID BENNER

A week and a half ago, The Chicken and the Kansas City Kings drew 5,969 fans to Market Square Arena. Tuesday night, The Bird and the Boston Celtics drew 12,634 to MSA.

Which just goes to prove Indiana fans still prefer a basketball player, especially when it's Larry Bird.

From the introduction of the native Hoosier, which drew a loud ovation from the patrons before the game, to his final three-point fling at the buzzer, the 6-9 Bird was the center attraction.

"I know I'm a draw here," the former Indiana State star said. "Fans realize I have a talent that they like. I play the way they like. A lot of my friends come to see me play and I get a lot of fan mail from people in the Indianapolis area. There are people out there who know me personally that have never met me, because they've seen me play so many times."

When he comes to Indianapolis, the distractions can add up with the friends calling, the media asking for time, countless autographs and favors. But he handles it well and is very polite with nearly every request.

"I like coming here, I look forward to it, but sometimes it can be tough to play here with the demands," he said. "Plus, the Pacers always play us hard. They want to show the fans they have a good club, too. This is one of the toughest games of the year."

That was proven Tuesday night, as the defending World Champions lost 90-87. But Bird still did his share, despite being hobbled by a sore ankle, scoring 16 points, (8-of-18 shooting), grabbing 11 rebounds and handing out three assists.

It is the all-around game—passing, shooting, defense, moving without the ball, rebounding—that is Larry Bird. He proves it night after night.

"I may be one of the best all-around players, but I'm not great at anything," Bird said. "I definitely have weaknesses. I turn the ball over a lot (in fact, Tuesday night he had eight errors). I don't always play good defense, things like that. I just try to be a consistent player."

One thing Bird avoids is comparisons and by being a member of the Celtics, there are many. Is he as good a passer as Cousy? Can he dominate a game like Russell? Can he turn around a game with his presence like Havlicek did? Is he as complete a player as Havlicek?

"I don't like to get into that," Bird said. "It's very gratifying to be compared to people like that, but people realize how I have my own style of play."

"I know one thing, he's a much better passer than I

Bird autographs a ball for a fan after ceremonies honoring him as the first recipient of the Hoosier Pride Award at the Claypool Court in Indiana. (John Warner)

(Indianapolis Star/News Photo)

"I know one thing, he's a much better passer than I was," said John Havlicek, who was doing color commentary for the Celtics Tuesday night. "He's an excellent passer. As for comparison, Larry and I have some of the same characteristics as far as getting the team involved.

"I do know he's definitely a guy you would pay to see."

Mainly because Bird looks at his profession realistically.

"It's a business, a big-money business," he said, "but it's also an entertainment. We're entertainers who are constantly in the public eye. Most importantly, we have to set a good example for kids, they are the main concern."

Bird admits that life in the NBA can be tough, a difficult transition from college.

"It's a long, long season, but that's part of the league," he says. "Everybody's got to do it. It's not like college where you play one or two games a week and have a chance to rest up a little bit. Sometimes you have to be ready to go the next night. It's tough to go out there and play every game well.

"But this has been fun for me."

And not too full of disappointment.

"The first year we lost to Philly, no excuses, they just beat us," he said. "Last year, we knew we had a championship caliber team and we proved it. The only disappointment is when we lose. A loss stays with me until the next game and makes me want to win all that much more. I hate to lose."

He's in the right place. The Celtics have that tradition of not losing very many and as long as Bird is in the Celtic green, it's doubtful they will. ■

Bird Keys East Stars Past West

February 1, 1982

BY DICK MITTMAN

Comedian Nipsy Russell's little poetic routine at the National Basketball Association banquet ended humorously. "And Larry Bird, why aren't you black?"

Russell was telling the audience that in a game dominated by black players this white dude from the hills of southern Indiana had become one of the most forceful performers in the NBA today. Nothing racial was intended, but instead it was meant as a tribute to Bird's many talents.

Yesterday after Bird had won the most valuable player award as the East nipped the West, 120-118, the players and coaches were talking about him being maybe one of the greatest—black or white—to ever play the game.

"I think he is one of the greatest," agreed teammate Robert Parish, whose 21 points and 10 rebounds certainly made him a candidate for the award that had been captured by black players the last eight years and 12 of the last 14.

The third-year pro from French Lick, Indiana so took charge of the game in the last six minutes that he stole away media MVP votes that were headed for Parish or the West's Gus Williams (22 points, nine assists).

East coach Bill Fitch called on his Boston Celtic star with 6:48 left in the game and the East leading by four. At that point, the Indiana State graduate, whose Celtics visit Market Square Arena tomorrow night to play the Pacers, had scored only seven points and sat on the bench for a goodly portion of the second half.

Bird immediately drilled a jumper from the side. He plunked a pair of free throws (after missing three in a row in the first half), then swished a falling backwards shot from above the key. He then hit another from there. A 10-footer fell and his last two free throws provided the winning margin.

But that wasn't all. In the final minute Speedy Norm Nixon got loose on a break, but Bird bothered him enough that his attempt at a tying lay-in rolled off the rim. Bird, of course, snatched the rebound.

"The best part about Larry Bird, " said Fitch later, "is that he would not have said a thing if I had not put him back in. He runs away from mistakes. He doesn't stand around and let mistakes get him down."

Fitch was asked if he saw any change in Bird since his arrival from Hoosierland.

"The first two years, Larry was the first to practice," replied Fitch, who got a victory in his first All-Star coaching experience.

"I've been waiting for the NBA syndrome (where a star expects to be pampered). The only thing now is he occasionally doesn't have a good practice.

"He needs a pick and four other people who play the same way. He is not a one-on-one player. He doesn't have to score to help you. He can set a pick or decoy. I don't think anybody is better. I can't say he is better than Doc (Julius Erving) or some of the players in the past. But I don't think you can get a majority to say there is anybody better."

West coach Pat Riley expressed the same sentiments.

"I want to compliment Larry Bird for his efforts," said Riley. "It doesn't seem to matter what the game is, a pick-up game, a regular season or World Championship game, he always plays with the same consistency."

Bird, as usual, was humble, passing out kudos to his teammates.

"I loved to see Robert (Parish) and Tiny (Archibald) on the court," he said. "A couple of times we ran the play we ran for the Celtics.

"When it goes down to the wire I want my team to get me the ball. It was the same today. I wanted back in. When I came back in I was ready to play basketball."

Rookie Isiah Thomas, who led Indiana to the NCAA championship last season, started for the East and scored 12 points and dished out four assists in 17 minutes before twisting an ankle that kept him on the sideline most of the second half.

"I didn't feel nervous," said the 20-year-old Isiah. "These guys made it very easy to play with them. I wish I had all these guys on my team."

Another rookie with Indiana connections, Kelly Tripucka, played 15 minutes and scored six points. ■

Bird won the MVP award as the East beat the West, 120-118, in the 1982 NBA All-Star game. (Rich Miller)

Bird Yearns For Hoosier Home

March 29, 1983

BY DICK MITTMAN

Larry Bird is in the tailend of the fourth year of a marvelous professional basketball career and he says, "Sometimes I wonder if I like it (basketball) as much as I did the year before."

But don't get the idea this means you won't see him playing his posterior off tonight when his Boston Celtics meet the Indiana Pacers at Market Square Arena.

"I think everybody gets tired of the season sometimes, living out of a suitcase and traveling," explained Bird, who is averaging 23.3 points and 11.2 rebounds for 70 games. "But when gametime comes I think it is a good game for me.

"As a whole, I still love to play in front of the fans, go out and put on a good show and I love to win. Because we're losing more this year than we ever have (48-22 to Philly's 59-11) makes no difference as far as liking it or not. At times it's tough on me. I hate to play when I'm injured.

"I hate to play with nagging injuries to my foot, my toe or my hand. I feel like I can't give 100 percent. I pulled a tendon in my foot one time and it was really impossible for me to run, but somehow I got out there and struggled for 25 minutes. One time I had an infected toe and it bothered me for a long time. It's something you can tolerate."

Bird, a small-town boy from French Lick, Indiana, has been living in Boston for four winters now, but he still maintains his low key lifestyle. He prefers hunting and fishing and says when he retires he'll probably make Indianapolis his home.

"If you want to make a big thing out of it, you can," he said about living in a metropolis. "I think everybody going to the big city thinks of all the limelight, all the people, all the things to do. That's fine if you want to do those things.

"Because I'm in a big city doesn't mean I love to do those things. I like to stay on my own, be private and do the things I've always done. I don't want to go out of my way to do anything else, because I really don't get an interest out of going to plays, doing things, sightseeing, things like that.

Bird pointed out that there are many ponds and lakes in the Boston area plus the ocean. He says he prefers to fish in private waters and plans "to catch a few" before returning home to Indiana after the season is finished.

He is having a new home built in French Lick but indicated his mother probably will live in it.

"I think when I retire and settle down," he said, "I'll be living in Indianapolis. A small town is great and Indianapolis is not a city, a big city, to me. It's very small and very pleasant.

"I don't think I'll be staying in Boston the rest of my life. I think Indianapolis has got more to offer to me than, say, something like French Lick."

Something that is much closer to the present is the threatened strike of the NBA players set for Saturday if something between the owners and the Players Association isn't worked out this week. The two sides resumed talking today.

Bird notes the prospect of a strike has played mentally on the minds of the Celtics.

"We're used to being first," he explained, "we're losing some games, we're not playing up to our potential and all of a sudden there's a strike.

"It's very tough because all of a sudden they're saying we might not be playing basketball for the rest of the year. And the playoffs are the most fun of the whole season. We're not going to be making any money and we're not going to be playing basketball, so we lose both ways."

Bird shares a laugh with longtime fan and former French Lick neighbor Mildred Quinn. (Charles A. Berry)

Pacers fans thought it was too good to be true when this picture appeared in the morning paper in 1984. And it was. Unfortunately, Bird was only borrowing the Pacers jersey for an impromptu workout at the Pacers' summer camp in Market Square Arena. (Jerry Clark)

Bird scores 53, Celts crush Pacers

March 31, 1983

SPECIAL CORRESPONDENT

The Indiana Pacers were crushed by the Boston Celtics, 142-116, before the 109th sellout crowd at Boston Garden Wednesday night.

The story of the game can be explained in two words: Larry Bird. The All-Star forward from Indiana State broke his career-high as well as the Celtics' individual all-time scoring game record by tallying 53 points. The previous record was 51 points by Sam Jones (against Detroit, October 29, 1965).

In only 33 minutes, Bird hit 21-of-30 shots, adding 11 straight shots from the charity stripe.

Bird wasn't trying to break the record, it just happened. After the game, he said, "I really didn't know how many points I had until Coach (Bill) Fitch told me I needed five more to break the record."

Break the record he did as the crowd went wild. Pacer Coach Jack McKinney said, "Bird's performance was simply awesome. We threw a lot of different things in his way to try and slow him down but nothing worked."

If the Pacers expected a repeat of Tuesday night, when the Pacers trounced the Celtics, 130-101, they were in for a quick disappointment. In the first quarter, the Celtics came out playing strong, aggressive basketball and led, 37-16, at the end of the period.

Bird was controlling the game, scoring 18 points and grabbing four rebounds in the first 12 minutes. Indiana responded with poor 26 percent shooting from the floor. The Pacers looked flat, grabbing only nine rebounds to Boston's 17.

Clark Kellogg, who scored 29 points Tuesday night, was held scoreless in the first half, missing four shots and grabbing only one rebound. Billy Knight and Herb Williams carried the Pacer scoring attack with 12 and 10 first half points, respectively.

The Pacers looked better in the second half, bringing their shooting percentage up to 54 percent, but it simply wasn't enough as Bird kept pouring in baskets. Knight, the veteran Pacer backcourt ace, kept the game respectable, scoring 25 points, but it just wasn't enough.

McKinney was not pleased with the officiating. Midway of the third quarter, he drew a technical foul from referee Bill Saar. He had been complaining about calls most of the game and Saar quieted his complaints with a technical.

The Pacers finished with a poor 43 percent shooting from the field and were outrebounded, 53-39. McKinney said that the fact that the Celtics flew home and practiced Wednesday tipped him off that his team might be in trouble.

At 19-54 on the season, the Pacers have little to look forward to, except perhaps 7-4 Ralph Sampson. Cleveland won Tuesday night, so they are again tied for last place in the Eastern Conference. ■

Bird broke the Celtics single-game scoring record with 53 points against the Pacers in 1983. (D. Todd Moore)

Mom Likes Pact

BY DICK MITTMAN

September 28, 1983—"It makes chills go down my back."

That's how Georgia Bird today described the $15 million contract her son, Larry, has agreed to with the Boston Celtics.

"That's a lot of money," said Mrs. Bird, contacted at her home outside French Lick. "I can't understand that much money. But like Larry says, it's there so why not get it?

"I think he's worth every bit of it. He's still my little boy and he'll never change. I never thought about him getting money like that (when he was younger) because I was wondering where the next meal was coming from."

When Larry was growing up with four brothers and a sister, Mrs. Bird worked as a waitress and cleaner to help support the family. Since Larry signed with the Celtics, he has built his mother a home on the "Grandma Bird land" outside French Lick.

"I worked a lot and, really, those were the happiest days of my life," said Mrs. Bird.

Larry worked, too, on a sanitation truck (he drove it) and for the gas company in French Lick after he quit Indiana University and before he enrolled at Indiana State. She said he worked two jobs while attending ISU.

"That was a good job, it paid good money," said Mrs. Bird of his sanitation truck duties.

Mom Georgia Bird watches her son with pride. (Charles A. Berry)

"When he went to I.U., he had nothin'. He didn't have any clothes. He shouldn't have went there in the first place. I know, because he told me that. I think Bobby Knight would have changed his style and he would have sat on the bench. Larry doesn't like to sit on the bench."

Larry has helped his family, particularly his mother, in many ways, but Mrs. Bird said her son prefers to keep that private.

"I'm still just me," she said. "I don't go out and buy expensive clothes. I'm kinda country."

Youngest son Eddie now is a sophomore at Springs Valley High School on 101 Larry Bird Blvd. and plays basketball. Jeff played high school ball when Larry first signed with Boston.

"At first it was terrible," Mrs. Bird said of the fan treatment of the younger Birds. "Even now when Eddie gets a foul called on him, the crowd cheers because he is a Bird.

"He's pretty good, but I don't think he'll be another Larry Bird. We don't need another one."

Mrs. Bird pointed out her son will be playing against the Indiana Pacers in Market Square Arena on his 27th birthday, December 7.

"I think he was built to be a Celtic," she said, although she admitted, "I would have loved to have seen him as an Indiana Pacer. He loves Indianapolis."

Unflappable Bird still improving

November 8, 1983

BY DAVID BENNER

He stands on the floor at Boston Garden, two hours before game time, and moves in a 15- to 20-foot perimeter around the basket. Jump shot after jump shot, basket after basket, the concentration of Larry Bird never wavers.

"It's something I like to do before a game, especially if we didn't play the night before," Bird relates a short time later. "You can always improve your shooting."

He moves on the floor of Boston Garden now, the game having started with Bird very much in it. Jump shot after jump shot, basket after basket. Only now there are teammates and opposition involved, so Bird—like an Olympic decathlete who's well-versed in everything— is hustling on defense, passing out assists and rebounding as if that's all he's supposed to do.

Jump shot after jump shot, basket after basket, the concentration of Larry Bird never wavers.

"If you work hard on all phases of the game a little bit, you're bound to get better on each one," Bird says. "It just takes a little more time. It's very hard to just work on one phase of my game because I want to be a consistent player."

He sits by the floor of Boston Garden a short time later, watching the game in front of him intently. The eyes never stray from the play, the face never breaks into a smile or a frown. Nothing but concentration and intensity, except for encouragement given to his mates on the floor.

"You've got to watch different things, even when you're on the bench," Bird says. "Those things come from watching your own team and the opposition, then you have to use them to your advantage."

Last summer, Larry Bird became a very rich man when he re-signed with the Boston Celtics, a year before he was to be eligible for free agency. The contract was hefty—"People around here think it was for $15 million (over seven years)," he says with a laugh. "I won't tell you how much it was worth, but it was a lot less than $15 million"—and will ensure Bird ends his career in Boston.

That's no real surprise considering his vast talents, which he has displayed the last four seasons in the National Basketball Association and will display again tonight in Market Square Arena when the Celtics meet the Indiana Pacers.

What is surprising is that in this day of holdouts, guaranteed salaries, cocaine and a general I-don't-care-I'll-get-them-tomorrow-night attitude in professional sports, there are some athletes who will take the extra step or steps.

Larry Bird is one of those. That's why he is out there two hours before game time. That's why he is early for practice and then tries to learn everything off it.

"The Boston Celtics took care of me for my life, so why should I come in here, sit back and say. 'Hey, look, I'm going to sucker-punch you guys. I'm secure, pay me. I'm going to lay back.'" Bird says.

"That's not what fans pay $15, $20 a seat for. They pay their money to see a guy come out here and play basketball. If you're not shooting or playing real well, they want to see you give 100 percent. That has always been my philosophy and I can't see myself changing now."

That philosophy originated in French Lick, Indiana, and was fostered at Springs Valley High School and Indiana State University. First an Indiana All-Star, then college player of the year, now all-pro.

He has been the league's rookie-of-the-year, all-NBA, All-Star Game MVP, second team all-defensive. In his four years, he has averaged 22.3 points per game (49 percent from the floor, 85 percent from the line), more than 10 rebounds per game, more than five assists per game, has been part of one world championship and is now one of the highest paid players in the game.

Sum it up and it condenses into superstar.

"There are so many so-called superstars everywhere, TV, radio, football, baseball," Bird says. "I don't see myself as one, other than the fact when I'm downtown and going around. People come up to me all the time and it gets monotonous because I like my free time like anybody else.

"If you're going to be a superstar, you've got to pay the price because if you go out in public, you're harassed all the time. That's one aspect of it where I don't like to be called a superstar.

"But when I'm on the basketball floor, I love for people to holler and scream for me because that shows me I'm doing my job very well."

Doing his job "very well," that's what keeps Bird going, day after day, night after night through the 82-game grind of the NBA season.

He is not obsessed with winning a championship—"That's a very tough thing to do, a lot harder than people realize," he says. "Only one in 23 wins it and those aren't good odds. The chances are slim and none"—but rather what he can do as an individual to help his team try to win the championship.

In other words, satisfaction must come from within.

"Going out and performing up to my potential every night is the biggest challenge I have," Bird says. "That doesn't mean what I do is for myself, but what I do is to contribute to the team.

"The way I look at it is, anybody in this league can come out and get 30, 40 points and not think a thing about it. But when a guy comes out and gets 25 points, 15 rebounds and 10 assists like Magic Johnson (or Larry Bird), that shows you right there a guy means a lot to his team.

"That's the whole part of the game."

Bird was known for his work ethic and his desire to keep improving as a basketball player. (Charles A. Berry)

Bird's intense focus and thorough preparation set him apart from most other NBA players (John R. Gentry)

Bird Saw Tough Times

December 29, 1983

BY DICK MITTMAN

Larry Bird is the greatest basketball player who almost played for Bob Knight at Indiana University.

He's also the greatest player who drove a garbage truck. And the greatest Indiana All-Star who didn't get to play a whole lot.

The year 1974 became a traumatic one for the blond superstar now of the Boston Celtics.

He was chosen as an Indiana All-Star, but then ran afoul of coach Kirby Overman, who kept him on the bench much of the game against Kentucky. When Overman tried to insert him near the end, Bird refused to go in.

This, however, didn't prevent Knight from recruiting the French Lick, Indiana forward. However, after only two weeks on campus Bird went home. Even today he doesn't know where he was headed at that juncture in his life.

College basketball, or any basketball, wasn't a driving desire at that time.

"The thing that surprised me the most, or bothered me the most, was how my family reacted to my leaving I.U.," he recalls.

"I finally made a decision I didn't want to be there and there was no sense being there, because I wouldn't be able to play basketball up to my potential and I wouldn't be able to go to school like I wanted to.

"And once I quit I.U., with all the negative vibes I got from people, I didn't want anything to do with that situation again."

He took a job driving a garbage truck in his hometown, "making good money," according to his mother. During that period also his life was further disrupted by the death of his father and a broken marriage.

Then-Indiana State coach Bob King and Bill Hodges (both now gone from the university) approached him about enrolling at the Terre Haute school.

"Once they told me I was going to a different atmosphere, a different type of place and they would help me through that adjustment period, I really didn't know what to expect.

"I really didn't know if my life was headed that way, but I was very happy with what I was doing. I was working. I played a little ball, but not much. But once I got back in the groove and got back up there and played against competition, I found out that's what I wanted to do.

"They weren't the only ones trying to recruit me. There was a whole bunch of other ones. It was just a matter of what I wanted to do in life.

"Once I decided to go to school, I decided I might as well make the most of it."

It is nearly a decade later and Bird is one of the premier players in basketball. At 27, he has a new contract valued at nearly $15 million over the next five years.

He owns a home in Boston, next door to his agent, Bob Woolf, but doesn't relish the city life. He still prefers hunting and fishing and playing softball as his favorite pastimes. And he intends to move to Indianapolis when he retires.

Marriage may not be too far in the future, as Bird has had a strong relationship going with a Carmel woman for several years.

"There's no doubt marriage is in my future," he assured.

"I'm very happy I found a person that I want. It's just a matter of getting the thing done. It's not that I don't want to do it, but since I went through a divorce early in my life and it wasn't a good situation, and I finally found the right person—and I've been with her eight years now so I know she's the right person—it's a matter of getting married when we feel like it's the right time.

"It's something I'm looking forward to."

Bird points out that the constant traveling of a professional athlete can be hard on a marriage.

"You've got to understand this is my job," he exclaimed.

"Like I say, you've got to find the right person. A lot of wives can't cope with that. And now that she knows what my life is all about, she expects me to be gone so much. Sometimes it's good for a relationship."

"You're not home for Christmas or your birthday, or you're not home at New Year's at times, but you've got to adjust to that. It'll be tougher when we have kids.

"When kids are growing up, it's very tough on them. Quinn Buckner's kids can't understand why he's leaving, Chris Ford's kids. They always want to know when you're coming back, so it's something I've always looked forward to but it's a tough situation."

Another psychologically tough part of the pro life is the loss of a close friend through a trade. Bird and ex-Pacer Rick Robey were extremely close friends but during the off-season Robey was dealt to Phoenix.

Bird has had to find another intimate chum and it is Buckner, the former I.U. star.

"When I first came into the league, Red (Auerbach, Boston general manager) told me a lot of things to expect in this league," Bird related.

"One thing he told me was when he was coaching that's why he didn't get close to the players' wives, because you never knew when you had to unload somebody. He told me the same thing about players: No matter who you got close to there was the possibility that he might be traded.

"It was very hard for me to adjust to the fact Rick Robey wouldn't be around. We were so close and I re-

Bird pounds the floor in frustration. (John R. Gentry)

spected Rick as a person and a human being, but I realized it was part of the game.

"Quinn has sort of taken his spot. You need people to lean on in this league, because when you're not playing well there are times when you need someone to lean on.

"Quinn went through this adjustment period for a long time and we talked about it. It's very easy to get through something like that if you've got somebody to talk to." ∎

Injuries badger Bird's summer

November 16, 1985

BY DAVID BENNER

Summers for Larry Bird are spent enjoying the good life. Play some golf, play some softball, spend time with friends, have a few beers, shoot a little basketball.

Last summer, however, was different.

Although Bird had an MVP year, although the Boston Celtics were once again in the National Basketball Association finals and although the Celts were improving their roster in the off-season, there was doubt surrounding the former Indiana State star from French Lick. First, it was a sore right elbow, then a sore back.

Normally, there wouldn't be much concern, but as we all know Bird has defied description as normal ever since he picked up a basketball. He's regarded by many as the finest player in the game, playing for one of the most visible teams in sports and his history of injuries has been nothing more than a short story—a broken ankle as a sophomore in high school.

All of a sudden Bird was big news at a time when he's usually no news at all.

"I wasn't worried about it," said Bird, who with the Celtics will meet the Indiana Pacers to-

night in sold out Market Square Arena. "Back in Boston, they were writing in the papers my career was over and all that. It was funny because here I am now still playing the game as hard as I did when I first came in the league. I did everything I could for the Boston fans and press and all of a sudden they're trying to get me to retire."

Of course, Bird was far from retired, but also far from healthy. First the elbow.

"I don't know what's wrong with it, they (the doctors) never did tell me anything," he said. "I've seen a lot of doctors, but they really didn't tell me what they would do. It gets stiff here and there, but it's not as bad as it was last year. Even in the finals. I think it was just tired and sore and stiff from all the needles they were sticking in it. It was the type of injury where they had to go in and drain it and my elbow wasn't used to that. Now it has calmed down, it just gets stiff, and I can work my way through it."

The back problem looked as if it could have been serious. Bird said it started bothering him "a little bit" at the end of last season and finally "it got to the point it was bothering me a lot. I had to quit doing everything."

The problem, Bird said, was a twisted vertebra that

The back problems that eventually ended Bird's career began near the end of the 1984-85 season. (Indianapolis Star/News Photo)

caused pressure on a joint and not back spasms as rumored. "I've never had a back spasm in my life," Bird said.

When Bird arrived for training camp, he was still in pain and his preseason playing time was limited. He made a brief appearance here in an exhibition game, but the next day flew back to Boston for therapy and after a week with the therapist, the pain began to subside.

Now, Bird says, "I'm 100 percent because when I'm playing I don't even think of the back pain. I play the same way I always did." Which is always hard and almost always well. A perennial All-Star, Bird enters tonight's game averaging 21 points a game and just un-

der 10 rebounds, numbers under the norm, for him. But it's all by design and by acquisition.

"I'm not going to score as much this year because last year I thought I hurt the team," he said. "Our guards weren't involved that much and this year I'm trying to keep the ball moving and make the guards take the outside shot because all of our guards can shoot.

"I won't get as many rebounds as I have in the past because we're a much better rebounding team. Bill (Walton) comes in and gets everything."

So, he says look for an increase in assists and turnovers since he'll be handling the ball more. And, no surprise here, also look for the Celtics to contend again. ■

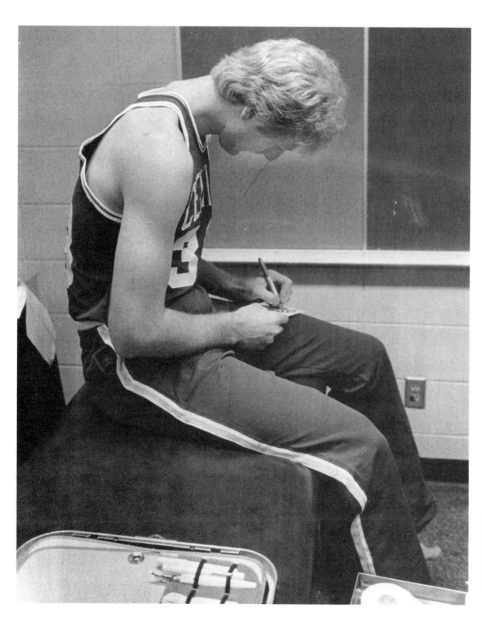

Bird writes a note to himself in the dressing room before a game at Market Square Arena. (Charles A. Berry)

(AP/Wide World Photos)

Despite the early stages of his back problems, Bird led the Celtics to NBA Championships in 1984 (above) and 1986 (right). The Celtics defeated the Lakers in seven games in 1984 and Houston in six games in 1986. Bird was named the MVP of both Championship Series.

(AP/Wide World Photos)

Bird knows need to sit

December 8, 1988

BY DICK MITTMAN

The pain in Larry Bird's ankles was so severe he had no other alternative but surgery.

"It was too much for me to play," Bird said during an interview at Terre Haute.

So for the first time since he was a junior in Springs Valley High School in French Lick, Bird, the Boston Celtics' superstar, is sitting on the sidelines for much of a basketball season.

The three-time National Basketball Association most valuable player underwent surgery to remove bone spurs from his Achilles tendons last month. He probably won't be back in a Celtics uniform until March.

"There's really not much I can do about it," he said.

"I felt there was a need for surgery. I felt that way for a while. Mentally, I can handle things like that because I knew it had to be done.

"I will miss a lot of games and be out a major part of the season, but I feel that's life. I've been very fortunate so far that I haven't had the major injury (an ailing elbow was previously his most serious injury). It's just too bad I had to have it now."

Bird, who observed his 32nd birthday Wednesday, said he had been playing with pain for some time. Last season he averaged 29.9 points, his highest ever, but in the playoffs it dipped to 24.5, lowest in six seasons.

He again won the three-point shootout at the NBA All-Star Game, but scored only six points in the game itself.

Bird started this season and won the MVP award in a preseason exhibition series with three European teams in Spain. He then played six regular-season games, averaging 19.3 points, before making the decision to have surgery performed.

Afterward, he returned home to French Lick to begin his recovery. Twice he appeared at the Hulman Center in Terre Haute to watch his younger brother, Eddie, a sophomore at Indiana State, play.

He sat in the front row of the arena with family members. He walks slowly but without a sign of a limp and wears large brown bag-like slippers around the casts on his ankles.

"I'm doing all right," he said after spending halftime signing autographs. "I'm feeling pretty good right now."

Bird received orders not to grant any interviews because the Boston media was upset with the Celtics that

Bird watches his younger brother Eddie play for Indiana State after undergoing surgery to remove bone spurs from both Achilles' tendons. (Indianapolis Star/News Photo)

he returned home and was not available to discuss his situation. He was to have a news conference in Boston today.

"I just wanted to come home and see Eddie play a couple of games and then get back and get with (the team)," he said.

"I wanted to get home because I hadn't seen my little brother play since high school. I just had a chance to see him one time, so I just think it was an opportunity for me to be able to do that."

Bird said his main objective is to relax and get healthy. He is lifting weights.

"I don't know what to expect," he said. "I can't do anything with my ankles. I'm just sort of laying back, working out as much as possible and I'll take it from there."

Finally, Bird was asked if he had read about the flak of the past week involving Chuck Person and the Pacers. He said he had.

"I'm all for Chuck," he said.

"I think Chuck's a great player. I just think right now he doesn't know what his role is, whether they want him to score or play defense. And I'm sure they want him to do a little bit of everything because that's what he capable of doing.

"If the Pacers are willing to get rid of Chuck, I think he could play on my team any time."

Bird charters road to recovery

June 24, 1989

BY CONRAD BRUNNER

For those who anticipate the demise of the Boston Celtics and their dominant star of the 1980s, Larry Bird has a few words of caution.

"I'll play good. I've had a lot of good dreams over the winter," Bird said. "I don't have no problem with that. I'll be back to normal early next year."

Bird will take a major step back on his road to recovery at 7:30 Sunday night at Market Square Arena in the Larry Bird Pro All-Star Scholarship Classic—commonly known as "Larry's Game"—when he returns to the floor for his first game appearance in roughly seven months.

With Bird out of the lineup for all but six games last season, the Celtics dropped from 57 victories and a berth in the Eastern Conference finals in 1987-88 to 42 victories and first-round playoff elimination.

If Bird is indeed able to return all the way from in-season surgery on both heels, the Celtics could be back, as well.

He has been on a rigorous conditioning schedule that includes running 3 miles a day, swimming and playing basketball for up to 90 minutes.

"If my feet tend to get better, I'll be in tip-top shape when I come back," said Bird. "Now, I'm trying to get my feet adjusted to playing basketball again. Once I get that done, I won't have any problems at all.

"I just have to stay in good shape, and I have to come to training camp in great shape because they're expecting a lot out of me this year."

Bird, who got clearance to play this week from Celtics president Red Auerbach, said he would try to play more than half of Sunday's game.

"I'm going to see how good of shape I'm in and see how sore my feet are going to get after the game," he said. "I can use that as a stepping stone to the rest of the summer. If everything's going fine, I can work harder the rest of the summer."

Though Celtics management originally opposed the idea of Bird playing Sunday night, Auerbach left the final decision with Bird.

"I would never go against their will," said Bird, a former All-American at Indiana State. "I'm sure some of the people in the organization would rather me not play, but I talked to Red...Red said, 'If you feel good, play.' He puts his trust in me to know if it starts hurting, to pull myself out."

Bird will team with Chicago's Michael Jordan and Dallas' Rolando Blackman on the white team. The red team features Detroit's Isiah Thomas, Atlanta's Dominique Wilkins, Cleveland's Ron Harper and the Pacers' Chuck Person.

Proceeds from the game will be used to provide college scholarships.

Left to right: Jack Ramsay, Larry Bird, Mike Woodson, and Magic Johnson enjoy a break after building up a lead in the 1989 Larry's Game, which raised scholarship money for in-state college aspirants. (Mike Fender)

(Mike Fender)

LARRY BIRD STORIES ABOUND, but here's one of the better ones as told by Cleveland Coach George Karl:

"The Larry Bird story I love is (New Jersey forward) Mike O'Koren's. He came into the Garden two hours before the game. He walked in and he goes, 'So, what's all this crap about Larry Bird being out here shooting two hours before the game? I'm here two hours before the game, where's Bird?'

"Just then, an usher said, 'He's already done. 'He's upstairs running laps.'

"Here's one of the highest paid players in the NBA with maybe the best work ethic in the league. That's admirable."

That's also another reason why Bird is voted by players, coaches and media as the best all-around player in the NBA.

World B. Free on Larry Bird: "Only one way to stop him. Kidnap him."

—May 5, 1985, David Benner

Recuperating Bird misses pigeons on the golf course

June 16, 1991

BY ROBIN MILLER

Lying on the couch watching television is not how Larry Bird likes to spend his summer, but it's probably going to make his winter much more enjoyable.

The Bird is currently grounded in Boston, recovering from back surgery on June 7, and he won't be able to fade a 5-iron or shoot a jumper until at least August.

"I'm walking five to seven miles a day, but that's about it," said Bird, who missed 22 games last season for the Boston Celtics and played in constant pain because of his bad back, "I can't sit, I've got to lay down and it makes for a long day.

"I don't know how long it will be until I can run, or play golf, or shoot a basketball, but it might be three months . . . that's how long I'll be in this (back) brace.

"I'm going to see my doctors in a couple of days and I'd like to get back home (French Lick, Indiana) as soon as possible, but I don't know if they (doctors) will let me sit on a plane."

The 34-year-old veteran was plagued by an inflamed bone that's attached to the vertebrae in his back and a swollen disk that put pressure on the nerve. His right leg and foot suffered— along with his game.

"People said back surgery should be a last resort and not to have it," recalled Bird. "All I know is I had pain all last year and I couldn't move very well.

"Right now I feel 100 percent and have no pain whatsoever . . . I feel like running, but I've just got to let that bone heal."

Obviously, the promoters of Larry's Game would like to see No. 33 running up and down the Market Square Arena floor next Sunday, but

that's impossible. Besides Bird, the fourth annual charity game between NBA players will likely be missing Michael Jordan and Magic Johnson.

"Michael told me last year he would be taking the whole month of June off and that was way before the Bulls won the title," said Bird, who hopes to be in attendance anyway. "I don't want to keep pressing him because I understand why he needs a breather.

"I know Magic is also cutting back his off-season

Golf was one of the things Bird missed after his back surgery in June, 1991. (Gary Moore)

schedule, but both of them have been real good to us. It makes it hard to have these games because those two are such big draws, but overall this will probably be the best talent we've ever had."

Bird was asked about the recent Michael/Magic Show in the NBA Finals.

"I didn't see hardly any of it," he replied. "I never watch much basketball. But I did see Michael hit that jumper over (Vlade) Divac to put the (third) game into overtime and I knew then it was over.

"I kind of thought the Lakers would win it all before (James) Worthy hurt his ankle. Without him, they didn't have a chance. But it's always nice to see somebody new win the championship. Michael certainly deserves it."

Even without Mike and Magic, Larry's Game will sport Charles Barkley, Dominique Wilkins, Shawn Kemp, Tim Hardaway, Ron Harper, Danny Manning, Rex Chapman, Kevin Duckworth, Scott Skiles, Ron Anderson and the Pacers' Reggie Miller.

"I'm really impressed with that kid (Miller)," exclaimed Bird. "When he came into the league, some guys thought he was sort of a sissy, or said he'd never be as good as his sister (Cheryl).

"But not only is he a helluva player, he's also one of the classiest kids in the NBA and during the next three or four years he's going to get better and better."

Larry usually spends the summer teeing it up with his buddies at Hulman Links or French Lick or Wolf Run and still hopes to get in some swings.

"Not being able to play golf is costing me a lot of money," he said with a laugh. "But right now I'd be happy just to walk around the course and drink beer." ■

Bird plays golf with friends regularly during the off-season. (Patty Espich)

4

1992

BARCELONA DREAMING

Bird an Olympic co-captain whose goal is 24-karat pure

June 28, 1992

BY BILL BENNER

He has heard the crowd's roar so many times. Back at Springs Valley High School. At Indiana State University.

And finally, with the Boston Celtics, the team he has led to three National Basketball Association championships.

But even Larry Bird, now 35, with so many victories, titles and magic moments behind, had to admit the sound he heard when he entered Portland's Memorial Coliseum Saturday was, well, special.

"It got me pumped up," Bird would say later.

The ovation was in response to the introduction of the U.S. men's Olympic basketball team during opening ceremonies for the Tournament of the Americas.

Bird and his long-time rival and friend, Magic Johnson, led the U.S. team onto the floor. As Team USA moves through this Western Hemispheric qualifying tournament and on to the Barcelona Olympics, Bird and Johnson—the men who have elevated and defined the excellence of professional basketball since 1979—will serve as co-captains.

"It's quite an honor, and to be able to share it with Magic is even more special, because of all we've been through the last 13 years," Bird said. "We finally have an opportunity to play together, and to be co-captains of the team that's supposed to be the best ever assembled."

But then a smile creased his face.

"That's one reason I'm glad I'm 35," he said. "If I wasn't, they probably wouldn't have given me this honor."

There were questions all through last winter and this spring that Bird would make it to this point.

A bad back limited him to just 45 games with the Celtics. It was the third season in the last four the fabled Hick from French Lick was unable to go start to finish.

Injuries and age are exacting their inevitable toll. Larry knows he's nearing the end, and the final chapters in his storybook career are being written.

But, barring an upset of cataclysmic proportion, Bird will bow out with the one significant achievement that appeared to have eluded him: an Olympic gold medal.

His sensational career at Indiana State unfortunately

came between the '76 and '80 Olympics. The U.S. sat out the '80 Olympics, anyway, because of Jimmy Carter's boycott.

So Bird never gave it a thought.

"Coming out of Indiana State, I was so caught up in the NBA game that all I ever thought about was the Boston Celtics and winning NBA championships," Bird said.

But time and circumstances change. The U.S. collegians suddenly were no longer able to win against international competition. Then the International Basketball Federation voted to allow NBA players to participate in the Olympics.

Could any team of the NBA's greatest not include Larry Bird?

The only one to even question it was . . . Larry Bird.

"Once I got the opportunity to play I didn't know how to take it," he said. "I didn't know whether it would be good or bad for me. But once I started thinking about it, I realized it was all positive."

So, Saturday, Larry Bird walked onto the floor as an Olympian. Today, he'll play as one when Team USA opens Tournament of the Americas competition against Cuba.

His back, he said, still bothers him—"I feel young, but my back feels old," he says—but not enough to keep him out of uniform or out of action. The fact that there is so much talent on the team will help, he said, "because I know I won't have to play 40 minutes a game.

"I've just been practicing hard enough to get in shape, to get my skills toned up."

Don't let him kid you. At the team's training camp in LaJolla, Calif., Bird was usually the last to leave at the end of practice.

When the ball goes up, he'll be ready. He figures he has to be—despite predictions the U.S. will roll uncontested to the gold medal.

"I've always taken the stand that on any given day, anything can happen," he said. "The shots don't drop, you get a couple of bad calls, it can go the other way. What we have to do is go out, force the issue, get the ball going, get our running game going. If that happens, I don't think we can get beat."

Larry Bird is all about one thing . . . winning. Always has been.

Michael Jordan says this Olympic experience is like a vacation. He brought his golf clubs.

But not to worry. Bird will bring the hardhat and lunchpail.

"Our ultimate goal is to win the gold medal," Bird said. "That's the reason I'm on this team. Second place means nothing." ■

Members of the U.S. Men's Basketball Team pose with their gold medals at the Barcelona Olympics. (AP/Wide World Photos)

Bird made dreamers the world over

From sandlots to subways, children longed to be him

November 1, 1992

BY BILL BENNER

The names of the boys, ages 11 and 8, were Victor and Ricardo and they were among the dozens of us sardined onto a steamy subway bound for the Barcelona suburb of Badalona.

American journalists covering the summer Olympic Games had nicknamed this particular ride the "subway to hell" because it required one transfer, 18 stops and 45 minutes on a crowded, un-air-conditioned car. It was a sauna on rails.

But to Victor and Ricardo, this was not the subway to hell.

It was the subway to heaven.

Because the ride this night was taking them—and hundreds of others—to see the U.S. men's Olympic basketball team, also known as the Dream Team.

In particular, though, Victor and Ricardo were going to see their all-time basketball hero.

And that was none other than the Hick from French Lick, Indiana, USA.

Larry Bird.

I suppose it was not until then that I fully realized we Hoosiers shared our quintessential Indiana hoopster not just with fans of the Boston Celtics, or of the NBA, but with basketball fans of the world.

"We see NBA games once a week," Victor's and Ricardo's father, Jose, explained to me. "The boys always want to know when the Celtics will be playing, so they can see Larry Bird. When they play basketball against each other, they always argue (over) who gets to be Larry Bird. Usually it is Victor, because he is oldest."

The boys are lucky on this night because their hero comes through. The Dream Team is playing Germany, and it proves to be Bird's finest outing in that USA uniform.

The pain in his aching back has eased. And Bird responds with the kind of game that thrills the Victors and Ricardos of the world.

He scores 19 points in 21 minutes. He hits three 3-pointers. He produces three steals and blocks a couple of shots. He has a pair of deft assists with no-look passes. He crashes to the floor in pursuit of loose balls.

It was one last, long look at the Legend. He would play again, of course, but not as long nor as well.

And when the gold medal finally was draped over his neck, there was a strong feeling that Bird's storied career—from Springs Valley High to Indiana State University to the Celtics to this final golden moment—was over.

A few weeks later, he confirmed the suspicion by announcing his retirement.

There couldn't have been a more fitting farewell for Larry Joe Bird than the Olympic experience.

True, he did not have to be the kind of player he had always been—the player who had transformed an average college team into a great one, or the player who had taken good Celtic teams and led them to championships.

But from the first day the Dream Team reported to training camp in LaJolla, California, Bird and Magic Johnson—Bird's alter ego in basketball—were the undisputed leaders of this all-galactic lineup.

And while many of the Dreamers packed their golf clubs and treated the Olympics as a vacation, Bird brought his hard hat and follow-me-boys work ethic. Typically, when the U.S. team practiced, he was the first player to arrive and the last to leave.

Even for a team so incredibly skilled and talented as this one, someone still had to set an example. It came from Bird and Johnson.

Another Bird story, and this one goes back to the beginning of his career, not the end. It was 1974 and Bird was a member of the Indiana All-Star team playing Kentucky in Hinkle Fieldhouse. Kirby Overman, coach of that team, played Bird sparingly. But with the victory safely in hand late in the second half, Overman motioned for Bird to go into the game.

Bird motioned back. Let someone else do the mopping up . . . he was staying put.

Afterward, I tried to ask Bird about his refusal to play, but he refused questions and departed the fieldhouse in tears.

I thought to myself, who does this kid think he is?

But obviously, he had a far better idea than any of the rest of us.

Bird was bound for Indiana University that fall, but didn't last long, and we've all pondered the possibilities of Bird playing for Bob Knight.

It was left for a persuasive, persistent assistant coach from Indiana State, Bill Hodges—a plain-talking, down-home guy Larry could relate to—to talk Bird off his garbage-truck route and back onto the road to one of the great careers of all time.

It finally came to an end, half a world away in Spain, in front of youngsters like Victor and Ricardo who related to Larry Bird in the same way Indiana kids did.

What he brought to basketball was universal. It needed no translation.

After the gold medal ceremony in Barcelona, a reporter asked Bird, "Will there ever be another Dream Team?"

"Nope," he replied with a smile, "because I won't be on it."

Truer words have never been spoken . . . even if he did speak them himself. ∎

Larry Bird jokes with teammates on the bench as the Dream Team crushes Cuba, 136-57 at the Tournament of the Americas, a tune-up for the Barcelona Olympics. (Jack Smith, AP/Wide World Photos)

ISC eyeing dream game for Larry

November 1, 1992

BY BILL BENNER

Everyone knew the U.S. Olympic men's basketball team—the Dream Team—would be absolutely nightmarish for foreign competition in last summer's Barcelona Games.

While several of the foreign teams had a couple of players who could hold their own—sort of—against the Americans' all-galactic lineup, none could hope to come close to competing against a team of such overwhelming depth and skill.

But as the U.S. steamrolled to its inevitable gold medal triumph, minds tended to wander . . . and wonder.

What if the Dream Team was matched against the best of the rest . . . an international all-star team?

What if the Dream Team had to play against a lineup that, say, had Yugoslavia's Vlade Divac at center, Germany's Detlef Schrempf and Brazil's Oscar Schmidt at the forwards, and Lith-uania's Sarunas Marciulionis and Croatia's Drazen Petrovic at the guards . . . with Croatia's Toni Kukoc as a super-sub.

Well, it could happen . . . emphasis on the word could.

A well-placed source—who asked me not to name names—within the Indiana Sports Corporation says the organization hopes to re-unite the Dream Team for an on-court farewell tribute to Hoosier and Boston Celtic legend Larry Bird.

The plans, still in the formative stages and pending approval and co-operation of the NBA, would bring together the Dream Team against a team comprised predominantly of foreign-born NBA stars such as the Indiana Pacers' own Schrempf, Petrovic and Marciulionis.

The game would be played in the Hoosier Dome June 29.

It would be the fourth and final Larry's Game, the scholarship fund-raiser that has been held in June in conjunction with the Sports Corp.'s Youthlinks golf tournament.

Bird, a member of the Dream Team, has since retired because of a chronic back injury. So has Magic Johnson, because of the HIV virus, although the source said if the game is approved, Johnson would be invited to play.

Two well-known figures in the Indianapolis sports and business community are scheduled to meet with NBA commissioner David Stern to seek league approval within the next few weeks.

"We want this to be the final Hoosier tribute to Larry," the source said. "It's my understanding that Larry already has given his approval."

If the game receives the green light, ISC officials—who already have reserved the Hoosier Dome—plan to use the NCAA tournament configuration that has ap-

Bird's time with the Dream Team gave fans from all around the world a final chance to see him play. (AP/Wide World Photos)

proximately 40,000 seats.

However, the source said, the ISC would consider using the entire seating by placing the floor in the middle of the Dome.

The first event held in the Dome—a game pitting Bob Knight's 1984 Olympic team against NBA all-stars—set the world indoor basketball attendance record of 67,000-plus.

The Sports Corp. wants to use proceeds from the game to permanently endow the Larry Bird scholarships, which go to Indiana high school graduates intent on attending in-state colleges but who wouldn't be able to do so without financial help.

Beyond NBA approval, there's another huge variable in the Sports Corp.'s plans—how many of the Dream Teamers and foreign all-stars would commit to playing.

The Sports Corp. is hoping, of course, that Bird's stature and appreciation of what he did to popularize the NBA—and therefore fuel escalating salaries and endorsements—would entice most, if not all, the Dream Teamers to take part.

Still, agents and general managers are skittish about their high-priced talent risking injury in these summer hoopfests.

As far as foreign-born talent, there currently are 16 playing in the NBA—including Schrempf and Rik Smits of the Pacers—but the Sports Corp. will try to attract only the top players and fill in the roster with such non-NBA international stars as the high-scoring Schmidt and Kukoc, a Chicago draft choice whom the Bulls still are eager to sign.

Suffice it to say that this plan has several major hurdles to clear before becoming reality. But if the Sports Corp. is able to pull it off, I've got to believe it would be a hot box office item as well as TV attraction.

And what better way to fete Larry Legend.

Yet, while this would only be a one-shot deal, my mind tends to wander and wonder again.

What kind of TV ratings and income could be generated by a three- or five-game challenge match between NBA and international all-stars in the non-Olympic years?

If I couldn't be there, I know I'd watch.

In the meantime, I'll hope Larry has his game June 29 in the Dome. Despite the obstacles, the men behind this effort have a history of getting things done. ■

Larry's Game, Bird's annual charity event, provided Bird with a chance to show off all his skills. Unfortunately, "logistical problems" made it impossible to bring about the hoped-for matchup between the USA Dream Team and an international dream team. (Mike Fender)

5

1992-1997

TIME OUT

BIRD'S FLIGHT OF GREATNESS COMES TO END

Hoosier legend's heart is still in it, but his back isn't

August 19, 1992

BY RICHARD D. WALTON

Georgia Bird says she could see her famous son was in pain. But when she'd urge him to retire from the game he loved, Larry told her he couldn't.

"He'd say, 'Oh, Mom, I need the money.'"

And if the Boston Celtics great wasn't joking to deflect concern about his nagging back injury, he was changing the subject.

"With Larry, you ask him a question and half the time he doesn't answer," Georgia Bird said. "The re-

porters think they have a hard time. They should be his mother."

On Tuesday, though, Bird took his mom's advice.

Saying, "I knew this day was going to come," he announced the end of his memorable 13-year pro basketball career at a news conference in Boston.

The self-described "Hick from French Lick"—known for his pinpoint passing, blue-collar rebounding and 3-point marksmanship—said his still-painful back forced his decision.

"He just couldn't carry on like that," his mother said from her home in West Baden Springs shortly after the announcement. Bird, who choked back tears during the news conference, said he will stay with the Celtics, advising management and making public appearances.

Injuries had limited his effectiveness in recent seasons, which frustrated Bird. Because here was a man who knew how to play basketball at only one speed:

All-out.

"I wasn't going to let an injury stop me from diving on the floor to try to do everything that I was capable of doing to win a basketball game," Bird said Tuesday. "And that's all I want to be remembered for."

Bird was a three-time league MVP and leaves the game having scored more than 21,000 points. But he will be most remembered for his team play, which paced the Celtics to three league titles and, before that, sent Indiana State University on an improbable run to the NCAA championship game in 1979.

His retirement, though a relief to Georgia Bird, also brings some sadness. Larry, she said, lived to play basketball. The sport helped him overcome a natural shyness.

"He always had a basketball in his hands," she said. "It seems like that was always his friend.

"I think that when he was on the basketball court before all those people, he felt safe; he felt secure."

Dubbed "Larry Legend" because of his knack for coming up with the winning play under pressure, Bird honed his game amidst the hills of his native southern Indiana.

"He'd play in all kinds of weather and on any court he could find," said boyhood friend Tony Clark of Terre Haute. The pair played together for the Springs Valley High School Blackhawks in French Lick.

By the end of his sophomore season, Bird was making eye-popping, thread-the-needle passes. His performance paced the team to a state ranking during his junior year. And when he sprouted 4 more inches to 6-7—he's now listed at 6-9—his teammates knew they were watching someone special.

"Probably the greatest thing about him, though, is he's as good a person as he is a basketball player," Clark said.

Bird's done charity work on behalf of the Terre Haute Boys Club, Clark said, and he never forgets a friend. Despite all his fame, "he's just the same old Larry."

Mike McCormick didn't know Bird well, but he covered his exploits at Indiana State for a Terre Haute weekly called *The Spectator*.

And, he recalled Tuesday, Bird was "the only basketball player that ever made me cry."

It happened during a late-season game at ISU's Hulman Center in Bird's sophomore year. He was within a few points of breaking the school single-game scoring record with just minutes remaining when a little-used teammate took the floor. He was a senior making one of his last appearances.

McCormick said the reserve shot and missed. Bird rebounded. Rather than put the ball back up in quest of the record, Bird took it away from the basket and gave it back to the sub.

Again, he shot and missed. Again, Bird rebounded and passed back.

"Just watching that happen made me a lifelong fan," said McCormick, now a Terre Haute attorney. "He was so totally unselfish.

"Tears rolled down my cheeks in the stands."

Dave Gavitt, the Celtics' chief executive officer, was quoted by The Associated Press as calling Bird one of

the top five players ever to play the game.

"God may have not granted him an all-world body, but from the shoulders to the top of his head and from his wrist to his fingertips, he played the game better than anybody's ever played it, and he played it with a heart five times as big as anybody else I ever saw."

People who know Bird, then, think it's only fitting that he went out a winner. He played, though only sparingly due to injuries, on the Dream Team that captured the gold medal at the Olympic Games in Barcelona.

Georgia Bird said "it meant everything" to her son to achieve that victory—and she has her own idea of a dream team:

One run by Larry Bird.

She'd love to see him return to Springs Valley High as coach, and take the team to great success in the basketball tournament.

"We'd finally get to the State!" she said. ■

His playing time limited by his back problems, Bird watches his Celtics teammates from the sideline. (Frank Espich)

BIRD'S BOSTON STATS

Regular Season

Year	G	FG	FT	Reb	Ast	Pts
1979-80 Boston	82	.474	.836	852	370	21.3
1980-81 Boston	82	.478	.863	895	451	21.2
1981-82 Boston	77	.503	.863	837	447	22.9
1982-83 Boston	79	.504	.840	870	458	23.6
1983-84 Boston	79	.492	.888	796	520	24.2
1984-85 Boston	80	.522	.882	842	531	28.7
1985-86 Boston	82	.496	.896	805	557	25.8
1986-87 Boston	74	.525	.910	682	566	28.1
1987-88 Boston	76	.527	.916	703	467	29.9
1988-89 Boston	6	.471	.947	37	29	19.3
1989-90 Boston	75	.473	.930	712	562	24.3
1990-91 Boston	60	.454	.891	509	431	19.4
1991-92 Boston	45	.466	.926	434	306	20.2
Totals	**897**	**.496**	**.888**	**8974**	**5695**	**24.3**

Playoffs

Year	G	FG	FT	Reb	Ast	Pts
1979-80 Boston	9	.469	.880	101	42	21.3
1980-81 Boston	17	.470	.894	238	103	21.9
1981-82 Boston	12	.427	.822	150	67	17.8
1982-83 Boston	6	.422	.828	75	41	20.5
1983-84 Boston	23	.524	.879	252	136	27.5
1984-85 Boston	20	.461	.890	182	115	26.0
1985-86 Boston	18	.517	.927	168	148	25.9
1986-87 Boston	23	.476	.912	231	165	27.0
1987-88 Boston	17	.450	.894	150	115	24.5
1988-89 Boston	Injured, did not play					
1989-90 Boston	5	.444	.906	46	44	24.4
1990-91 Boston	10	.408	.863	72	65	17.1
1991-92 Boston	4	.500	.750	18	21	11.3
Totals	**164**	**.472**	**.890**	**1683**	**1062**	**23.8**

NBA HIGHLIGHTS

NBA Rookie of the Year, 1980

All-NBA First Team, 1980, 1981-88

NBA Most Valuable Player, 1984-86

NBA All-Defensive Second Team, 1982-84

NBA Finals MVP, 1984, 1986

NBA All-Star Game MVP, 1982

All else pales when compared to titles

November 1, 1992

BY DAVID BENNER

The trophies, plaques and other honors are reminders that collect dust along with occasional gee-weren't-they-great memories. They age with some explanation.

The rings, however, are reinforcements that command respect. They just display with definition.

Larry Bird was an Indiana All-Star in high school. He led surprising Indiana State to the 1979 NCAA basketball championship game before losing to Michigan State. He won three National Basketball Association MVP awards and was a 12-time NBA All-Star selection.

Special stuff, but shelf stuff.

Larry Bird was part of three world championships—1981, '84, '86—as a member of the Boston Celtics.

Significant stuff. Sincere stuff. Accomplishments that truly define.

"Winning championships is all I care about," Larry Bird once said. "The other stuff, you guys (the media) control. I can control winning."

To Bird, this was what his existence as a competitor was all about. It is also the most definitive element of his career, simply because to him it meant the most. Mold the form of greatness any way possible, but when the profile is done, it is incomplete without championship rings.

"It is an absolute criteria for great players," Celtics president Red Auerbach said.

Then Larry Bird, without question, was a great player.

What the 6-9, 220-pound forward had accomplished with ISU was surprising, legendary and certainly noteworthy. It still remains as a wonderful time for a team,

school, community and state, something Bird acknowledged in 1989 when that team gathered for a reunion.

"I do so many of these things, you can't get caught up in them," he said. "But this one's special."

However, it was short of the standard Bird wanted and expected, which was to have the team he played for finish as champion. It is what helped make him different, it is what made him meet the criteria of truly great players, one who excelled on the floor and also had the ultimate team success to show for it. It probably helped him succeed as a pro.

Bird's skills were obvious and—despite his mind games of too slow, can't jump, no quickness—he had talent. One does not get drafted as a junior eligible with the sixth pick overall in the first round of the 1978 NBA draft by one of the most storied franchises in league history without some ability.

But taking that ability, which is so similar to so many in professional sports, and raising it a notch to become a champion required something special.

"I never dreamed he would be that highly motivated an individual," admitted Auerbach.

Yet that's what made Bird—and his main rival in the '80s, Magic Johnson—so special, the desire to win championships.

"He's a winner and I'm a winner," said Magic. "That's what makes us different. We do whatever is possible to win. Larry knows how to do it and what it takes to do it."

That end-all was Bird's passion and it manifested itself in a number of subtle and not-so-subtle ways during his 13-year NBA career. He took on everyone—opponents, fans, media, coaches, management, friends,

> As the Celtics left the Spectrum floor in defeat, a Sixers' fan yelled at [Bird]: "Hey Larry, we'll see you back here for Game 6." Bird, not missing a step or an opportunity, shot back: "You've got a better chance of seeing God."

teammates, referees, himself.

Given a challenge to the goal, he took a personal approach to the challenge. For example:

It was May 19, 1985, and the Philadelphia 76ers had just defeated Boston 115-104 in Philly to cut the Celtics' lead in the best-of-7 series to 3-1. The next game would be in Boston and a sixth game, if necessary, would be played in Philadelphia.

As the Celtics left the Spectrum floor in defeat, a Sixers' fan yelled at him: "Hey Larry, we'll see you back here for Game 6." Bird, not missing a step or an opportunity, shot back: "You've got a better chance of seeing God."

It's uncertain if the fan met his maker but it was certain again Bird could meet his match. The Celtics won the series in five games.

The fan, tossing out a seemingly innocent ember, had lit Bird's competitive fire, which could burn into an inferno, particularly in the playoffs when the 82-game regular season was over and the title hunt was on.

For Indiana Pacers' fans, the 1991 playoffs are vivid. Bird's bad back, which eventually forced his retirement last summer, left him day-to-day, yet he played. In a deciding Game 5, his face crashed to the floor—chasing a loose ball—and he left the game in the second quarter, only to return in the third and lead a Boston comeback to victory.

"Truly amazing and courageous, truly the leader of the Celtics," said Boston coach Chris Ford.

That's because the playoffs were Bird's time—just remember the steal of Isiah Thomas' inbounds pass that led to a Boston victory over Detroit in 1987—and his numbers would increase when postseason play began. They weren't dramatic jumps but over the course of his career, his play left him first among the Celtics' all-time playoff leaders in scoring average, assists and second in rebounding only to Bill Russell.

His greatness as a player and winner was never more evident than in the postseason.

Said Bird, "In the playoffs or a championship series, you have to do everything you can to help the team. If you can make that extra pass, get the big rebound or a big basket. Whatever I can do to help the team, I've got to do it. I can't worry about scoring 30, 35 points a game.

"Whatever it takes, I'll do it because I'm the type of guy I feel can make things happen out there. Whatever it takes."

Whatever it takes. A key phrase to Bird, a principle that could alienate teammates and during his career, he did. Not because Bird was a perfectionist, but because his personal standard—winning the title—was a team standard. Anyone who didn't adhere, didn't measure up to Bird.

"I've played awful hard for these guys and they've played awful hard for me over the years and, of course, when things aren't going well, people will say some things," he once said. "That stuff happens. I've said some things under certain circumstances, but my whole goal was to win a championship."

It was more action than talk. Whether coming back from numerous injuries or losing weight or building strength to absorb the marathon NBA schedule as he grew older or running laps two hours before game time or shooting for hours alone during the summer and season, Bird's purpose was solitary.

"If you win a championship, as soon as that season is over, you forget about that one and want another one," he said. "You don't care about it after you get it, you want another one.

"It's a very tough thing to do, a lot harder than people realize. Only one in 27 win it and those aren't good odds, slim and none."

Yet those odds can be overcome and Bird did it. How?

"Going out and performing up to my potential every night was the biggest challenge," Bird said. "That doesn't mean what I did was for myself, but what I did to contribute to the team. That's not what fans pay $15, $20 a seat for. They pay their money to see a guy come out and play basketball.

"If you're not shooting well or playing real well, they want to see you give 100 percent."

That led to what we all saw the last 13 seasons in the NBA. Bird establishing himself as one of the all-time greats not only through personal accomplishments but through team accomplishments by giving 100 percent.

It all led to the rings. Significant, sincere, the brand of success and greatness.

"He wants to win, whether it's softball, golf, basketball, playing cards," said Bob Heaton, a teammate of Bird's at Indiana State. "He's very, very competitive. He sacrificed about anything to be the best he could be."

The most succinct way of summing up the challenges, the competitiveness and the desire to win for Bird comes in one word: championships. ■

Bird addresses the crowd during "Larry Bird Night" at Boston Garden. (Boston Globe Photo)

No playing and no coaching, but Bird staying busy after NBA

November 1, 1992

BY ROBIN MILLER

He hasn't touched a basketball in several months and doesn't plan to even shoot around this year, but Larry Bird is still very much a part of the Boston Celtics.

The 12-time NBA All-Star still has a contract with the pro club he rescued back in 1979 and his official title is special assistant to Celtics president Dave Gavitt.

And while Bird no longer performs miracles on the parquet floor in Boston Garden, he'll continue to work for Red Auerbach—the man who was smart enough to draft him as a junior at Indiana State.

"It's not hard work . . . I watch tapes, do a little scouting and attend some functions," said Bird recently from his Boston home. "It's off and on all year but still not something that's permanent.

"In the beginning I didn't want to be involved but Dave (Gavitt) told me I could take off and do whatever I had to whenever I wanted, so that helped make my decision.

"I just didn't want to be committed the whole time."

But don't think Larry Legend's first year away from the court will be a quiet one. He's still in demand for endorsements and public appearances.

"It's been crazy, things coming in every day," he continued. "The next two months I'm loaded and it's kind of amazing really . . . nothing's really changed except now I've got so much free time and I can pick and choose."

Bird is booked and also has a hotel/restaurant/sports bar in Terre Haute, The Boston Connection, a Ford dealership in Martinsville and some plans for something in Indianapolis.

"It's a little premature to talk about, but I should have something to announce pretty soon," he said of his Indy business venture.

As for building a home in Indianapolis, Bird isn't sure but definitely plans to commute between his Boston and French Lick residences.

"I've been at the Celtics' camp this week and I'll be coming home next week . . . I haven't seen my little boy but a couple of days in the last three weeks," said Bird of his 1-year-old son, Connor.

Bird doesn't see coaching in his future.

"I don't think so, you're just too committed," he said. "A coach has to deal with everyone every day and I don't want that hanging over me.

"Besides, I never know what I'm going to do day-to-day. I change my mind all the time."

One thing Bird can't change is his persona—or popularity.

"Oh yeah, out here it hasn't changed much," said Bird of his admirers. "It's funny though, because if I'm not standing out in my yard here they won't stop and they never come up to my house. But at home (French Lick), people still drive up to the gate and hang around.

"It still amazes me," he said with a chuckle, "because if they really knew me, they probably wouldn't want to talk to me."

At 35, he's looking forward to a healthy retirement after enduring a fractured face, bone spurs, broken bones and back surgery.

"I've been taking it easy to let my back rest so I can travel," said Bird. "I haven't been jogging in a week and I've put on a few pounds so I need to get home and get in shape."

He knows watching big-time basketball, instead of playing it, for the first time in 17 years won't be easy.

"I know I'll miss it but I've had a great life the past 17 years," he said. "And there's still a lot of things to enjoy."

Retirement gave Bird an opportunity to spend more time on his golf game. (Rich Miller)

Fans keep sending messages on card at Hall

November 1, 1992

SPECIAL CORRESPONDENT

Retirement is a bittersweet event for almost everyone. For sports figures, with their careers so public and so brief, it is even more so. Larry Bird's retirement was a surprise to no one, and he went out a winner, with an Olympic gold medal around his neck. Yet many fans still aren't ready to let go.

The Indiana Basketball Hall of Fame found that out quickly this fall as suddenly virtually every visitor wanted to see everything the museum has on the "Hick from French Lick."

Most of Bird's memorabilia, in fact, is in his restaurant in Terre Haute, the Boston Connection. The Hall of Fame does have one of Bird's high school jerseys, on loan from the restaurant. That, and a Celtics' warmup and a collection of photos, magazine covers and game programs are now on display.

But in response to a visitors' desire to see more of Bird, the Hall has developed a huge, larger-than-life retirement card and let visitors leave a message of their own for Larry.

The messages have become as interesting, as an exhibit, as any collection of photos and objects in the museum. Many are endearing statements of how much this player and role model meant to his many fans, from across Indiana and around the world.

Certainly half the 500-odd signatures collected in the first six weeks on the giant 8-foot-by-8 foot card are simply that. About 100 have added their hometown, while 100 others have written a personal message.

Many are simple statements of "Thanks for the memories," and "You're the greatest." But others are real attempts to establish some kind of spatial or temporal relationship to Larry Legend.

Thanks to one class Indiana high school basketball, everyone who ever played in the state can say they once played in the same "league" as Bird. Maybe that's what

motivated people who signed their names and "Danville Warriors 1935," "ECR '66" and "Big Daddy" Jay County '86."

Bird's career generated a lot of Hoosier pride, eliciting comments like "Thanks for showing everyone how to do it right the first time," and "You were the best, a credit to Indiana."

Several French Lick natives already have signed the card, including the painstakingly rendered signature of 4-year-old Woody Ent.

People from outside Indiana usually make a point of the fact, as evidenced by signatures from Largo, Florida; Cliffside Park, New Jersey; Accokeek, Maryland; North Branch, Mich.; and "Vicki from Brooklyn, your biggest fan."

International visitors, in particular, had personal statements. Barcelona's Ana Jara followed Larry back to the USA and wrote, "Nice to see you in Barcelona." Pedro Reimzo drew a Brazilian flag above his name. And Australian Larry Dohee wrote, "Congratulations on a superb career. If you decide to come back, play for the Adelaide '36ers!"

Some visitors have made interesting stretches to establish a connection. One visitor indentified himself as "a brother of an ISU alum." Then there was the couple from Redkey who wrote, "Thanks, Larry, for your attitude and pride. Our kids have blonde hair and fondly call you 'Uncle Larry.' A job well-done."

Other connections are more immediate. Hall of Famer Del Harris, visiting the museum with his father, recalled that as coach of the Houston Rockets, he had been the opponent in Bird's first NBA game. Later, Harris also was the opposing coach in Bird's first NBA championship series. "I signed it anyway," Harris said with a smile. ∎

> Many are simple statements of "Thanks for the memories," and "You're the greatest." But others are real attempts to establish some kind of spatial or temporal relationship to Larry Legend.

A King Retires

August 19, 1992

EDITORIAL

The announced retirement of Larry Bird, Indiana's reigning king hoops, means a special era of basketball is ending. There is no doubt the kid from French Lick took the professional sport to a new level. In the process he became a legend.

Like all genius, his talent was extraordinary to watch but hard to explain.

Fans pondered how he seemed to have a thousand eyes. In so volatile and fast a game as basketball, where both his teammates and opponents moved in such myriad patterns—about-faces, forward, backward, sideways, feints, leaps and zig-zags—he had an uncanny ability to see the whole floor and know everyone's location on it.

His passes were marvels of timing and precision. His rebounding was relentless and awesome. And his shooting, well, he was simply among the best that ever played the game. He could consistently flick or float in a three-pointer from virtually any place on the floor and hit nothing but net.

In his 13-year National Basketball Association career with the Boston Celtics, Bird was named rookie of the year in 1980, the NBA's most valuable player in the three consecutive years of 1984, 1985 and 1986 and led the Celtics to NBA titles in 1981, 1984 and 1986.

It's too bad he didn't play for the Indiana Pacers.

He did play for the Indiana State University Sycamores, and he put them on the national basketball map, taking them to the National Invitational Tournament in his junior year and then winning 33 straight games in his senior year. That is when the world discovered Larry Bird.

It was a fitting cap on his career that he played on this summer's U.S. "Dream Team" that took the gold medal at the 25th Olympiad in Barcelona.

Painful back injuries had plagued him for the past two years, but Bird did not let them slow his game any more than he let his popularity and riches compromise his sense of hard work and humility.

Boston Celtics executive vice president David Gavitt called him "the greatest player I have ever been associated with." He will stay in Boston as Gavitt's assistant in the front office.

Bird has often said he would like to return to French Lick some day, and maybe he will. Whatever he does, we wish him well. He'll always be Indiana's very own Larry Bird. ∎

Bird's number is up

March 16, 1993

EDITORIAL

Larry Legend, they called him. The nickname, in part, was supposed to be slightly mocking, a gentle jab at the man's incredible sense of self-assurance. But it also was a genuine tribute, because he is a legend, one of those sports figures who seem to defy human limitations.

Larry Bird did just that.

Even though he didn't look like a basketball player—he was slow, couldn't jump very well and even was a little overweight in his early years—Bird dominated the court and dictated the way the game was played. He had a fierce desire to win and a drive to constantly refine his skills.

As is the case so often in life, that desire and that drive were rewarded. Larry Bird led the Boston Celtics to three championships. In his prime, he was the finest basketball player alive.

He retired from the game last summer. And, on Thursday night, the Celtics retired his number—the highest tribute a player can receive.

It was a moment Larry Legend deserved.

Larry Bird to be marshal of '500' Festival Parade

May 11, 1993

BY REBECCA BUCKMAN

This year's "500" Festival Parade will feature the usual group of soap opera stars, but there'll be at least one big name up-front: Larry Bird, who's scheduled to be grand marshal.

Bird, the recently retired Boston Celtics star and a native Hoosier, will preside over a parade that boasts a new route, expanded seating and a determined effort at crowd participation.

Ticket-holders for the May 29 event, sponsored this year by Delco Electronics, are expected to get involved in the festivities by brandishing certain props —such as a tiara and a kazoo—at appropriate times during the procession.

Spectators will don their tiaras, for instance, when the float carrying the "500" Festival princesses passes by. They'll blow their kazoos for the bands and wave U.S. flags for political officials and others, said Elizabeth Kraft, executive director of "500" Festival Associates, which organizes the parade.

"Great parades have a hook," she explained at a news conference Monday. "And we (Indianapolis) can do crowd participation better than anybody."

Kraft said the "hook" of giving each parade-watcher a bag of goodies to use would be similar to the stunt performed by the crowd at the opening ceremonies of the 1987 Pan American Games here.

People sitting in bleachers at that event, held at the Indianapolis Motor Speedway, held up large plastic cards to spell out greetings and create designs.

Parade spectators also should bring along inserts from the May 28 *Indianapolis News* and May 29 *Indianapolis Star*. They will be things people can wear around their necks—sort of like bibs—as "costumes," such as

Grand Marshal Larry Bird oversees the 1993 "500" Festival Parade in Indianapolis. (Patty Espich)

checkered flags and race drivers' uniforms.

Kraft said those unable to afford the $10 for a parade ticket still could participate near the route by buying a newspaper and wearing the inserts. "It's really important that people have a quality parade experience, ticketed or unticketed," she said.

Spectators can gawk at Bird and other celebrities like Lee Greenwood, who will sing his tune "God Bless the U.S.A." to kick off the event at 11:45 a.m.

Others slated to attend are Craig T. Nelson of the TV series "Coach"; Crystal Bernard, who plays Helen on TV's "Wings"; Dr. Joseph Allen, a NASA astronaut; and Lorenzo Lamas, former star of TV's "Falcon Crest" who now stars on "Renegade."

Lamas' wife and co-star on "Renegade," Kathleen Kinmont, also will participate in the parade.

Daytime TV actors including Antonio Sabato Jr. from "General Hospital"; Karen Witter from "One Life to Live"; and Paul Anthony Stewart from "Loving" will attend as well. ■

Coaching job not for ailing Bird

May 20, 1993

BY CONRAD BRUNNER

The back problem that forced Larry Bird's premature retirement as a player apparently will prevent him from becoming a head coach. Sources close to both Bird and the Pacers told *The News* today the club had discussed the possibility of Bird filling the vacancy created by Tuesday's firing of Bob Hill, but were told his lingering back pain would prohibit any such move, for now.

"We're trying to make contact," club president Donnie Walsh said. "The only negative we've heard is that his back may prevent him from doing it."

Bird's agent, Bob Woolf, said he had no knowledge of any contact between the Pacers and his client.

The agent did say he believed Bird was "more interested in getting himself better physically" than moving into a new line of work.

Bird, who has served as a special consultant to the Boston Celtics since his retirement last summer, recently sold his Boston home and has set up a residence in Naples, Florida.

One source said Bird did not rule out the possibility of becoming a coach, but not this year.

"He had interest," said the source, "but his back is too bad."

Walsh said he has moved into the early stages of candidate contact and evaluation.

Though he has no timetable for hiring the new coach, Walsh said he "would prefer" everything to be settled before the June 30 draft.

"There's going to be a lot of action," he said, "and you'd like your coach to be involved."

He has sought permission from Cleveland to discuss the job with coach Lenny Wilkens, who still has one year remaining on his contract with the Cavaliers. Other possibilities include L.A. Clippers coach Larry Brown, former Atlanta coach Mike Fratello, and former Chicago coach Doug Collins.

It is clear from the nature of Walsh's list his first preference is to bring in a marquee name.

"There are people calling me now," he said. "If they're assistants, I'm telling them we're looking for high-level guys right now.

"Other than that, what we're doing is making sure the people I want to talk to, I have the right to talk to."

Lisa Eltzroth sold 14 commemorative boxes of Wheaties in three days. (Patrick Schneider)

Wheaties' price for the Bird, if not the birds

March 16, 1993

SPECIAL CORRESPONDENT

A quest for cereal—800 boxes of Wheaties, to be exact—drove Pete Gallagher and his son, Richard, all the way to Boston.

Their success is certain to delight Terre Haute area souvenir hunters.

Hoosiers hungry for the face of favorite son Larry Bird on the famous orange cereal box can buy theirs at Midwest Sports, 13 Meadows Mall, Terre Haute.

The price: $15 each.

The store opens at 11 a.m., and the boxes go on sale at noon.

"We're charging $15, which isn't bad since you also get the Wheaties," said the elder Gallagher, whose son owns Midwest Sports.

"Yeah, we'll make a few bucks, but the people in Terre Haute and Indiana will have a chance to get what people can buy only in Boston."

Gallagher said that for some reason General Mills, which produces Wheaties, will sell the boxes with Bird at a wholesale price only to stores in the Boston area.

"I think people in Indiana have a right to buy these, too," said Gallagher.

The first week of March, a store in French Lick had boxes of the Bird-cover Wheaties, too. They apparently sold out in a day. ■

6

MAY 8, 1997

INDIANA CALLING

More mature Bird flies home to Indiana

Following nearly two decades of trying, the Pacers get their man

May 9, 1997

BY CONRAD BRUNNER

The Indiana Pacers' flirtation with Larry Bird goes back to the final months of Larry Brown's tenure—with the Denver Nuggets.

Nearly two decades later, they finally got their man.

Bird's decision to return to NBA active duty as the Pacers' head coach brought to an end a pursuit that began when Bird was a junior at Indiana State, and Brown was holding his first NBA job.

With the third pick in the 1978 draft, the Pacers had the opportunity to select Bird.

Preparing for their third NBA season, the Pacers were in financial trouble, and in immediate need of help up front after losing power forward Dan Roundfield to Atlanta through free agency.

They had scouted Bird extensively, but had two concerns: keeping a competitive team on the floor in 1978-

79, and the strong possibility of being unable to come up with enough money to sign Bird, if they drafted him.

"I saw him several times, and you could tell he was going to be a player," said Bobby "Slick" Leonard, then the Pacers' head coach. "But I don't think there's any scout that thought he would be as great as he turned out."

The Pacers instead used the pick on Kentucky forward Rick Robey. Boston used the first of its two first-round picks, sixth overall, on Bird.

Leonard has no regrets when he looks back on the decision. He blames the high cost of entering the NBA in 1976—a $3.2 million entry fee, an $800,000 settle-

Bird, Walsh talk about coaching vacancy

SPECIAL CORRESPONDENT

*April 27, 1997—***BOSTON CELTICS LEGEND LARRY BIRD** met with Indiana Pacers president Donnie Walsh over dinner in Indianapolis on Saturday night, and had what Walsh told WRTV-6 were "preliminary" discussions about the team's head coaching vacancy.

Coach Larry Brown, under contract to the Pacers, is expected to announce his decision about his future early next week. Brown has had discussions with the Celtics and Philadelphia 76ers.

Pacers announcer Slick Leonard was Indiana's coach when the Pacers passed up Bird in the 1978 NBA Draft. (Paul Sancya)

ment with Kentucky Colonels owner John Y. Brown, no draft choices in 1976 and no television revenue for the first two years—for handicapping the surviving ABA teams.

"Let's think what might've been had we gotten a decent shake from the NBA when we first went in," he said. "They tried to pulverize us and, in that period, I was sweating out if we could pay the secretaries in the office. It was unbelievably tough."

"I don't look at what might've been. We were in no position as a franchise to wait on a player a year and, even then, if we had drafted him, would we have been able sign him?"

It was their first shot at Bird, but not the last.

A decade later, the Pacers made an attempt to acquire Bird. They offered Chuck Person and the second pick in the 1988 draft to Boston. Luckily for the Pacers, the Celtics turned it down.

That pick turned out to be center Rik Smits. Bird,

hobbled by injuries, would miss nearly as many games (142) as he played (186) in his final four seasons.

Looking for a replacement for Bob Hill in 1993, franchise representatives approached Bird about the coaching job. But Bird, who retired after the 1991-92 season because of back problems, was in no mood—or physical condition—to take on the grind.

The Pacers hired Brown, and quickly made a move that would've rankled Bird by trading All-Star forward Detlef Schrempf (who was pushing for a new contract) to Seattle for Derrick McKey.

"I can imagine if I took that job and the first day, I walked in and they told me they were going to trade Detlef because they couldn't pay him," Bird said later that season. "I'd just turn around and follow him out the door."

Following Brown's resignation two weeks ago and Boston's decision to hire Rick Pitino, Bird finally walked through the Pacers' open door. ■

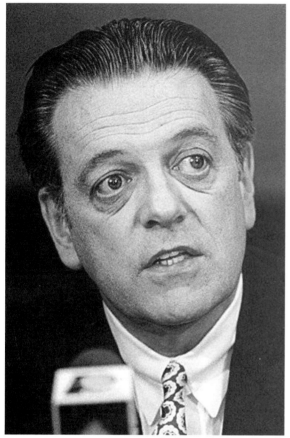

(Indianapolis Star/News)

When Donnie Walsh (left) and the Pacers were unable to acquire Bird from the Celtics in 1988, they used their first-round draft pick to acquire center Rik Smits (below).

(Kelly Wilkinson)

A WELCOME HOMECOMING

*In the town that spawned a superstar, Larry Bird's neighbors are
sure he's right man to lead Pacers.*

May 11, 1997

BY PHILLIP B. WILSON

The down-to-earth folks in Larry Bird's hometown have all the answers regarding their basketball hero's return to the state to coach the Indiana Pacers.

Most haven't spoken to Bird in a long time. But you can call it small-town intuition, the type of insight that develops from decades of friendship and admiration.

Ask anyone around here how Bird can be as good a coach as he was a player. Hard work, they'll tell you.

Why would Bird want to trade his Naples, Florida, winter home for a life on the road? He's bored.

What will Bird's Hoosier homecoming mean to the Pacers' fandom? The team can count on as many as 3,000 converted Boston Celtics fans from a certain rural community in southern Indiana.

Will coaching tarnish the image of Larry Legend? That's easy. The friendly folks of French Lick are convinced of three certainties in life: death, taxes and that Bird will always be just good, old Larry.

"Down here, he's not Larry Bird, the basketball player, to us," said police chief Tom McCracken. "That's why he likes to come home. We let him be just Larry."

"He's common. And he's never changed," said Eddie Kelloms, who runs Eddie's Service automotive and convenience store on the outskirts of town.

Kelloms, like so many of Bird's acquaintances, was unfazed by Thursday's announcement that Bird would join the Pacers. He acted no differently than if Bird himself walked into the shop to buy something, which he is known to do when he's in town each summer. Bird still has a home in the area.

Store patron Morris Rominger couldn't help but add his two cents: "Larry's pretty young to just sit on a beach the rest of his life. When you're that age, you run out of leisure things to do."

The town seems to take pride in maintaining Bird's rather private hometown existence. There is but one visible trace of his history—a Larry Bird Boulevard sign in the shape of a green basketball along the street that leads to his alma mater.

The town council has kicked around the idea of constructing a statue of the future Hall of Famer, but it's an ongoing discussion.

The Southridge Raiders high school girls' basketball team carries the "Spirit of Larry Bird" for good luck. (Mike Fender)

The bottom line, as Silver Springs High School principal Larry Pritchett says, is that "he does no wrong here."

Transfer that faith to the Pacers, who need a new outlook after a disappointing 39-43 season, and it's a no-lose situation, according to several residents.

"It's going to draw a lot of interest from the southern part of the state, and it will be good for the Pacers. I can't see how they can go wrong," McCracken said.

"We need somebody to drive those Pacers," said Bill Combs, while sipping a beer at the Colonial Bar on Front Street.

Nobody appeared to be more ecstatic about the news on this day than Virginia Stone and Marilyn Wilson, who rejoiced while working at the Village Market antique and collectibles shop on College Street.

"Hoosiers are lucky. They're real lucky," Stone said. "I'm glad to see him back. 'Hoosier returns home.' What else can you say? The people of French Lick will be tickled to have their boy home."

"Indiana needs him," Wilson said.

Bird's former high school coach, Gary Holland, smiles at the suggestion that his onetime Indiana All-Star may not be prepared for the job.

"He'll succeed. There's nothing Larry can't do if he sets his mind to it," he said. "I'm happy for him. He'll make a great coach, just like he was a great player. He made everybody better as a player and he was a coach on the floor. That's what will make him good."

Bird's nephew, 6-3 Silver Springs freshman John Goughenour, agrees.

"He just understands the game so much and he knows what to do," the red-haired relative said. "The players will listen to him. He'll get the most of his players."

But make no mistake, Bird has the benefit of the doubt from both young and old here.

"I like him because he's a good coach," said 6-year-old Springs Valley Elementary pupil Melanie Evans, albeit somewhat prematurely.

"He'll make a real good coach," said Jesse Rominger, 90, while sitting on a Front Street bench. "He did a lot of coaching when he was playing, you know. That's how come they won so much." ■

Ex-ISU coach Hodges says Bird will do fine

BY BILL BENNER

May 11, 1997—Some say Larry Bird has coached before. They say he was, essentially, a player-coach when Indiana State University reached the NCAA tournament's championship game in 1979.

"Yeah, I've heard that, too," said Bill Hodges, the Sycamores' coach in that magical 33-1 season that ended with a loss to Michigan State.

"There's no doubt that he showed what a great leader he was that year," continued Hodges who, as an ISU assistant, persistently recruited Bird after he dropped out of Indiana University.

"But as far as X's and O's and what to do, he wasn't into that kind of stuff. He just did whatever you told him to do and made sure that everybody else did what you told them to do."

Hodges said Bird's innate hoops knowledge is unsurpassed.

"He understands the game better than anyone I've ever seen and, in his mind, he's always been a step or two ahead of what's going on," Hodges said.

"I think he'll be as good a coach as there is in the NBA. The one hump he might have to get over is the way kids are today. The X Generation of players is such a me-oriented group and one of the reasons I'm getting out of coaching is I couldn't deal with that anymore. Too many players want the rewards without paying the price.

"But if he can motivate guys to practice and play as hard as he did, there shouldn't be any problem."

Another positive trait Bird has, according to Hodges, is his ability to measure people.

"He has great intuitive judgment and can judge people really well," Hodges said. "I think that will really help him as he decides who to hire and who to draft."

Hodges anticipates a happy reunion between Bird and Pacers legend—and current scout—Mel Daniels. Daniels was an assistant at Indiana State during the Bird era.

Bird's ISU teammates confident he'll raise Pacers to new heights

May 11, 1997

BY RICHARD D. WALTON

Their names meant little outside Terre Haute. To a nation, they were "the rest" of Larry Bird's basketball team.

But the other players on Indiana State University's miracle 1978-79 team know Bird—and they know just what to expect from the new Indiana Pacers coach: Straight shooting.

Bird, his former Sycamores teammates said, will leave no doubt about the effort he wants from the Pacers and

will sit down any player not giving it.

Anyone drawing a paycheck may hear, "to hell with you—if you ain't gonna play, we'll get you out of here," said Bob Heaton, a small forward on the ISU team that won 33 games, losing only in the national championship game to Michigan State.

Bird will be fair, expecting nothing from players that he didn't do himself, said former ISU reserve Tom Crowder of Cayuga.

Of course, Crowder added with a chuckle, Bird "did everything."

From taking shooting practice before games to running stairs alone in the gym, Bird did whatever it took to improve.

Crowder recalled well Bird's pursuit of perfection.

During one practice at ISU, he said, Bird missed a couple of shots and then kicked the ball into the second tier of the Hulman Center stands.

"Nobody said a word," Crowder said. "We just got another ball."

At ISU, Bird was a quiet leader.

The French Lick native seemed uncomfortable speaking in public and avoided the media.

But former ISU teammate Brad Miley said he watched Bird grow adept at press relations after he turned pro.

Miley, who works for a beverage wholesaler, saw no problem, either, with Bird relating to Pacer players.

"He's the kind of coach you want to play for—someone with high expectations," Miley said.

Former ISU guard Carl Nicks wondered how Bird's hard-driving style will mesh with the big egos of today's NBA. Even so, Nicks said Bird should have "instant respect" from players and believes Bird's dedication could rub off on the Pacers.

Bob Heaton, a former teammate of Bird's at Indiana State, says Bird could become the next Pat Riley. (Indianapolis Star/News Photo)

"I think Larry has the ability to bring back the old, traditional way of basketball," said Nicks, who works with disadvantaged children in Georgia.

While Nicks was surprised Bird wanted to coach, Steve Reed, the point guard on Indiana State's '79 team, said Bird just couldn't stay away from the game he loved. Bird, Reed said, "was born and raised with a basketball under one arm."

Reed, president and CEO of Columbia Women's Hospital-Indianapolis, predicted Bird will bring a new level of excitement to Indianapolis.

Heaton, a life insurance agent, said Bird could become the next Pat Riley, the successful player-turned-coach. Still, Heaton worried about the high failure rate of NBA coaches.

He recalled that former Indiana University player Quinn Buckner lost his job as coach of the Dallas Mavericks after players rebelled at his disciplinary style. Heaton said he would hate to see Bird meet a similar fate.

"Let's remember Larry Bird as a superstar legend that he was as a player," Heaton said.

Yet, his former college teammates said, it is precisely that memory that may push the Pacers to heights they have never reached before. ■

> **Bird will be fair, expecting nothing from players that he didn't do himself, said former ISU reserve Tom Crowder of Cayuga. Of course, Crowder added with a chuckle, Bird "did everything."**

Bird's ability to handle, motivate and inspire the NBA's new "x-generation" has been one of the main keys to his success. Here, Bird shares a laugh with NBA free agent Steve Turner at the Pacers' rookie and free agent camp. (Paul Sancya)

Hiring Bird produces more sales for Pacers

May 10, 1997

BY MARK MONTIETH

May 10, 1997—More tickets, merchandise and advertisements sold. More advertisements bought. More media coverage.

More of everything.

The hiring of Larry Bird produced a noticeable increase in activity around the Indiana Pacers' office Friday, the day following the announcement that he would replace Larry Brown as coach.

"This helps quite a bit," said Wendy Sommers, the team's director of advertising. "It gets everyone in the office excited and gives us a fresh start."

It's difficult to imagine a better coaching candidate for the Pacers from a business standpoint. That Bird's hiring comes in the wake of the team's first losing season since 1992 and its first season without a playoff appearance since 1989 provides an added boost.

Mike Henn, the team's director of ticket sales, said his department received 20 to 25 orders for various season ticket packages Friday. Many of them were clearly linked to Bird's signing.

Henn also cited a handful of accounts that were considering canceling their order, but jumped off the fence and back into the fold. "I've got to believe Bird's a factor there," he said.

The Pacers averaged 15,530 fans last season—a 5 percent drop from the previous season—and sold out only 10 of 41 home dates.

To help improve on that number, the Pacers will take out advertisements in newspapers in Indianapolis and Terre Haute next week, and perhaps in small southern Indiana towns as well.

Bird's impact on merchandise sales is more difficult to estimate, because there are not items directly related to a coach as there are for players.

"It's kind of a convoluted situation right now, because he's not a player," said Rich Kapp, the team's director of merchandise. "We're trying to work out details right now."

The Pacers broadcast 30 games last season on WTTV-4 and 30 more on the Fox cable network. Only one was televised nationally by NBC and one other on TNT.

Larry Mago, the team's director of broadcast production, said it is possible more games will be televised locally, with the cable package offering the greatest room for potential growth.

Pacers games were broadcast on 28 radio stations across the state last season, including Terre Haute.

"I would expect we can add a few more stations and fill in some of the areas we're not as strong in," Mago said.

The press conference for Bird Monday gives a hint of what might come. It will be broadcast live on local television and radio stations, as well as Sports Channel New England. A live audio feed will be available on the Pacers' internet home page, which can be accessed through the NBA's web site, NBA.com.

Bird's hiring has spurred demand for Pacers tickets and for team merchandise. (Paul Sancya)

During the summer between his junior and senior years, Larry Bird grew from a good 6-3 player to a great 6-7 star for Springs Valley. In his senior season, Bird averaged 30.6 points and 20.6 rebounds per game and earned a scholarship from Indiana's Bob Knight. (Courtesy of the Indiana Basketball Hall of Fame)

1974 Indiana All-Star Basketball Team. Front: Jim Krivacs, Southport; Wayne Radford, Indianapolis Arlington; Steve Collier, Southwestern; Roy Taylor, Anderson; Larry Bird, Springs Valley; Ron Smith, Elkhart Memorial. Standing: Kirby Overman (coach), New Albany; Larry Moore, Hammond; Tony Marshall, Anderson; Charlie Mitchell, New Albany; Walter Jordan, Ft. Wayne Northrup; Wayne Walls, Jeffersonville; Don M. Bates (game director) The Indianapolis Star.

Although best known for leading the Indiana State basketball team to the NCAA Finals, Larry Bird was also a hard-slugging first baseman for the Sycamores' baseball team. (Greg Griffo)

In the greatest individual matchup in NCAA Finals history, Indiana State's Larry Bird lends a helping hand to Michigan State's Magic Johnson. But, it was Johnson's team that handed Bird's Sycamores their only loss of the season, a 75-64 defeat in the Championship game. (AP/Wide World Photos)

Boston's Larry Bird shows off the trophy he won as MVP of the 1984 NBA Finals, which the Celtics won in seven games over the Lakers. Bird was also named the league's MVP for the 1983-84 regular season. (Sean Kardon, AP/Wide World Photos)

Boston star Larry Bird (center), is flanked by teammates Sam Vincent (left) and Rick Carlisle (right) as they celebrate through the streets of Boston after the Celtics' 1986 NBA Championship over the Houston Rockets in six games. (Paul Benoit, AP/Wide World Photos)

With the game on the line, few players have ever done it better or with more confidence than Larry Bird. (Indianapolis Star/News)

Indianapolis Star/News artist John Bigelow created this sculpture of Larry Bird, which was auctioned through the Star/News InfoLine for $2,500. These proceeds were donated to the Star/News Season For Sharing campaign, which assists needy children, and homeless, hungry and elderly people in Central Indiana. Bigelow's sculpture is 29.5 inches tall and was made with Crayola airdry model magic modeling compound and acrylic paints. (Ariana Lindquist)

(Paul Sancya)

The Pacers' seven-game series with the Bulls in the 1998 NBA Eastern Conference Finals was so intense that it had each team's superstar (Reggie Miller, left, and Michael Jordon, below) going all out to save every possession.

(Rich Miller)

New Pacers coach Larry Bird faces the media at Market Square Arena before the start of the 1997-98 NBA season. (Mike Fender)

Mark Jackson and Chris Mullin congratulate each other in the final seconds of the Pacers' playoff win over Cleveland. (Matt Kryger)

Indiana center Rik Smits battles with Chicago's Michael Jordan and Dennis Rodman in Game 3 of the 1998 NBA Eastern Conference Finals. The Pacers' strength on the boards was one of the keys to their dramatic 107-105 victory over the Bulls. (Paul Sancya)

When Larry Bird first stepped onto the court as the Pacers' new head coach, many wondered if he could transfer his playing excellence to the coaches' box. 58 regular season wins later, a Coach of the Year trophy, and a tough seven-game series against the World Champion Chicago Bulls left no doubt that Larry Legend could indeed excel on the coaching level. (Paul Sancya)

The Shot of the Season. Reggie Miller's three-pointer with 5.9 seconds left in Game 4 against the New York Knicks at Madison Square Garden sent the contest into overtime, where the Pacers pulled out a 118-107 win and took a commanding 3-1 series lead. (Paul Sancya)

Back Home Again

Larry Bird's return to Indiana sparks a media frenzy, reinforcing his status as a Hoosier legend.

May 13, 1997

BY BILL BENNER

A whale of a player jumped back into life in the fishbowl as a coach Monday. Needless to say, it made for quite a splash.

So welcome back, Larry Bird. This mob's for you.

Dozens of minicams and microphones were wielded by nearly 100 reporters—possibly the largest media group ever assembled without the lure of a free meal—who gathered in Market Square Arena late Monday afternoon.

Local newscasts and accounts from the real world were interrupted for live television and radio reports of Bird's first public utterances since accepting the Indiana Pacers head coaching job last Thursday.

'Twas the Hoosier twang heard 'round the world.

And suddenly, the question "Can he coach?" became almost secondary to this one: "Can he handle the media crush?"

Although certainly not of this magnitude, similar scenes will follow Bird as he returns to an active role in basketball.

Always a private person even as he evolved from the shy "Hick from French Lick" into "Larry Legend, worldwide superstar," Bird now is very much a very large public persona again.

And coaching, ironically, is only part of being an NBA coach. Sometimes it's not even the biggest part, especially when you are Larry Bird.

Is he ready for it?

For instance, when a reporter reminded Bird, "NBA coaches speak to the media every day," he retorted, "I heard they used to."

Bird was kidding. At least we think he was.

But there can be no doubt that he is placing himself, his wife, Dinah, and their two young children, 6-year-old Connor and 4-year-old Mariah, under an intense microscope.

Particularly so in Indiana.

"This is a little different," he said, squinting through the TV lights at the horde.

"I haven't had this in a few years, but it's part of it. The last week was pretty hectic, but I think we handled it pretty well and hopefully we can handle it going forward.

"It's tough on me. I don't particularly like being in the public eye. But this is something I want to do. I want to see my team succeed and I want another opportunity to win a championship, and that's what it's all about."

Bird also must know that although he was rarely—if ever—criticized as a player, he will be fair game as a coach. As much as he is greeted by adulation in his return to his home state, he also is greeted by a fair amount of skepticism.

While many hope he will succeed as a rookie coach, there are those who believe he will fail and are waiting with all the I-told-you-sos.

Larry Bird answers questions from the media at the press conference announcing him as the new head coach of the Pacers. (Steve Healey)

"Being a coach of a team, you take all the pressure," Bird said. "If you win, the players should get the credit, and if you lose, the coach should get the grief. I understand that. I've been patted on the back all my life. Now I'm taking a chance on becoming a good coach, hopefully a great coach."

Yet if Bird handles future media demands nearly as well as he handled Monday's, he will encounter little difficulty.

No matter what question was tossed his direction, his responses were right on target for an audience lapping up his words in their cars and living rooms.

Bird's words were heartfelt, humorous, earnest, enthusiastic and confident. Most of all, he was plainspoken.

He talked about "coachin'" and "reboundin'" and "runnin'"—dropping the "ing" the way many Hoosiers do.

And just so you know, "re-tar" in Birdspeak is not something you do to the driveway, but something you do when you quit working. As in "retire."

He also referred to "them times" and "them years"

> "I've been patted on the back all my life. Now I'm taking a chance on becoming a good coach, hopefully a great coach."

with the Celtics. So an English professor he's not. Bird was hired to coach basketball, not teach grammar, and he left little doubt he can be a terrific communicator.

Bird also responded to the issue of his presence as an impetus for a new downtown arena. Though denied by all as a factor in his hiring, it is a factor nonetheless.

"When I talked to (Pacers President Donnie Walsh), he talked to me about coachin'," said Bird. "He didn't talk to me about sellin' tickets or buildin' new buildings. I'm very aware it could possibly help if we have a great year this year or next. And I never could shoot in this arena, so I'm all for tearing it down.

"I'm sure they'll get one. They need it, and they deserve it."

Finally, the questions wound down. Bird shook a few hands, then disappeared behind a curtain, where Pacers Reggie Miller and Fred Hoiberg awaited.

Yes, it was quite a scene, one not likely to be duplicated until Steve Alford returns to coach at Indiana University.

"I want to make Indiana proud," said Bird.

Monday, he took the first steps. ■

Accepting the Pacers' coaching offer meant accepting the intense media scrutiny that comes along with the job. (Rich Miller)

Coaching will offer Bird a new chance to compete

May 13, 1997

BY CONRAD BRUNNER

He could've stayed in Boston as the Celtics' general manager, a lofty and comfortable position that offered the ability to take credit for recruiting Rick Pitino.

He could've stayed in Naples, Florida, playing golf with his buddies, raising his two children, Connor and Mariah, and enjoying the good life with his wife, Dinah.

Instead, Larry Bird has given it all up for coaching, a job former Celtics coach Red Auerbach described as "a 15-hour day and travel and responsibility and aggravation and emotional ups and downs. . . . What would he want that for?"

The answer, to Bird, is pretty simple: to win.

"Everybody always asks me, 'Why do you want to do this?' And my answer is, I've always been very competitive," said Bird, 40. "I've been laying around for five years. I found out that 35 is too young to retire. I love the NBA, I like the competition, I like everything about it. And this is one way I can get right in the middle of it.

"If you want to compete in the NBA, you can be a player or a coach. That's the only way. I'm too old to play, so the only option I had was to coach, and I'm very thrilled about this opportunity to come here and see if I can do it."

This isn't what Bird had in mind when he ended his playing career in 1992. This isn't the end result of some master plan.

This is an opportunity to get back to work, to get his hands dirty in the workshop, and, ultimately, to build something new.

He sought advice from more than two dozen friends and colleagues, then ignored half of it.

"I talked to a lot of different people, probably 25 or 30, and it was split," he said. "After I ran everything by 'em, I asked 'em direct: Do you think I should get into this or should I stay away from it? And I have to tell you, it was probably 50-50. But at least I got some good input.

"I made the decision like I always do: myself. My heart was in it to coach. I wanted to be the Pacer coach in the worst way."

He leaves a sizable piece of that heart in Boston, where he played 13 seasons, won three championships, three MVPs and dozens of other individual honors. Though he has been on the Celtic payroll as a "special assistant," a job as nebulous as its title, Bird wasn't really involved until this year, when chairman of the board Paul Gaston asked him to put together a list of candidates to succeed outgoing coach M.L. Carr.

Bird did not put himself on that list. He approached Rick Pitino and Larry Brown. When Pitino accepted the job, Bird saw a new era dawning in Boston and figured it could happen here as well.

"This is my home state, and this is coaching," he said. "Rick Pitino will do a fine job in Boston. He's one of the top coaches in the country. He's proved that he's worth everything he gets. I have a lot of respect for Rick.

"But I didn't want to be there, sitting behind Rick and the people he brought in. I wanted to be involved, I wanted to be out there being competitive every night, and this is the place I wanted to do it."

He knows other great players have trod this path before him; in fact, he is the 15th former Celtics player to become an NBA head coach. Only a handful have made the transition with distinction.

"I think when guys make the commitments sometimes, maybe their hearts weren't in it. I don't know. I can't speak for 'em," he said. "My heart's in this. I want to win. I crave winning. Whether I'm going to be a great coach or not, I don't know that yet. I feel I'm gonna be. I feel I've got the tools and the knowledge of this game to do well."

It isn't a no-lose situation for Bird but, clearly, that isn't what he wants. He passed up a couple, after all, to take this job.

Bird's got high hopes

Pacers' rookie coach has a lot of confidence in himself to get the job done

May 13, 1997

BY MARK MONTIETH

Larry Bird has yet to coach a game in the NBA, but it's immediately apparent his style will be drastically different from that of his predecessor with the Indiana Pacers.

Whereas Larry Brown was a persistent teacher who instructed on virtually every possession of every game, Bird hopes to get more results by coaching less.

"I'm going to sit down and keep my mouth shut," Bird told more than 100 media representatives from across the nation Monday during his introductory news conference at Market Square Arena. "I think the coaches are taking over too much of the game. A lot of times coaches try to coach too much.

"If your guys are prepared and you have them in good shape and they know what your game plan is . . . stay back and let them play. If you've got a good point guard, which I know we do, who can call the plays and get the ball to the people we need to get it to, I can just stand over there and act like I'm coaching."

Bird doesn't intend to take a passive approach to coaching the Pacers, who have signed him to a contract that pays an estimated $4.5 million per season with a share of ownership. Bird believes he knows what needs to be done, and how to get his players to do it.

His style of play? Simple. Get the ball off the boards and run whenever possible. Be prepared to play a half-court game when necessary. Get the ball in the hands of shooters. Play good defense. And be the best-conditioned team in the league.

Other than that—and Bird admits he'll need help from experienced assistant coaches to handle the Xs and Os—it's a matter of competing.

"I expect them to come out to win; not just to play, but to win," he said. "There's probably times we won't get along as well as we'd like, but you don't take coaching jobs to make friends. You take coaching jobs to be competitive and win, and that's what I intend to do.

"I'm young and I'll probably make some mistakes. I just hope when I'm writing the plays out in the final seconds of a game, I don't put myself in the plays. I'm new at this game, but I feel I can get the job done. I have a lot of confidence in myself."

Pacer guards Fred Hoiberg and Reggie Miller attended Monday's news conference as observers, but Bird has not had an opportunity to speak with any of his players. He has played against some of them and studied them more this past season while mulling over the job opportunity that appeared likely to become available to him. Aside from more offense—a need Pacers president Donnie Walsh already has acknowledged—Bird believes he can win with what he's got.

"I like the team because I feel they can compete," Bird said.

"I'm not going to be happy missing the playoffs. Our intention is to get in the playoffs and win. We have

When you have confidence in your backcourt (Reggie Miller, left, and Mark Jackson, right) Bird told reporters that his philosophy is to "stay back and let them play." (Erin Painter)

a solid ballclub here. There's a couple of spots we have to improve on, but I think we have a good enough team to get where we want to get."

Although much has been said about superstars who did not succeed as coaches, Bird said he believes he has the patience, the work ethic and the thirst to win. He recalled playing with teammates who lacked ultimate dedication, and said he understands not everyone will love the game as he did. But he hopes his example will rub off on the players.

"The players that play for me are going to work hard, they're going to do the things necessary to win," he said. "I don't expect these kids to stay around for an hour and a half, two hours after practice and shoot. I do expect them to work on their weaknesses. Dale Davis, I

expect him to shoot 100 to 150 free throws every day of the week. That's a must. If we're in the final game of the playoffs and we need that game to move on, do you keep him in the game or do you take him out? I'll feel a lot better keeping him in the game if I know he's shot 100 to 150 free throws every day."

Bird said he has no idea how long he plans to coach. His contract is open-ended, providing the opportunity for him to move into the front office after his coaching career ends.

"If I really enjoy it and the players like me, I'll probably do it as long as we can win and be competitive," he said. "There's no timetable for me. If everybody's happy, I think we should continue to do it. I'll be the first one to know if I can't handle the job." ∎

Front-office role is in Bird's future

May 13, 1997

BY CONRAD BRUNNER

LARRY BIRD DIDN'T REVEAL MUCH when asked about his new contract with the Indiana Pacers, except to say, "I signed it."

But both Bird and team president Donnie Walsh confirmed Monday the deal includes a future front-office position in coming years.

Not that Walsh—the team's general manager since 1986— is ready to step aside, just yet.

"I'm going to be here for a while, with Larry in the position he's in," said Walsh. "Then, down the road, we'll take a look at it. Any time you're in one place for so long, you run the risk of having your thinking become stale, and I don't want that to happen here. I do know I can't think of anybody I'd rather leave it to than Larry Bird."

For the time being, Bird will have his hands full learning to be a head coach.

"I've got a lot of work to do," he said. "I've got to get some assistant coaches, I've got to find a place to live. . . . Geez. Is this (news conference) about over with?"

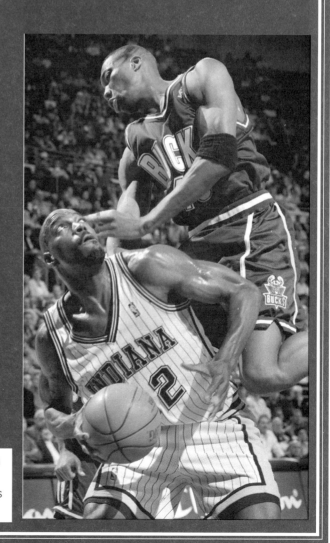

In order to keep Dale Davis and his ferocious rebounding on the floor in the late stages of a game, Bird expects Davis to improve his free-throw shooting by taking 150 practice shots every day. (Matt Kryger)

7

MAY-OCTOBER 1997

SHAPIN' THE FUTURE

Bird is intent to look into Pacers' hearts

May 14, 1997

BY MARK MONTIETH

On his first full day as the coach of the Indiana Pacers, Larry Bird wore his job like a well-tailored suit. Displaying the confidence of a veteran and the enthusiasm of a rookie, Bird met the team's front office employees, huddled with team president Donnie Walsh and trainer David Craig to go over various details and squeezed in a few media interviews.

Although he's worked for the Boston Celtics for the previous 18 years, Bird began referring to the Pacers as "we" several weeks ago, when he began seriously considering the job. It rolls off the tongue easily now.

Coaching the Pacers promises to be a brave new world for someone who has spent the past five years tucked away in Naples, Florida, a place Bird calls "the greatest place in the world." Not only will he give up 80-degree winter days, he'll give up much of the privacy he cherishes for himself and his family.

Still, Bird will be surrounded by family and friends in central Indiana, and he'll always have his home in French Lick, where he's spent many of his summers since graduating from Indiana State in 1979. Fittingly, the Pacers figure to have a more home-spun flavor under his reign. Practices will be open to the media, and he'll invite the public—particularly children's groups —to watch on occasion. Training camp, conducted in Chapel Hill, N.C. under former coach Larry Brown, will be in Indiana, perhaps even Indianapolis. "I always liked the idea of staying home," he said.

He likes the idea of returning home, too. Bird sat down with a reporter and columnist from *The Indianapolis Star* and *The Indianapolis News* Tuesday to discuss the challenges ahead.

Q. You're returning to public life now, and doing it in your home state. You're going to get a lot of attention from fans, and you're going to have to deal with the media. Do you cringe when you think about that?

A. "Not as much as I used to. It's not that I get mad at the people, but I've never understood it. I've never understood autographs. The best thing about retirement was living in Naples and nobody bothering me. That was the best.

"But I'm 40 years old and I've been out for five years. I still think I've got something to give to this game. I think I've got the opportunity of a lifetime, coming back home and coaching a team I've respected, an organization I've always respected. I know I've got to put up with the other stuff. I don't

really feel comfortable with it, but I'll adjust to it and do it."

Q. What do you want to discuss when you sit down with your players?

A. "I want to find out, really deep down in their hearts, if they want to win a championship. There's some guys in this league who don't want to win. Some guys just want to play the season and get the hell out so they can go on down the road and have fun. A lot of guys don't want to dive on the floor because they're afraid they'll get hurt and might hurt a future contract. I want to find out if these guys really want to dig down deep and try get to the next level."

Q. You had a chance to watch the Pacers some this past season when it appeared you might take over as coach. What were your impressions of them?

A. "I could tell the players didn't have the fire they had the year before. Something was missing. I remember reading a quote from Larry Brown about having a very important game, and they went out and played terrible. Maybe they tried too hard, I don't know. Things like that scare me.

"But I do believe in these guys and what they're capable of doing. Hopefully I can get them motivated enough to not be in the position to fight the last six or seven games of the season to get in the playoffs. Our goal is to get in the playoffs and advance after we get in there."

Q. What are the Pacers' greatest needs?

A. "This team needs one more scorer. You have Rik Smits and Reggie Miller, but if you shut those two guys down . . . is Dale Davis capable of getting you 18 points a night? I don't know. Is Tony Davis? You look there and you don't see it, consistently. But if we get one more player . . . you look at Chicago and they have three players who can score. That's what you need to win in this league."

Q. Did you follow the Pacers as a kid, during their glory years in the ABA?

A. "I remember watching them on TV and seeing Dr. J flying through the air and dunking. That was back in '74. I was up in a friend's room watching the game and couldn't believe it. I never had aspirations of playing pro ball then. That was so far away for me, I could care less. All I

Bird says he's looking for players who are willing to give the extra effort required to be a champion. Antonio Davis shows that effort by finishing his play with an exclamation mark. (Kelly Wilkinson)

wanted to do was go to college and play a little bit. But watching them games was unbelievable.

"I had gone to a game in Louisville when I was in the seventh grade. I had no clue it was a professional game. A guy took my brother and I down there and dropped us off. We had the worst seats in the house, which was fine. I sat there and these people were going absolutely berserko. The place was rocking. I mean, rocking.

We were heading home and the guy who picked us up said, 'Well, how'd you like that game?' I said it was something else for a college game. You've got to understand, I had never gone to high school games or anything. And I said, 'The pro games are even better, aren't they?' He said, 'You didn't know that was a pro game?' I had no clue."

Q. The Pacers had the first pick in the draft in 1978, after your junior year at Indiana State. You met with Bobby "Slick" Leonard, the coach at the time in Indianapolis, and talked about coming out then, but you decided to return for your senior season. The Pacers, of course, passed you over in the draft that year, and you went to the Celtics. Was that a disappointment?

A. "If I remember right, I was p——— off at the time. I knew absolutely nothing about Boston. Nothing. I knew (Bill) Russell played for them and they won a lot of championships, but

that's about it.

"It would have been a hell of a lot easier to make the drive up here than pack my car and go all the way to Boston. Of course things turned out great and Boston was probably the best place for me.

"Slick told me the Pacers couldn't afford to pay me much, but he wanted me to come out. I said, 'Hell, I'm going back to college.' My mom wanted me to stay in college and I wanted to get my degree.

"The next thing I know, I was playing golf and somebody said they heard the Boston Celtics had taken me in some kind of draft. That night I watched it on TV. Nobody from Boston had called me or said anything to me. It was really strange.

"But everything turned out all right." ∎

> "I want to find out, really deep down in their hearts, if they want to win a championship. There's some guys in this league who don't want to win. ... I want to find out if these guys really want to dig down deep and try to get to the next level."

As a player, Bird's trademark was his commitment to doing whatever was necessary to win—diving for loose balls, boxing out opponents, making the extra pass. As a coach, he expects no less from his Pacers. (Paul Sancya)

Bird won't let Rose wither on the pine

May 15, 1997

BY BILL BENNER

Just when did Larry Bird begin to evaluate the Indiana Pacers with a critical eye?

"Back in 1980," Bird said during an interview in the Pacers' Market Square Arena offices Tuesday, the day after he was officially introduced as the team's new coach.

"I've always followed them. I've always wanted to see them do well. I always wanted to play against them in the playoffs. I've just always followed this team."

But Bird's scrutiny has been particularly keen over the past couple of months as his interest in coaching the Pacers came closer to becoming reality.

He reiterated Tuesday what he said during his news conference Monday. He believes the pieces and personnel are in place for the Pacers—out of the playoffs this season just two years after reaching the Eastern Conference finals—to return to contending status.

He also acknowledged the obvious: that a change—or two—in the roster will have to be made.

But if his comments Tuesday are any indication, two names that won't appear on the list of expendables may surprise you.

Jalen Rose and Fred Hoiberg.

"I've got big plans for Jalen Rose," Bird said of the 6-8, 210-pound, Michigan product who just finished his second season as a pro.

"I'm going to play him in different positions. He's got to be on the floor. I think he's a plus when he's out there.

"I love Jalen Rose. He's a utility player, like a baseball player that can play all the positions. That's the way I see Jalen. Me and Jalen will get along fine because I like the way he plays."

Bird intends to give Jalen Rose lots of playing time to take advantage of the matchup problems Rose creates with his size and versatility. (Matt Kryger)

That was, of course, an opinion not always shared by Bird's predecessor, Larry Brown. Brown, too, liked Rose's versatility, but Jalen's lack of skills on the defensive end led Brown to move Rose out of the rotation as often as not.

Although still not a stopper by any stretch, Rose became a better defender as the season progressed and, in April, Brown rewarded Rose with consistent, meaningful minutes.

Rose responded with his best overall play of the season, scoring in double-figures in six of Indiana's last nine games, shooting .495 from the floor (even with an 0 for 8 against Detroit in the finale) and averaging more than three assists.

"Jalen Rose just needs time," Bird said. "You have to find time for him. He might not be happy if he's not starting and playing 38-40 minutes a game, but you've got to find time for him. I'm going to play him."

Another player Bird has bigger plans for is backup shooting guard Hoiberg (Hoe-berg, in Bird's pronunciation) who is as revered in his hometown of Ames, Iowa, as Bird is in French Lick, Indiana.

Under Brown, Hoiberg saw limited action early but, like Rose, had his playing time increased as the season wore down.

Bird said he is concerned about how much players will work on their skills this summer. Hoiberg's effort, however, isn't something Bird feels compelled to check on.

"I don't have to worry about Fred," Bird said. "He's going to be there. And he's going to get some time. I'm not going to let him sit on the bench for 10 or 12 games in a row, then bring him in. If that guy's there every day, he deserves some time.

"I'm not going to say he's going to start in front of Reggie Miller. I'm not that stupid. Reggie's a hell of a basketball player. But there's a place for a guy like Fred on my team and there always will be." ■

Bird, Mullin form dream team

August 14, 1997

BY BILL BENNER

They're not clones but the Indiana Pacers' newest coach and newest player, Larry Bird and Chris Mullin, could be described as twin sons of different mothers.

As they hoisted Mullin's No. 17 Pacers jersey Wednesday at a news conference in Market Square Arena, Bird and Mullin shared more than a grip on the same fabric. They also shared a grasp on how a quickness-impaired, gravity-challenged fellow in constant need of 30 SPF sun block can not only survive, but thrive in the above-the-rim world of the NBA.

The two Barcelona Dream Teamers made their marks based on the lost art of the jump shot, deft passing and an uncanny sense of knowing where to be, and when, on the basketball floor.

And when it comes right down to it, all Bird is asking Mullin is to be to the Pacers what Bird was to the Celtics: a small forward who plays big and makes those around him better.

Granted, the 6-7 Mullin is no Bird—who is?—but he's not far behind, especially when the primes of their careers are compared.

Now, at 34, with injuries and illness marking four of his previous five seasons, Mullin is no longer in that prime. And those unknowns—can he remain healthy, can he approach his previous productivity, can he be the offensive relief valve for Reggie Miller and Rik Smits?— make Mullin's acquisition for Erick Dampier and Duane Ferrell a high-risk, high-reward deal that gambles the future for the present.

Then again, in this what-are-you-doing-for-me- now world, that may be the way to go.

Mullin has been at the top of Bird's wish list since Larry took the job in May. Donnie Walsh finally was able to seal the deal and Mullin feels like he's 13 years old with the keys to the gym again.

(Paul Sancya)

New Pacer coach Larry Bird has made it clear that he expects important contributions from Jalen Rose (above) and Chris Mullin (below).

(Mike Fender)

3 on a bench: Bird chooses quality over quantity

October 31, 1997

BY MARK MONTIETH

Y ou don't have to look hard to find assistant coaches in the NBA. They're everywhere, over-flowing benches and forcing injured players, seldom-used players, trainers and others onto the floor and into makeshift second rows.

Most teams have three assistants. Some, including the Chicago Bulls, have four. And that's not including the scouts, video specialists and other clipboard-toting extras who fill out a basketball staff.

Indiana Pacers coach Larry Bird, on the other hand, has gone for efficiency.

He hired Dick Harter, Rick Carlisle and nobody else to be his bench assistants, preferring the quality company of two over the crowded confusion of three.

The beauty of it was that he didn't so much hire assistants as he unwrapped them—a staff-in-the-box shipped directly from Portland, already proven and ready to plug in and play. Harter and Carlisle had worked for the Trail Blazers for the past three seasons and already had established mutual respect and chemistry.

Another Blazer employee, video coordinator Dan Burke, followed them, completing the package deal that has made Bird's transition easier.

"I got very lucky," Bird said.

"They like working together and they stay out of each other's way. Dan, Rick and Dick have been perfect so far."

Perfection will be difficult to maintain, but if the reputations of Harter and Carlisle are deserved, Bird can rest assured he got two of the best. Some would say the best.

Sports Illustrated will feature Harter in an upcoming issue as the NBA's top assistant coach. Carlisle was listed as the best assistant in the Eastern Conference by a Boston reporter in a recent issue of *The Sporting News*.

The respect of peers is more meaningful, and they

have that, too. Harter had coaching offers from five other NBA teams besides the Pacers, Carlisle from four.

They chose Indiana largely because of Bird and the freedom he promised them. It's unlikely any set of Pacer assistants has ever been as involved as they are.

"I've been in this league now for 18 years and every time I've been around assistant coaches they've never done anything," Bird said.

"I don't want them sitting on the sidelines with their arms folded, like I've seen assistants do in the past. We're in it as a team, and the players know that. It's just like I want my team to work."

Harter, 66, won better than 60 percent of his games over an 18-year-period as the head coach at Rider, Penn, Oregon State and Penn State. He then moved into the NBA, where he has served as an assistant to Chuck Daly in Detroit (three years), to Jack Ramsay with the Pacers (two years), as the sacrificial first head coach of the expansion Charlotte Hornets (two years), as a television commentator in Detroit (one year), as an assistant to Pat Riley in New York (three years) and as an assistant in

With assistants Dick Harter (left) and Rick Carlisle (right), Bird has surrounded himself with a veteran coaching staff. (Paul Sancya)

Pacers assistant Rick Carlisle diagrams a play with head coach Larry Bird.
(Paul Sancya)

by the Nets, in November 1988, when he accepted Fitch's offer to work as an advance scout/assistant coach.

He stayed with Fitch and the next Nets coach, Daly, before moving on to Portland. His role and reputation grew at each stop, particularly relating to offense, and he's now considered throughout the league as a virtual lock to become a head coach.

A BOND IN BOSTON

Bird and Carlisle had become friends during their playing days in Boston and kept in touch after Bird's retirement.

When Bird began talking of getting back into the game a few years ago, Carlisle sent him a notebook of scouting reports. When Bird was deciding whether to accept the Pacers' offer, Carlisle was one of the people he consulted.

So it was no surprise that, when Carlisle and Harter washed ashore in the wake of P.J. Carlesimo's firing in Portland, Bird immediately went after Carlisle . . . who in turn recommended Harter . . . who in turn told Bird that two should be enough.

"I told Larry when we sat down, 'I don't know if you're going to hire me or not, but my advice is to hire two guys and really use them,'" Harter said.

Bird has, and the combination of rookie head coach and veteran assistants appears to be working.

Bird is clearly in charge, but he has no insecurity about his authority. Harter and Carlisle have meaningful voices, and the freedom to exercise them. It's appropriate that Bird sits between them on the bench, lending one ear to each.

"When you put a new staff together, sometimes it takes a year to get comfortable, because you don't want to step on peoples' toes," Carlisle said.

"Dick and I are beyond that. Larry and I have known each other for a long time, and Larry and Dick have hit

Portland (three years).

Harter describes his experience as the head coach of the Hornets as "a death wish," and while he would consider another head coaching opportunity if the situation was right (a veteran team and a stable front office), he's happy as an assistant. Having built a reputation as one of the game's top defensive minds, he has unique security.

Carlisle, 37, was a teammate of Bird's for three seasons in Boston. He also played one season for Rick Pitino in New York, then caught on with Bill Fitch in New Jersey.

His coaching career began the day after he was cut

it off fabulously. There's no messing around. We get right down to business."

DAILY DEBATES

The trio gets along well enough that they can disagree now and then. Many of the debates center around the team's performance and progress.

Bird, while demanding, is an optimist who doesn't hesitate to offer praise. He realizes there will be bad practices and bad games, but he says he can't imagine the team shifting into reverse after such a promising preseason.

But Harter and Carlisle, hardened by their experiences in the NBA, point out the negatives and wonder how the players will deal with adversity. Bird smiles when recalling the almost daily point-counterpoint.

"I'll say, 'Hey, we had a great practice today,'" Bird said. "And they'll say, 'No, we had an average practice.' I'll ask why and they'll come up with a few little things. I'll say, 'If you're going on two or three little details, yeah, we had an average practice.' But I look at the total picture. That's what I have to do."

Carlisle and Harter respond with knowing smiles.

"The longer he's in this, the more he's going to be just like us," Carlisle said. ■

Bird and assistant Dick Harter bark out defensive assignments. (Matt Kryger)

8

1997-98 PACERS

NOTHING REGULAR ABOUT THIS SEASON

Team heads into camp on the run

Coach Larry Bird has vowed to begin the season with players in top shape

October 3, 1997

BY MARK MONTIETH

Larry Bird wanted his first Indiana Pacers team to have a running start heading into training camp. It appears he has gotten it, literally.

Most of the 20 players who open training camp this morning at the Disney Institute in Orlando have participated in the team's informal workouts at the Indiana Basketball Academy for the past few weeks. The voluntary sessions included non-voluntary running, either on the court or on the North Central High School track.

It's all part of Bird's plan to have the "best-conditioned team in the league," a vow he made when he was named the Pacers' coach last May and has repeated since then.

"I can't tell you exactly what kind of condition they're in, but I know next week they'll be in a lot better condition," Bird said Thursday. "If they're in shape we'll be able to move along more quickly.

"The one thing we won't have on this team is a lot of guys with a beer belly. They're going to be slim; they're going to be able to run; they'll be able to jump. I'm not here to kill these guys, but I know if you want to be in top condition, you have to run."

From all appearances, most of the players are nearly there already. Former coach Larry Brown had the same emphasis and issued written warnings to his players throughout the summer to report in shape. Not many heeded Brown's message, though.

"Most guys came in just a few days before camp last year," third-year guard Fred Hoiberg recalled. "That may have been why we got off to a slow start. Those early games can't be made up for later, especially the home losses."

Brown tested his players by conducting a timed mile run on the first day of camp last year. Another former Pacers coach, Jack Ramsay, conducted a two-mile run, with fines for those missing cutoff times, in the mid-1980s.

Bird won't go to that extreme because he knows from personal experience how difficult distance running can be for basketball-sized athletes. He'll keep his conditioning program confined to the basketball court.

"You get guys who have been in the league for 12

years and have had two knee operations or a back operation and start (running long distances). It's tough," Bird said.

Bird, however, has logged plenty of miles. He has been an avid runner since his days at Indiana State. He once ran a 5:08 mile, which is exceptional for someone standing 6-9 and weighing more than 200 pounds, and routinely knocked off 5:20 miles in preseason workouts. He recalls with nostalgia running three or four miles, scrimmaging with his teammates, doing situps and then closing out the workout by shooting.

"I enjoyed it, because I was a good runner," he said. "But the big guys always had problems. I felt sorry for them. I used to say, 'You can't break six minutes? You're dogging it.' But I'd see the pain on their faces and realize how hard it was."

Bird continued running throughout most of his NBA career. He often participated in races through the streets of Boston, acting as a celebrity starter on many occasions. He'd fire the starter's pistol and then take off with the rest of the elite runners in the front of the pack—for awhile.

"I had to watch out because there were some big-time runners out there," he said. "You'd have three or four thousand people come up on you. You'd have to stay out of the

way or they'd run you over."

His longest race was 8.5 miles, with about 14,000 fellow competitors. He had only completed about half of the run when the leaders crossed the finish line, and he paid a stiff price for his daring adventure.

"It about killed me," he said. "From that I went down to five (miles). Everything on me hurt...my ankles, my knees, my back."

Bird continues to run today. A morning person by nature, he's often up about 5:30 a.m. and out the door soon thereafter. He's mapped out a 3.3 mile course in his neighborhood and tries to run it four or five days a week.

"When you're running, anything negative that can go through your mind will; it drives you crazy," he said.

"Every once in a while I'll get up and go, 'Well, I'm running 15 minutes behind schedule. If I don't get this done, maybe I won't run today.' Then all of a sudden you go, 'Hey, get your butt out there and run.'"

Words for his players to live by for the next week. ■

Before starting practice, Bird often begins his day at 5:30 a.m. with a 3.3 mile run. (Mike Fender)

Pacers to open under microscope

Large media contingent is poised to dissect Larry Bird's coaching debut.

October 31, 1997

BY MARK MONTIETH

OPENING NIGHT

Who: Indiana Pacers at New Jersey Nets.
Tipoff: 7:30 p.m.
TV: WTTV-4
Radio: WIBC-1070 AM

It should be the final significant first of Larry Bird's coaching career with the Indiana Pacers.

After an offseason of landmark moments—his hiring, his first draft, his first day of coaching at rookie camp, his first summer league game, his first day of training camp, his first preseason game—Bird finally gets to do what he was hired to do in the first place.

Coach an NBA game. One that counts.

A large media contingent will be on hand for the Pacers' opener at New Jersey tonight to report the story of the legendary player who gave up warm weather, country club golf and his cherished privacy to coach his homestate NBA team.

Along with the usual group from New York City and surrounding cities in New Jersey, representatives from two Indianapolis television stations, a radio station and a Boston newspaper will cover the moment.

That media contingent, along with a near-sellout crowd of about 19,000, will also witness a vigorous pre-game promotional effort designed to emphasize the new in New Jersey.

A new mascot, a new dance team, a new $1.4 million lighting system, a new video, a new logo and new uniforms will be unveiled. To help set the

Rookie head coach Larry Bird grimaces as his Indiana Pacers fall 97-95 in the season opener to the New Jersey Nets. (Corey Sipkin Photography, New York)

mood, boxing announcer Michael Buffer ("Let's get ready to rumble!") will be on hand.

"It will be the most animated type of presentation the Nets have ever put on," one team official said Thursday.

Just what Bird needs. More hype.

The former Boston Celtics great, who hasn't been directly involved in an NBA game since the end of the 1992 season, already has received visits from media members representing newspapers in New York, Los Angeles, Chicago, Philadelphia, and Washington D.C.; magazines including Sports Illustrated and Esquire; and television networks ESPN, CNN-SI and TNT.

The Pacers' media relations department had a revolving list of interview requests that topped out at about 35 over the summer, many of which Bird was unable or unwilling to meet. He's also turned down invitations to appear on Late Show with David Letterman, The Tonight Show with Jay Leno, Charlie Rose's PBS program, ESPN's Up Close and a Roy Firestone ESPN special, as well as various network radio talk shows.

He's taken a businesslike approach, patiently answering every question that comes his way after practice or games but declining to take time out for those who want special arrangements.

"I don't like it, and I never did," Bird said of the media interest. "But it's part of it."

And he knows it will follow him every step of the way as the Pacers tour the NBA.

The incessant Bird-watching could be a negative for the players, who will be scrutinized more closely than otherwise because of their coach. Or it could be a positive, distracting some of the attention from them.

Or, it could be neither.

The attitude of many of the media members on hand for Bird's debut on Friday was succinctly defined by the reporter who called his office from the press room beforehand. "Hey, it's me," he said. "I'm at the Bird game."

The media crush surrounding Bird's coaching debut has also increased the media's scrutiny of the players. (Paul Sancya)

Bird recalls past as he steps into coaching

November 1, 1997

BY MARK MONTIETH

Larry Bird's first NBA game as a player came 18 years ago in Boston. Friday, in the moments leading up to his first game as an NBA coach, he saw little comparison between the two events.

"When I was excited about playing professional basketball and seeing how good these players really were," Bird told about a dozen reporters gathered behind a curtained-off area outside the Pacers' locker room. "It's different."

Bird said he recalls his debut, against Houston "very vividly," as he remembers all of his games. He says he "played average" but couldn't remember how many points he scored in that game. One Boston reporter who covered the game recalled him scoring about 18 points.

Bird was one of the most scrutinized players in the NBA during his 13-year playing career because of his success and figures to be one of the more watched coaches this season. That, however, doesn't seem to faze him.

"I could care less," he said. "As a player I could care less, and as a coach, I could care less. That's your guys' job. I wish you luck with it."

The fun, Bird said, will be the challenge of equaling the success he had as a player.

"That's why I'm in this," he said. "I want to accomplish things that people said I couldn't accomplish. I'm the type of individual who really doesn't listen to the outside.

"I just want to do my job and work hard at it and learn as I go. But it's difficult. I'm in a game where there are a lot of great coaches. But I want to win a championship; that's my ultimate goal."

Other thoughts from Bird:

On what he enjoys most about coaching: "The practices. Working these guys hard and seeing how they're going to react to it."

On his approach to conditioning: "I wouldn't put these guys through anything I wouldn't go through. Seeing them react to what I have to say about conditioning is mind-boggling at times. But it's the truth. I won't lie to these guys. I'll tell them exactly how I feel about the game and what they have to do to prepare themselves."

On whether he's a better shooter than his players: "No, not even close. After five years (of retirement), I've gotten a little rusty."

On the expectations of his home-state fans: "They're probably not expecting any more than I am out of these guys. If I don't do well, I'm sure they'll find somebody else."

Although he still practices regularly, Bird says his five years of retirement have left his shot a little rusty. (Paul Sancya)

Little things mean a lot for Bird

Pacers Coach hopes better mental conditioning will help win games in the closing minutes

November 14, 1997

BY MARK MONTIETH

When Larry Bird was putting the Indiana Pacers through all those grueling preseason workouts, he had a simple, deal-closing sales pitch: It all would pay off in the fourth quarter of close games.

"Now they're probably thinking, he doesn't know what he's talking about," Bird said Thursday, poking a ray of humor through the cloud hovering over his team.

It turns out physical conditioning hasn't been a problem for the Pacers. It's more the mental conditioning that has brought about the myriad of small mistakes that have caused their 2-5 record heading into tonight's game against the Miami Heat.

Indiana's two victories have come by a total of 25 points. The five losses have come by a total of 21, and all of them were winnable in the final minute. Bird's repeated message to his players is that little things make the big things happen, but the Pacers haven't done enough of those little things to get a close win.

"A lot of people would rather get beat by 15 or 20, because you could name so many things," Reggie Miller said. "But when you're losing by two or three points a game, you have to look at yourself and think, 'Damn, if I hadn't let him go baseline that time, or if I had hit my free throws in the fourth quarter or if I had blocked out that one time. ...'

"It's a break here, a rebound here, a turnover there. If we turn that around. ... But if ifs were fifths, we'd all be drunk."

Bird has been pleased with his players' effort and attitude since the start of training camp. He calls them "the best guys in the league." But their effort and attitude hasn't always carried over into the games, where lapses in concentration on the part of a few for relatively brief stretches have forced everyone to pay a stiff, ultimate price.

That mystifies Bird, given the favorable math that the games offer.

"We were out here today for two hours," Bird said following Thursday's practice. "To stay focused for two hours is tough, I'll admit that.

"But when the game comes, all I'm asking is for a couple of our guys to play 35 minutes; the rest of them don't even play 30 minutes. Now come on, just play hard for 28 to 30 minutes on game nights. That's a lot easier than practices. It's like a day off. Why can't they give it to me during games? That's all I ask."

That, and for his players to greet the final ticks of the clock with open arms. Bird looks into the eyes of his players in the latter moments of games and sees insecurity. He'd prefer serenity.

"When I played and the game got close and there were two or three minutes on the clock, I always felt this calmness come over me," Bird said. "But it's hard for me to get into their heads and ask these guys how they feel. Guys react differently.

"I really enjoy it. That's why I got back into this. When it's close like it was (in Wednesday's loss to the Atlanta Hawks), I still

Bird sculpture auctioned to Indy man for $2,500

11/08/97—Sid Blazek of Indianapolis is the proud owner of the Larry Bird sculpture auctioned by The Star and The News with proceeds going to charity.

Blazek, an avid Pacers and Larry Bird fan, outbid 48 others who left bids on the Star-News InfoLine.

Blazek bid $2,500 for the sculpture, created by Star-News staff artist John Bigelow for the cover of the NBA Preview section published October 31.

The donation will go to the Star-News Season For Sharing campaign, which assists needy children, the homeless, hungry and elderly in Central Indiana. The fund will actually grow by $3,750, however, because the Robert R. McCormick Tribune Foundation donates 50 cents for every dollar contributed to the holiday fund.

Bigelow's sculpture of Bird, the Indiana Pacers' new coach, is 29 ½-inches tall, and was made with Crayola airdry model magic modeling compound and acrylic paints.

feel that calmness, and I really like it. Because I have trust in these guys that they'll pull it out."

The challenge is transferring that feeling to the players.

"Boy, I wish I could," Bird said. "I don't think you can do that. I think it's all in the individual makeup." ■

Bird says transferring his legendary mental toughness to the players is his greatest challenge as a coach. (Erin Painter)

Bird's hands-off approach

Pacers prosper under coach's cool courtside manner

December 26, 1997

BY MARK MONTIETH

Leaning back on the bench clasping a knee, or standing along the sideline with his hands stuffed in his pockets, Indiana Pacers coach Larry Bird often appears closer to a yawn than a shout during games.

State basketball fans accustomed to the more aggressive demeanor of college coaches such as Gene Keady and Bob Knight, or notable NBA coaches such as Rick Pitino and Pat Riley, might wonder if the rookie head coach already is tired of his new job.

Bird isn't feeling boredom, however; he's trying to give freedom.

"I'm into every one of these games, although I might not show it," said Bird, whose 17-9 team plays Orlando at Market Square Arena tonight.

"A coach is sort of a leader, and if you're hollering and screaming at everybody, I think it takes something from them. I've always said it's a players' game, and the players should be putting on the show. I'm not going to be screaming and yelling at them all the time; that's not my nature. I played for coaches who were screamers, and I didn't like it."

Bird takes the Theodore Roosevelt approach: walk softly and carry a big stick. Twenty-six games into his rookie season as a coach, he has been called for just two technical fouls, one of them in Tuesday's loss at San Antonio.

Bird doesn't scold players during games, and he doesn't fill timeouts with frantic dialogue. Other than calling an occasional play, or making a joke, he says little to the players during games. But he's blunt with them during private moments and demands the same effort in practice, win or lose.

"He'll let you know if he's upset with something; he just flat out tells you," Rik Smits said.

"But he lets you play and learn from your own mistakes. He doesn't make you feel bad about taking your shots."

Mark Jackson probably has been most affected by Bird's style. As the point guard, he takes pride in being a leader, but he found it more difficult to lead under former coach Larry Brown's anxious, talkative coaching style. Bird says less and gives him looser reins. Jackson believes his league-leading assist-to-turnover ratio might be an indirect result of Bird's approach.

"Coach Bird tells me to call the shots and run the show," Jackson said. "He respects what I've done in this league. He trusts me with the ball and with the offense.

"Sometimes he calls something, but even then he says, 'Hey forget what I say if you want. If you feel something, go ahead and do it.' It just boosts the confidence level of everyone on the floor. You're not looking over there if you make a mistake. It's almost like a quarterback being able to step to the line and reading an audible and not being afraid to make a change.

"Coach Brown allowed me to call the plays, too. The difference was the yelling in the midst of it. Everybody pretty much froze and was afraid to do things. It affected the whole offense."

Bird's demeanor has brought a major change to huddles during timeouts, too. He spends the first few moments with his assistant coaches. All three then take turns addressing the players. Dick Harter discusses defensive assignment, and Rick Carlisle goes over the offense. Bird is an overseer.

"Whenever he says something, people are attentive because he doesn't say a lot," Fred Hoiberg said. "He doesn't play around with us and tell us what we want to hear, he tells it like it is. And when the players respect the coach, they're going to listen to what he says.

"It's quality over quantity." ∎

BOSTON ALL AFLUTTER OVER BIRD'S RETURN

Celtics fans may end up cheering Pacers' coach in the heavily hyped matchup on national TV

January 18, 1998

BY MARK MONTIETH

Joe Qatato knows how the fans in Boston will feel today.

"They'll be in an uproar," he said. "They'll have that feeling you have when chills are running up your spine."

Qatato spent 17 years working for the Celtics in a variety of part-time positions. Many of those duties put him in contact with Larry Bird during Bird's playing career, and the two developed a close relationship. So when Bird called him early last June to offer a position with the Pacers as an assistant to the training and administrative staffs, he said yes "in a heartbeat."

If Bird can inspire that kind of loyalty in a team employee, it only figures the fans who cheered his legendary 13-year playing career will be excited by his return to Boston today. The team Bird coaches, the Indiana Pacers, meets the team he played for, the Boston Celtics, at the sold out FleetCenter in what is probably the most hyped and anticipated game of the NBA season to date.

"The fans loved him so much," Qatato said. "It's going to be a weird crowd. They'll give him a standing ovation, and I think they'll watch how the game goes to see who's in the lead.

"If the Pacers are winning, they might change and root for the Pacers."

NBC will broadcast the event as the opener of a double-header that kicks off its nationally televised Sunday games—one of just two appearances for the Pacers this season. ESPN radio also will air the game nationally, and almost 400 media members—about double the normal turnout—have received credentials.

Today's game sold out well before the season be-

gan, and marks the ninth full house in 21 Celtic home games. Indiana's next trip to Boston on April 12 also is sold out.

Bird's 25-11 Pacers and Rick Pitino's 17-19 Celtics are two of the NBA's most surprising teams, each compiling eight more victories than at the same stage last season. Only San Antonio (15 more wins) and Phoenix (12) have improved more.

But the game itself is a subplot, and to a lesser degree so is the halftime ceremony to retire the number (00) of former Celtics center Robert Parish.

> **"Deep down I want to win that game so bad I can almost taste it."**

The main attraction will be Bird, who won three NBA Most Valuable Player awards and led the Celtics to three league championships during his career.

Bird vividly recalls the day he drove from Terre Haute to Boston to begin his NBA career. It was in Boston, he said, that he grew from boy to man. He enjoyed his time there immensely.

But he doesn't agree with the notion that today's game represents a homecoming for him. He came home, he said, when he took the Pacers' job.

"Them days are over," Bird said of his career with the Celtics. "I'm moving on. My pride and everything else is in Indiana now. We're going there to win a ballgame."

Bird, as usual, will do as much as possible to avoid the hoopla. His only social plan after the Pacers' arrival in Boston late Saturday afternoon was to stop by a small dinner gathering for Parish, his teammate for three championships. Nor has he allowed himself to get caught up in the scramble to provide complimentary tickets for long-lost friends, common when NBA players or coaches return to cities where they played. He's giving his allotted four to Dan Dyrek, a Boston physical therapist "who kept me in the league for four years," and has left it at that.

Throughout last week, Bird continually referred to today's matchup as "just another game on the schedule." Following Friday's victory over Sacramento, however, he admitted to special feelings for it.

"Deep down I want to win that game so bad I can almost taste it," he said.

His players will feed off the special atmosphere. The national television audience and the hype surrounding the game make it special for them, too, and they hope to present themselves and their coach in a positive light.

"It's almost a win-one-for-the-Gipper attitude," Reggie Miller said.

Bird and his players are grateful they have a veteran team that should be able to handle the distractions. Each of Indiana's starters has been in the league a minimum of six seasons and has playoff experience. The most experienced Boston starter, Andrew DeClerq, is in his third season.

"We understand the microscope that we're all going to be under," Mark Jackson said. "I'm sure their team will be motivated, and I'm sure coach Pitino will make it a rah-rah thing with the fans. But it's a great opportunity for us to showcase our skills in front of a sold out house and in front of the nation."

Several factors dampen Bird's sentiment for returning to the scene of his glory days. The Celtics' front office underwent a thorough makeover after Pitino was named coach, the day before Bird accepted the Pacers' offer in May. Bird would find few familiar faces if he walked through the Celtics offices today. The players are foreign to him, too. The only current Celtic he played with is Dee Brown, and the only two he played against are Pervis Ellison and Dana Barros.

More importantly to him, the Celtics no longer live in the house where he grew up. Bird played in the historic Boston Garden, not the more modern but less personable FleetCenter, which became the team's home two years ago.

"When they switched over, I switched off," Bird said. "I'm happy for the fans because they have a better place to view a basketball game, but the prices are too high. I have no attachment to that place whatsoever."

Bird also left the Celtics with a slightly sour taste in his mouth. Paid as a consultant, he never felt his opinions on player personnel matters were held in much regard during the five years following his retirement from the court.

"I was in a lot of meetings and had a lot of say, but they did a lot of things I didn't know they were going to do," he said. "It's their team and I was only there part of the time, I understand that. But I was very disappointed when I left there with the type of team they had."

Bird likes the team he has in Indiana just fine. And the fans in Boston are learning to like the Celtics again. Today, with their former hero working for the opposition, they'll have two teams to cheer. ■

Indiana 103, Boston 96
January 18, 1998

PACERS

PLAYER	MIN	FGM-A	3PM-A	FTM-A	OFF	DEF	TOT	AST	PF	PTS
D. Davis	24	3-3	0-0	0-0	2	7	9	2	1	6
Mullin	22	4-8	1-1	4-4	2	4	6	1	1	13
Smits	28	11-18	0-0	3-4	2	5	7	0	6	25
Miller	39	6-14	2-5	6-8	0	4	4	0	1	20
Jackson	31	4-8	1-1	0-2	1	1	2	13	1	9
Rose	26	7-10	0-0	6-7	0	0	0	5	1	20
McKey	24	1-4	0-0	2-2	1	2	3	1	5	4
A. Davis	20	0-2	0-0	2-4	0	2	2	0	1	2
Best	17	2-3	0-0	0-0	1	0	1	2	3	4
Hoiberg	9	0-2	0-0	0-0	0	0	0	0	3	0
TOTAL	**240**	**38-72**	**4-7**	**23-31**	**9**	**25**	**34**	**24**	**23**	**103**

CELTICS

PLAYER	MIN	FGM-A	3PM-A	FTM-A	OFF	DEF	TOT	AST	PF	PTS
Walker	45	5-18	0-2	6-9	3	5	8	6	3	16
McCarty	17	2-3	0-0	0-0	0	2	2	1	2	4
DeClercq	29	5-9	0-0	7-8	6	3	9	0	3	17
Mercer	35	8-16	0-0	5-5	1	2	3	3	6	21
Billups	24	6-14	1-4	1-1	1	1	2	2	4	14
Brown	22	3-4	0-0	0-0	0	3	3	1	0	6
Barros	21	4-6	2-3	0-0	1	2	3	6	1	10
Knight	16	3-5	0-0	0-0	2	2	4	0	1	6
Minor	14	1-6	0-0	0-0	1	1	2	2	1	2
Bowen	7	0-1	0-0	0-0	0	1	1	0	5	0
Thomas	7	0-0	0-0	0-0	0	1	1	0	1	0
Edney	3	0-0	0-0	0-0	0	0	0	0	0	0
TOTAL	**240**	**37-82**	**3-9**	**19-23**	**15**	**23**	**38**	**21**	**27**	**96**

HOOP DREAMS

*Larry Bird makes a triumphant return to Boston,
and the frenzy created by the Celtics fans shows that he may be our
new coach, but he's their legend.*

January 19, 1998

BY BILL BENNER

It may have been the most heralded arrival here since Paul Revere galloped through the streets on horseback and informed the populace that the British were on their way.

Only this time, Bostonians were happy—indeed, elated and ecstatic and even euphoric—to see this particular enemy coming.

Larry Bird—former Boston Celtics legend, current Indiana Pacers coach—was back in Beantown. He was greeted by a media and fan frenzy that turned the occasion of Sunday's regular-season National Basketball Association game between the Pacers and Celtics into something more closely resembling the seventh game of the NBA Finals.

"The biggest victory I'll have, probably forever, coming back here for the first time," Bird said afterward.

That his Pacers won it, gutting out a 103-96 victory in the closing minutes, brought enormous relief and immense pleasure to Bird.

"The biggest victory I'll have, probably forever, coming back here for the first time," Bird said afterward. "I wanted my team to play well and they did. I'm so happy.

"The guys knew how bad I wanted this game today. Coming in here and winning is the ultimate."

Ultimately, the Pacers will have to quickly put this one behind them. Another road game, at New York on Wednesday, beckons for the 26-11 team, which has ascended to the top of the Eastern Conference.

But even the media mecca of the Big Apple will seem tame compared to Sunday's environment.

National television (NBC) and radio (ESPN), about 20 TV stations from Boston, New England and Indianapolis, and dozens of reporters representing cities from New York to Chicago to Los Angeles chronicled Bird's return.

And, of course, a sellout crowd in the FleetCenter—adjacent to the old Boston Garden, where Bird played—was there to offer its roaring approval of the man who led their beloved Celtics to three championships in a glorious 13-year playing career.

"This was a lot like when Michael came back against us at our place... the magnitude, the press, the ambiance," said Pacers' guard Reggie Miller. He was referring to Michael Jordan's return to basketball in a game against the Pacers in Indianapolis in March 1995.

That Bird's return coincided with halftime ceremonies for the retiring of former teammate Robert Parish's number (00) turned the game into a Celtic lovefest.

But there was no question who was most adored by the sellout crowd of 18,624.

Bird's first appearance just before tipoff provoked a prolonged ovation and the first of several "Larry! Larry! Larry!" chants. Camera-toting fans crowded for shots, and some hoisted children on their shoulders for a closer look at the legend.

Bird also was greeted by numerous signs —"Clone Bird" read one; another stated "The Bird's Back in the Nest"—while the organist saluted him with a rendition of Back Home Again in Indiana.

During a third-quarter timeout, the video screens offered the message: "Larry, you may be their coach, but you're our legend." It was preceded by a video highlight reel of famous Bird plays as a Celtic, all done to the

Larry Bird waves to the Boston crowd as he takes the bench just before game time. Bird called the Pacers' 103-96 victory over the Celtics "the biggest victory I'll have, probably forever." (Pat Greenhouse/The Boston Globe)

tune of Lynyrd Skynyrd's Free Bird.

The crowd went nuts, cheering almost as if its No. 33 was back in uniform, performing his magic once more.

Even the Pacers got caught up in it.

"We were looking, cheering from the bench," said Jalen Rose. "That's all we were talking about. We weren't even listening in the huddle."

Some of the Boston fans were so enraptured by Bird's presence that they taunted the officials on his behalf. When referee Terry Durham talked back to a complaining Bird, one fan yelled, "Hey, Terry, don't be giving Larry none of your lip!"

"It was fun but strange," said Bird. "I just wanted to get the game over with and go home. I wanted to get in a shell and just hide. I'm a little embarrassed by how the fans treat me here."

Initially, Bird had downplayed the importance of his return. But as the event grew closer, his feelings grew as well. After Friday night's victory over Sacramento in Indianapolis, Bird finally admitted he wanted to beat Boston "so badly I can taste it."

Reminded of that quote Sunday, he smiled.

"Now I can taste it," he said.

Yet, he insisted repeatedly that the credit should go to his team: to Rose, with another inspired performance off the bench; to Derrick McKey, who came up with big defensive stops against the Celtics' Antoine Walker; and to Miller, who came out of a gamelong shooting slump just in time to drain a critical 3-pointer.

"It's a players' game," Bird said. "All I do is stand there and watch. I want this team to get the accolades they deserve, and I'm happy just to be a small part of it."

Finally, someone asked Bird what the best part of his return to Boston was.

He didn't hesitate.

"Winning," he said. ■

IT'S OFFICIAL:
Bird Will Coach East at All-Star Game

January 26, 1998

BY MARK MONTIETH

He'd rather spend the time with his family in Florida, and he's no fan of all-star games anyway.

Larry Bird, however, has the honor of coaching the East team in the NBA All-Star game on February 8 in New York City. Take it or leave it.

Utah's 101-94 victory over Chicago Sunday afternoon dropped the job in the laps of Bird and his assistant coaches, Dick Harter and Rick Carlisle. Although the Pacers are a half-game behind Chicago in the Central Division standings, they have the best winning percentage (.700) in the Eastern Conference—and that's the NBA's criteria for determining the coaches.

Bulls coach Phil Jackson said he was relieved not to have to coach the All-Star Game again following his team's loss to the Jazz, and Bird all along has been blunt about his desire not to work the game.

But while Bird was unavailable for comment Sunday, everyone within the Pacer organization expects him to go.

"Larry Bird lives up to his obligations," Pacers president Donnie Walsh said.

"It's a helluva tribute to the coaches and our players. It's a great honor for our franchise."

A 12-time All-Star Game participant as a player, Bird becomes the first Pacer coach to work an NBA All-Star game. Bob "Slick" Leonard coached the 1970 ABA All-Star Game.

With the starters for the game announced Sunday, the league's coaches now can vote for the seven reserves for each team. That group will be announced Tuesday or Wednesday, depending on when the ballots are tabulated.

Unlike Bird, Harter and Carlisle are enthused about coaching the game.

Harter, who's in his 14th season as an NBA coach, including two as a head coach, worked the game at Salt Lake City in 1993 as a member of Pat Riley's New York Knicks staff. He was so excited about this opportunity that he was pacing the floor in his home Sunday during the final minutes of Utah's victory.

"Larry will appreciate it more as the years go on, particularly if he stays in coaching and sees this isn't easy," Harter said.

Carlisle, a player or coach in the NBA since 1984, has never been to an All-Star game, but looks forward to the experi-

NBA STANDINGS AT THE ALL-STAR BREAK
EASTERN CONFERENCE

Atlantic Division

	W	L	PCT	GB
Miami	30	17	.638	-
New Jersey	27	21	.563	3 1/2
New York	25	21	.543	4 1/2
Washington	25	24	.510	6
Orlando	23	25	.479	7 1/2
Boston	22	25	.468	8
Philadelphia	14	31	.311	15

Central Division

	W	L	PCT	GB
Indiana	33	13	.717	-
Chicago	34	15	.694	1/2
Charlotte	29	18	.617	4 1/2
Atlanta	29	20	.592	5 1/2
Cleveland	27	20	.574	6 1/2
Milwaukee	24	23	.511	9 1/2
Detroit	22	25	.468	11 1/2
Toronto	11	36	.234	32 1/2

ence—especially since it's in New York City. He grew up in upstate New York, played one season for the Knicks and spent five years across the Hudson River with New Jersey as a player and assistant coach.

"I have to admit I'm a little surprised it worked out, but it goes to show you if you keep playing hard, good things happen," Carlisle said.

Harter reminded Bird of the significance and rarity of coaching an all-star game—particularly as a rookie—following Indiana's win over Boston Saturday, and believes Bird will warm to the task.

"Larry has a true dislike for all-star type of competiton; a lot of us purists do," Harter said. "But you have to balance that with the All-Star game being a great showcase for the NBA. And it's great for the Pac-

ers and Donnie Walsh."

Bird's players had delighted in kidding him about having to coach the All-Star Game, but are happy for him—and not particularly surprised that he pulled it off.

"The way he attacks a challenge, nothing he accomplishes is a surprise to me," said Chris Mullin, a five-time All-Star selection. "If he wanted to be an actor, I wouldn't be surprised if he won an Oscar for his first movie."

Larry Bird is the seventh first-year coach to work the All-Star game since it was first held in 1951.

Bird, the All-Star MVP in 1982, becomes the third person to be named NBA All-Star MVP and coach. Bill Sharman and Lenny Wilkens were the others. ■

Eastern Conference coach Larry Bird attends the pre-game ceremonies at Madison Square Garden for the 1998 All-Star game. (Linda Cattafo, New York Daily News)

Bird won't duck his All-Star duties

Saying, "I've got to do what I have to do," Pacers coach will take family to New York during break.

January 27, 1998

BY MARK MONTIETH

When Indiana Pacers coach Larry Bird walked onto the Market Square Arena court for practice Monday morning, his players interrupted their stretching to stand and cheer for him.

"You got me," he said with a smile.

Bird's players took devilish delight in sticking their coach with the job of coaching the Eastern Conference team in the NBA All-Star game. Their 28-12 record and Utah's win over Chicago on Sunday did the trick.

And Bird, his protests to the contrary, will do it.

"I'd enjoy a few days off, but I think it would be pretty selfish of me not to go," said Bird, whose team plays Washington tonight at MSA. "I represent the Indiana Pacers now. I'm not a player. I've got to go do what I have to do."

Bird had hoped to fly with his wife and two children to his home in Naples, Florida, for the All-Star break. Instead, he'll take them to New York for the February 8 game at Madison Square Garden.

It will mean more time in the limelight for a private man who would rather be on a golf course, but Bird couldn't turn his back on the NBA or the Pacers.

"The (All-Star experience) is a lot better than it used to be," said Bird, who played in 12 All-Star games dur-

ing his career with the Boston Celtics. "We don't have banquets anymore, and they do a good job of setting things up and taking care of you.

"But there's a lot of people. Every time you move, somebody's got something to sign. It makes it annoying and something I don't like to do. But I'm very honored to represent the Pacers."

Bird, at least, will be compensated for his trouble. The coaches, players and trainers from the winning All-Star team receive $12,000 each. The losers get $6,000.

Bird, who will be joined on the East team's bench by his assistants, Dick Harter and Rick Carlisle, played in enough All-Star games to know how they are coached. Design a couple of plays to be run between fast breaks, and turn them loose.

"You sit back and let them do what they do best, and that's play basketball," Bird said. "You give them a couple of plays and pat them on the back and tell them good luck. But when it comes down to the fourth quar-

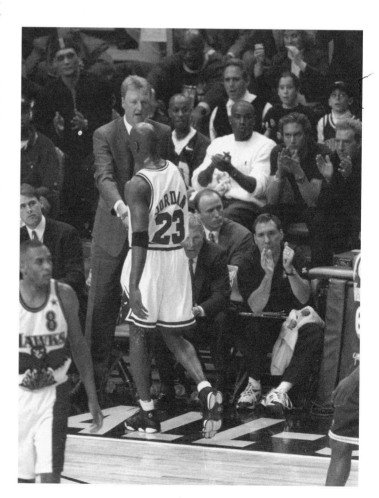

Legend to legend. Two of the game's greatest joined forces to lead the East All-Stars to a 135-114 triumph over the Western All-Stars. (Linda Cataffo, New York Daily News)

1998 All-Star Game, Madison Square Garden
Sunday, February 8, 1998

Final	1	2	3	4	T
West All-Stars	25	33	33	23	114
East All-Stars	33	34	34	34	135

BOX SCORE—All Star Game 1998

West

PLAYER	MIN	FGM-A	FTM-A	OFF	DEF	TOT	AST	PF	PTS
GARNETT	21	6-11	0-0	1	3	4	2	0	12
MALONE	17	2-4	0-0	0	3	3	2	1	4
ONEAL	18	5-10	2-4	2	2	4	1	2	12
BRYANT	22	7-16	2-2	2	4	6	1	1	18
PAYTON	24	3-7	0-0	2	1	3	13	0	7
BAKER	21	3-12	2-2	6	2	8	0	1	8
JONES	25	7-19	1-2	7	4	11	1	1	15
ROBINSON	22	3-4	9-10	2	4	6	0	1	15
RICHMOND	17	4-11	0-0	0	1	1	2	0	8
KIDD	19	0-1	0-0	0	1	1	9	2	0
DUNCAN	14	1-4	0-0	1	10	11	1	0	2
VAN EXEL	20	5-14	2-2	1	2	3	2	0	13
TOTALS	240	46-113	18-22	24	37	61	34	9	114

East

PLAYER	MIN	FGM-A	3PM-A	FTM-A	OFF	DEF	TOT	AST	PTS
KEMP	25	5-10	2-2	2	9	11	2	2	12
HILL	28	7-11	0-0	0	3	3	5	1	15
MUTOMBO	19	4-5	1-2	1	6	7	0	3	9
P HARDAWAY	12	3-5	0-0	0	0	0	3	0	6
JORDAN	32	10-18	2-3	1	5	6	8	0	23
T HARDAWAY	17	3-8	0-0	0	1	1	6	0	8
WILLIAMS	19	2-3	0-0	3	7	10	1	2	4
R SMITS	21	3-7	4-4	2	5	7	4	3	10
MILLER	20	6-8	1-2	0	0	0	0	2	14
RICE	16	6-14	0-0	1	0	1	0	0	16
S SMITH	16	6-12	0-0	2	1	3	0	0	14
WALKER	15	2-8	0-0	1	2	3	3	0	4
TOTALS	240	57-109	10-13	13	39	52	32	13	135

ter, they want to win the game. Hopefully you'll have the best players on the court then."

The league's 29 head coaches voted Monday for the All-Star reserves. They were to select two guards, two forwards, one center and two players of any position, but could not vote for their own players. The selections will be announced today or Wednesday.

Any selected player unable or unwilling to participate in the game will be replaced by one named by NBA commissioner David Stern. The head coach determines who starts in place of an injured player voted to the starting lineup by fans.

Bird, then, might have to decide who starts in place of Orlando guard Anfernee Hardaway, who was voted to the East starting lineup. Hardaway has been out since having knee surgery on December 10, and is not expected to play.

Bird hopes to be joined at the All-Star game by some of his players. Reggie Miller, Rik Smits, Mark Jackson and Chris Mullin were on the fan ballot. Miller—who will participate in the 3-point shooting contest—finished fifth in the voting for Eastern Conference guards, Hardaway included, and was second among shooting guards. Smits finished fifth among centers, but Patrick Ewing—who finished second—is injured.

"Seattle and L.A. (Lakers) probably will have three representatives from their team, and they're supposedly the best from the West," Miller said. "Why can't we have three from the best in the East?"■

In victory and defeat, this season's Pacers show admirable character

February 2, 1998

BY BILL BENNER

As the Indiana Pacers head into the second half of the NBA season with the best record in the Eastern Conference, the most amazing thing may not be their 31 victories.

It's their 12 defeats.

There's not a clunker among 'em.

There's not one night among the grind that is an NBA schedule during which the fellas reported for duty but never really went to work.

There hasn't been one blowout. The Pacers' worst defeat of the year was by just 12 points, 91-79 at San Antonio, and it is one of only two double-digit losses the Pacers have suffered. The average margin of defeat has been six points, and there hasn't been one game in which the Pacers have gone into the last 3 minutes without a chance to win.

Even the Chicago Bulls' 72-10 team in 1995-96 had a bad night, a 32-point drubbing by the Knicks. And their average margin of defeat in those 10 losses was 7.7 —above Indiana's current rate.

Certainly, the Pacers have had bad stretches during games, but coach Larry Bird can recall only one game in which he was disappointed with his team's wire-to-wire effort.

"Portland," says Bird, recalling the final game of the Pacers' four-game road trip in December. "I thought the guys packed it in on me. "We were way down and I called a 20-second timeout. I told them that they ain't foolin' me, I know they packed it in and were ready to go home and if they don't get it going, I'm going to put guys in there who will at least give me an effort.

"I'll be damned if we didn't come back and take the lead. Now we still got beat (93-85), but at least they showed me a lot of character."

And character—reflected in resiliency, tenacity, mental toughness and constant focus on tomorrow's challenge rather than yesterday's achievement—has become the hallmark of Bird's bunch.

By all accounts, there are no cliques, hidden agendas or unhappy campers. No one is pouting even if he's not playing.

"There's this feeling that we're here to win together," says Chris Mullin, the Golden State exile who can't wipe the smile from his face.

Adds point guard Mark Jackson, "I've been on teams that won, but you had little cliques here and there, or this guy or that guy was mad because he wasn't playing.

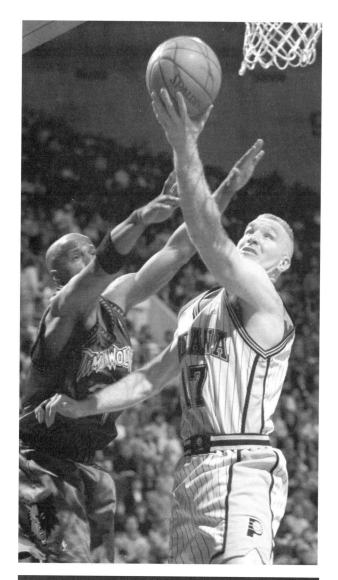

Chris Mullin's steady leadership off the bench is one of the reasons the Pacers are atop the Eastern Conferencee standings at the season's midpoint. (Paul Sancya)

We don't have any of that."

Credit goes to team president Donnie Walsh for assembling the pieces of the puzzle that fit so well together. There have been any number of bad actors available that would have made the Pacers more talented individually, but wouldn't have made the Pacers better collectively.

"It's as much the character of the team as it is the talent," says Mullin. "A lot of teams have the talent, but they go away from playing with each other. One guy tries to take over. That's not our team, whether we're up or down."

And so the Pacers roll along, winning most and being competitive in all. Sure, for the money they're making, they should be ready to give the maximum every night out, but that's not human nature and it's especially not NBA nature.

It is, however, Larry Bird's nature.

"I think they knew I've got a good judgment and feel for the game," Bird says. "Being a player, I know how easy it is sometimes (to slack off). But if you want to be a great team, you've got to fight through all that stuff. You've got to keep hammerin' and focusing yourself."

And Bird, speaking with unchallenged credibility, is there to remind the troops whenever that focus wanders.

Still, the Pacers can't get ahead of themselves. February's schedule is as tough as they've faced. It begins with six of the next eight games on the road, including trips to Seattle, Chicago, Miami and Atlanta.

"I wouldn't be telling these guys they're great because they're not great," says Bird. "But they can be. If they listen, they can be a great basketball team—if they really put their heart and soul into it." ■

During the grind of an 82-game schedule, one of Bird's most difficult tasks has been to keep his team focused on the challenges at hand. (Kelly Wilkinson)

The Rivalry Lives

BIRD HAS NOTHING BUT PRAISE for Miami coach Pat Riley, who coached the Los Angeles Lakers in their classic championship series with the Boston Celtics in the mid-1980s.

But he professes no desire to sit down with Riley and talk coaching, although Riley has worked in New York and Miami since Bird completed his playing career in Boston.

"Can't," Bird smiled. "Never will. He's a Laker. Don't have time for him.

"That's the way I remember it. He might be with Miami now, but he's one of them Laker guys."

Pacers Achieve Total Domination

February 28, 1998

BY CONRAD BRUNNER

If the Indiana Pacers had lapsed into a midseason slumber, they awakened with a start.

Not to mention a middle and a finish.

Escaping the clutches of a two-week minislump, the Pacers treated the Portland Trail Blazers like an offending alarm clock, shattering them against the Market Square Arena floor in a historic 124-59 victory Friday night.

The margin of victory was not only a Pacers franchise record, it was the second-largest in NBA history. Portland's point total represented another franchise record, and tied for the fourth-lowest in league history.

It also was the first time a team had its point total more than doubled by an opponent.

"I was hoping we'd break out sometime," said Pacers coach Larry Bird. "Portland's a very good team with a lot of talent and depth, but we played as good as we can play."

In matching their victory total for last season, the Pacers (39-17) spanked a Portland team coming off its most compelling victory of the season, a 106-101 conquest of the Bulls in Chicago on Wednesday night.

After that game, the Blazers enjoyed glowing visions of how good they can be. After this one, they had quite a different view.

"I lost a lot in Toronto," said heralded new acquisition Damon Stoudamire, "but I don't know if I ever lost like this."

It was a heartening performance for reasons well beyond the record book for the Pacers, who had lost four of seven and the top spot in the Eastern Conference.

The defense was dominant (forcing 22 turnovers while holding Portland to .333 shooting, a season low), the offense efficient (shooting a season-high .636 while placing eight players in double figures) and the board work aggressive.

Indiana entered the game tied for 24th in rebounding, while Portland was second. Yet the Pacers outrebounded the Blazers 48-28, with Rik Smits' 12 leading the way.

"We needed a game like this and we got it," Smits said. "We all worked together and, hopefully, this is beginning of a new season. We feel more good things are to come."

Mark Jackson led the Pacers with 18 points, hitting 4 of 5 3-point attempts. Jalen Rose had 13, while Smits, Dale Davis and Antonio Davis had 12 apiece. Reggie Miller added 11 and Travis Best 10.

"I keep telling these guys they have a great opportunity to do something this year if they listen to us and give the effort," Bird said. "Tonight we got that."

Bad passes found their way into shooters' hands. Airballs turned into putbacks. Loose balls became fast breaks. Mismatches worked out to be advantages. Broken possessions ended with made 3-pointers.

Everything went right for the Pacers from the opening minutes. The game amounted to little more than a

---

Biggest blowouts

68- Cleveland 148, Miami 80, Dec. 17, 1991.

65- Pacers 124, Portland 59, Feb. 27, 1998.

63- L.A. Lakers 162, Golden State 99, March 19, 1972.

Fewest points

57- Milwaukee vs. Boston, Feb 27, 1955; Philadelphia vs. Miami, Feb 21, 1996; Orlando vs. Cleveland, Dec. 4, 1996.

59- Portland vs. Pacers, Feb 27, 1998; Sacramento vs. Charlotte, Jan. 10, 1991; Cleveland vs. San Antonio, March 25, 1997.

Mark Pope and Larry Bird share a laugh during practice. (Mike Fender)

protracted run.

An 18-2 start grew to a 29-6 bulge. A 33-14 lead at the end of the first quarter quickly became 49-15 as Portland missed its first nine shots and committed seven turnovers in the first 7 minutes of the second period.

A 59-29 halftime lead swelled to 84-43 on Jackson's fourth 3-pointer of the game. the margin broke 50 when Rose hit a 3-pointer to make it 99-48, and went beyond 60 on Mark West's dunk with 1:13 left.

The final margin was the game's largest; the buzzer was the only thing that could stop the Pacers on this night.

"They're a good young team but they're still young," said Antonio Davis. "I don't think they're able to understand, when things go wrong, you have to fight back through this. They don't have guys to tell them to relax, settle down, don't try to get it all back in one possession. We've got a lot of guys like that. our coach is like that.

"What happened? I still don't think we know."

Against the Bulls, Portland played like blazers. Against the Pacers, they merely trailed. ■

LARRY BIRD: MAN OF LETTERS

Coach's volume of mail rivals team's stars, and it brings requests for calls, tips on beating the Bulls

April 2, 1998

BY EILEEN AMBROSE

The Indiana Pacers had been on the road, so Larry Bird's mail was left untouched for nearly two weeks. By then, it was 3½ feet high.

It used to be worse, says Joe Qatato, who worked for the Boston Celtics and is now Bird's special assistant.

As a Celtics player, Bird drew five times the volume of mail he does now. "I would have to take it home with me," says Qatato, whose duties with the Boston team included opening and sorting No. 33's mail.

In his first season as coach of the Pacers, Bird has re-energized players and fans alike. Although there's no precise count, Bird gets more mail than his predecessor, Larry Brown, and his load of letters rivals that of the team's star players, such as Reggie Miller and Rik Smits.

There is so much mail the Pacers don't have enough staff to keep up, so the bulk of it is handled by a New Jersey company that specializes in answering fan letters to sports teams.

FanMail Inc. has been handling Pacers' correspondence for three years, says president Budd Nesi, who got the idea for his company when the Florida Marlins stiffed his 8-year-old daughter after she wrote them.

The Pacers have been averaging 12,000 to 15,000 pieces of mail each year, although volume is up about 20 percent this season due to Bird and the team's improved performance, Nesi says.

That's respectable, but nowhere near the 75,000 pieces of mail each year sent to the most popular team, which Nesi declines to identify.

Most of the mail to the Pacers and other teams comes from kids.

"One of the things that comes through is how these kids view professional athletes as role models. They admire them for more than just the way they play, but for the kind of people they think they are," Nesi says.

The company sends Pacers fans a game schedule, stickers, a basketball card of Bird or the player they had written and a letter from the team with its updated statistics.

Each fan's name and address is entered into a database that the team can tap into later, say when a player wants to contact youngsters about a basketball camp, Nesi says.

Based on mail volume, Miller and Smits are the most popular Pacers. But Bird is right up there with them, Nesi says.

Before Bird's mail is passed along to FanMail,

A pile of letters to Larry Bird sits on the desk of Pacers employee Joe Qatato. He is responsible for reading Bird's mail and sending responses. (Gary Moore)

Despite Bird's enormous popularity, Pacer star Reggie Miller is still the fans' favorite Pacer when measured by the volume of mail. (Rich Miller)

though, it is first opened at Market Square Arena. Sometimes Bird assists, but mostly it's Qatato wielding the letter opener and zipping through hundreds of envelopes in an hour or two twice a week.

"I've done it for such a long time. I know where to look. You don't look at the beginning. You look at the middle and the end. That's when they get to their point," he says. "It's almost like speed reading."

Personal mail or letters from coaches and players are set aside for Bird to read. Celtic jerseys, *Sports Illustrated* magazines and basketballs sent in to be autographed are also retrieved for Bird to sign.

Organizations seeking an item for auction will get a photo of the coach rubber-stamped with his signature.

Bird gets plenty of requests for autographs as gifts for bar mitzvahs, weddings, birthdays and anniversaries. You can get on the wrong side of the coach, though, by seeking autographs with the intention of turning around and selling them.

Letters come from all over the country and the world.

A fan from the Philippines, for instance, writes:

"I have always enjoyed reading your quotes because they are quite funny. I myself am a very funny person although I'm sure that you are finding that very hard to believe so I guess you just have to trust me on that one."

Often correspondents want to meet Bird. A Canadian teacher asked Bird to telephone her colleague:

"You could call collect. I'd pay for the call. Five or ten minutes of your time is all I ask. Ruth deserves a thrill."

The coach has little time for meetings or calls, something which Qatato sometimes telephones fans to explain.

Not surprising, Bird gets unsolicited advice on how to do his job.

For example, Nicole from Indianapolis, writing in a childlike scrawl, suggests "a few tricks" on how to beat the Chicago Bulls:

"I think you should have Mark West out on Scottie Pippin. I don't really understand how matchups go, but if this sounds good, please use it. Now about that notorious Dennis Rodman..."

For the most part, the correspondence is pure adulation, such as the note from Kate:

"Dear Larry Bird, I really like you. What's your middle name?"

For Kate and the other inquiring minds, it's Joe.

Sometimes the answers are more obvious. Take 8-year-old Daniel's simple question:

"My dad looks just like you. ... You're the best coach a team can have. Did you use to play basketball on the Boston Celtics?"

Contrary to its name, fan mail can be ego-bruising. Writes one child:

"I am a big fan of yours. I was wondering if you would please get this card autographed by Reggie Miller."

Qatato says he gets a lot of paper cuts in his job. But he is greatly relieved the coach doesn't have e-mail. "Thank God. That's all I need," Qatato says.

Just the same, Qatato doesn't really seem to mind the mailbags and says he does what he can to get fans a quick and satisfying response.

"If it wasn't for the fans, where would we all be?"

FIRST TIME'S A CHARM

Beneath Larry Bird's stoic demeanor lies a novice coach who has tasted instant success by earning his players' respect.

April 23, 1998

BY MARK MONTIETH

He tosses it out casually, a parenthetical thought that's guaranteed to change the course of the conversation.

"I have a lot of things I could improve on," Indiana Pacers coach Larry Bird said recently. "If I'm back next year, I'll work on them and go from there."

If he's back next year? What does he mean by that?

"If I'm back next season. That's what I mean by it," he said, shrugging.

"I'll sit down with some guys on the team and talk to them and see how they reacted to everything we've done this year and go from there."

Would Bird really drop out of the coaching rat race after one lap? Would he take his single, shining season, in which he led the Pacers to an NBA club-record 58 victories, coached the East in the All-Star game and was a strong candidate for Coach of the Year honors, and call it a career?

Probably not. Bird has said —half-jokingly, it seemed —that if the Pacers manage to win the NBA championship this season he'll let assistants Dick Harter and Rick Carlisle take over. Nobody really expects him to exit that quickly, but he has repeatedly emphasized that he won't do it for long. And people do believe that.

Coaching satisfies Bird's thirst for competition, but it also places him in his least favorite location: the public

> It's not about [Bird] becoming famous again, or rich again, or successful again. It's about him passing on what he learned about winning championships to his players, so they can experience the thrill, too.

eye. He loves the game-day adrenaline, the practice preparation, the interaction with the players, the raw challenge of it all. He could happily do without putting on a tie for game nights, answering the same questions from the media and hearing fans shout his name in arenas around the country.

"This is the right job for me, because it's a small market," Bird said. "And I've got a good team and a bunch of good guys. But I'm not going to do it for very long because I'm not cut out to do this."

Bird has been asked often this season if coaching is fun for him. He always replies that it's "interesting," and "different." Although he handles all his job obligations smoothly, he remains a private person in a public position. His stamina for it might come down to which force burns brightest: his passion for competition or the spotlight of the public's attention.

Of course his protests might be idle threats, like all those claims that he wouldn't coach in the All-Star game. But Pacers fans would be wise to enjoy the team's version of Camelot while it lasts, just to be safe.

Bird is serious, however, about letting his players determine his coaching future. And as silly as that notion might sound, it reveals one of the primary reasons for his success: He's in it for them. It's not about him

Bird passes the knowledge of what it takes to win on to his star player, Reggie Miller. (Kelly Wilkinson)

becoming famous again, or rich again, or successful again. It's about him passing on what he learned about winning championships to his players, so they can experience the thrill, too.

If they don't happen to like how he's going about it, they won't have to ask him twice to leave. But if he's hoping his players give him an out, he can forget it. Reggie Miller, for one, has said he'd quit if Bird quit—which makes Bird laugh. Mark Jackson, meanwhile, seems to speak for everyone.

"If it's a question of whether we like him, he'll be back, because we love him," Jackson said. "He's made it fun once again and put us in position to win this thing. That's all we can ask."

It's not only what Bird has done that has made the Pacers successful, it's what he hasn't done. He doesn't nag the players, as Larry Brown did toward the end of his four-year run here. He doesn't suck up to the players, as Bob Hill did. And he doesn't try to steal credit from the players, as Dick Versace did.

Above all, Bird has communicated well with his players, an ironic trait for a private man. He can be blunt in his criticism, but

he's sensitive to their feelings. He'll challenge a player privately, but he won't raise his voice or embarrass him in front of his teammates. Most of all, he gives daily doses of confidence.

One of Bird's assistants, Harter, 66, was a head college coach for 18 years, head coach of the Charlotte Hornets and an NBA assistant under Jack Ramsay, Chuck Daly and Pat Riley. He says he's learned a few things from the rookie coach, mostly about patience. Most of

Bird's calm demeanor has had a positive effect on his players. Even his occasional outbursts at the officials have been rare. Bird received only three technical fouls during his team's 82-game regular season. (Rich Miller)

all, he's been impressed with Bird's knack for dealing with the players.

"I think he has a nice ability to say what he wants to say in a few words, which is very important in this league," Harter said. "He's very honest and very blunt. Yet he certainly can appreciate the players' ups and downs, so he hasn't been too severe. All that has added up to being an ideal type of leader."

When he coached the Eastern Conference All-Stars, Bird warned his players about the much-hyped matchup between Michael Jordan and Kobe Bryant. They were going to have to be ready, Bird said, because Jordan was playing against a man half his age and might need help. Jordan, although sick, wound up winning Most Valuable Player honors. At times this season, when a player hasn't been performing to his potential or appears distracted by outside interests, Bird has called him into his office and asked him if he really wants to be here. And when Miller hit big shot after big shot, Bird gave him credit but added, "That's why we pay him so well."

Bird's approach is instinctive. He hasn't buried his head in coaching manuals or management books, nor has he read the books on success written by coaching peers Riley and Rick Pitino. He simply knows how he liked to be treated as a player, and he coaches accordingly.

"I just know to get the best out of people you have to push the right buttons," he said. "It's more common sense than anything. I know when I played I didn't like people screaming at me. It seemed coaches got more out of me when they talked to me. And if you're honest with your players it goes a long way.

"These guys know I respect them. That's the reason I came here, because it was the type of team I wanted. I knew to get the most out of them I had to give them confidence, and I had to manage them."

For Bird, managing has meant dishing out stern discipline, quiet consolation and straightforward explanations at the proper times.

When Dale Davis and Travis Best were late—just barely—for a flight to an exhibition game in Nashville, Tennessee, in October, Bird left them on the runway. Best, who sat out the game because it was a repeat offense, paid a costly price. Bird had decided to start him in the season opener at New Jersey but changed his mind after that incident.

But when Best missed a running jumper at the buzzer in a one-point home-court loss to Phoenix on January 6, Bird called him away from his postgame interviews and told him not to worry about it. The play had not been executed properly, he had taken a good shot under the circumstances, and the loss wasn't his fault.

> **Bird's biggest regret about coaching the Pacers is that he didn't do it sooner.**

And when Rik Smits missed seven games late in the season because of sore feet—a vague condition that could have raised suspicions about his dedication at such an important part of the season—Bird, who had played with severe back pain at the end of his playing career, became an advocate for his center.

"Some of these guys might have gotten p—— off that Rik sat out for two weeks, but they haven't had the injuries Rik had," Bird said. "So you have to manage them through that."

Bird's biggest regret about coaching the Pacers is that he didn't do it sooner. He could have had the job four years ago, when it went to Brown, but the timing wasn't right then. He still felt the back pain that ended his playing career, and he wasn't feeling the boredom that ultimately drove him off the golf courses.

This team, with a starting lineup that averages 32 years of age, appears to have a small window of opportunity. Bird wonders now what would have happened if he had taken the job the first time it was offered.

"That's probably one mistake I made in my life, not taking over when I was a little younger," he said. "Not that Larry Brown didn't do a hell of a job, it's just that if you're going to get into something like this, you don't want to get in when your players are a little older. To have had them back three or four years ago would have been something to see." ■

NBA 1997-98 FINAL STANDINGS

EASTERN CONFERENCE
Atlantic

	W	L	PCT	GB	HOME	ROAD	CONF
Y-Miami	55	27	.671	-	30-11	25-16	35-18
X-New Jersey	43	39	.524	12	26-15	17-24	26-27
X-New York	43	39	.524	12	28-13	15-26	25-27
Washington	42	40	.512	13	24-17	18-23	24-29
Orlando	41	41	.500	14	24-17	17-24	22-30
Boston	36	46	.439	19	24-17	12-29	22-31
Philadelphia	31	51	.378	24	19-22	12-29	16-37

Central

	W	L	PCT	GB	HOME	ROAD	CONF
Z-Chicago	62	20	.756	-	37-4	25-16	42-11
X-Indiana	58	24	.707	4	32-9	26-15	41-12
X-Charlotte	51	31	.622	11	32-9	19-22	31-22
X-Atlanta	50	32	.610	12	29-12	21-20	33-19
X-Cleveland	47	35	.573	15	27-14	20-21	29-24
Detroit	37	45	.451	25	25-16	12-29	24-29
Milwaukee	36	46	.439	26	21-20	15-26	19-34
Toronto	16	66	.195	46	9-32	7-34	7-46

WESTERN CONFERENCE
Midwest

	W	L	PCT	GB	HOME	ROAD	CONF
Z-Utah	62	20	.756	-	36-5	26-15	38-13
X-San Antonio	56	26	.683	6	31-10	25-16	31-19
X-Minnesota	45	37	.549	17	26-15	19-22	29-22
X-Houston	41	41	.500	21	24-17	17-24	29-23
Dallas	20	62	.244	42	13-28	7-34	12-39
Vancouver	19	63	.232	43	14-27	5-36	14-37
Denver	11	71	.134	51	9-32	2-39	9-42

Pacific

	W	L	PCT	GB	HOME	ROAD	CONF
Y-Seattle	61	21	.744	-	35-6	26-15	38-13
X-LA Lakers	61	21	.744	-	33-8	28-13	41-10
X-Phoenix	56	26	.683	5	30-11	26-15	36-15
X-Portland	46	36	.561	15	26-15	20-21	33-18
Sacramento	27	55	.329	34	1-20	6-35	18-34
Golden State	19	63	.232	42	12-29	7-34	15-35
LA Clippers	17	65	.207	44	11-30	6-35	14-37

Y - Clinched Division Title
X - Clinched Playoff Berth
Z - Clinched Conference Title

9
1997-98 PACERS
PLAYOFFS: TO THE LIMIT

Indiana's success almost predictable

BY MARK MONTIETH

Someone knew. Back in October, someone with the Indiana Pacers took a marker and wrote "58" in the win column next to the team's name on the large standings chart on the back wall of the locker room.

Someone knew something or else was doing an uncanny impression of Nostradamus. A team that had won just 39 games last season, now led by a formerly great player who had never coached a basketball game in his life...who could have guessed what was to follow?

Not Larry Bird, who is a leading candidate to win Coach of the Year honors. When he met with his team on the first day of training camp in Orlando, Fla., he posed a slightly lesser, but still daunting, challenge.

"I told them they had to win 55 games to get a home-court advantage," Bird recalled.

His players went him three better, setting a franchise record for winning percentage (.707) and securing home-court advantage for the first two rounds of the playoffs.

They won six more games than any other NBA Pacers team. They won 26 road games, five more than the NBA franchise record. They won 19 more

games than last season, when they failed to make the playoffs for the first time since the 1989-90 season.

And they enter the playoffs talking openly of winning a championship.

All with a rookie coach.

• • •

As a former player, Bird understood the inevitable quirks that all teams encounter in an 82-game NBA season. But as a memeber of three championship teams, he understood the need for a consistent effort, and the need to be playing the best at the end of the regular season. His team did just that, winning seven consecutive games—including consecutive road victories over Atlanta, Boston and Chicago—before losing Saturday's finale at Cleveland, when the starters were rested most of the game.

"They've done some things this year that I'm very proud of," Bird said. "You have to try to be consistent, because that on-off button doesn't always work like you want it to. They've done a good job of elevating their game for the playoffs."

And now they start over. With 58 victories behind them.

To be No. 1, you've got to prove it in the playoffs. (Paul Sancya)

Goodbye to Cleveland

Pacers' rebounding advantage yields hard-fought win over Cavs, triumph in Round 1 of playoffs.

May 1, 1998

BY MARK MONTIETH

On a night when baskets nearly had to be hand-woven, the Indiana Pacers had to rely on their weakest link to survive.

Having been outrebounded by 33 over their last four games with Cleveland, the Pacers won the battle of the boards, and the war of their first-round playoff series, with an 80-74 victory over the Cavaliers at Gund Arena Thursday.

Their 3-1 series win moves the Pacers into the second round against the winner of the New York-Miami series, which concludes with a fifth game on Sunday. The earliest the Pacers could open the second round is next Tuesday, at Market Square Arena.

The victory ended Indiana's six-game losing streak at Gund Arena, and continued Cleveland's streak of playoff frustration. It was the Cavaliers' fourth straight first-round exit from the playoffs.

Like so many times during the regular season, pride made the difference for the Pacers. They hit just 11 of 26 shots in the second half and committed 25 turnovers overall. But they made the plays that had to be made to avoid what would have been

their first back-to-back losses since December 10.

"If they do get defeated, they want to come back and show they're not that bad," Pacers coach Larry Bird said. "They were focused like you have to be in the play-offs."

Focused on rebounding, more than anything. Indiana outrebounded the Cavs 35-29 and outscored them 14-5 on second-chance points. Antonio Davis did most of the dirty work, grabbing nine rebounds—including a game-high six off the offensive glass that were critical to the outcome.

"I have visions of Antonio Davis flying through and keeping balls alive," Cleveland coach Mike Fratello said. "We were reacting instead of acting and being the aggressors. It was like we were nailed to the floor and the ball was over there. We never got to it."

"He played his game," Bird said of Davis. "He had a couple games here where he didn't play up to his potential, but tonight he was there. We needed everybody."

Indiana had to dig deep for this one. They were called for 35 fouls and sent Cleveland to the

---

No. 3 Pacers (58-24) vs. No. 6 Cavs (47-35)

Key players: Pacers—Reggie Miller (19.5 pts), Rik Smits (16.7 pts, 6.9 reb), Chris Mullin (11.3 pts), Mark Jackson (8.3 pts, 8.7 ast). **Cleveland—**Shawn Kemp (18.0 pts, 9.3 reb), Wesley Person (14.7 pts, 192 3-pointers), Zydrunas Ilgauskas (13.9 pts, 8.8 reb), Brevin Knight (9.0 pts, 8.2 ast, 2.45 stl).

Season series: 2-2. The home team won every game, and neither team reached 100 points in any of the games. Each reached 90 just once.

Pacers edge: Experience. Despite having missed the play-offs last season, the Pacers still have almost all their players remaining from the team that went to the Eastern Conference finals in 1994 and 1995.

Cavaliers edge: Unpredictability. Coach Mike Fratello will concoct a few schemes to try to neutralize the Pacers' advantages. The Cavs also have Kemp, a proven big-game player.

Story line: How good a coach is Larry Bird? He'll be able to compare himself to one of the best in the business.

Prediction: Pacers in 5.

foul line 35 times. The Cavs, however, cooperated with 12 missed free throws, which offered more than enough opportunity for them to force a fifth game in Indianapolis on Sunday.

Reggie Miller led the Pacers with 18 points, but was hounded into 7-of-16 shooting and eight turnovers. Smits added 17 in 26 minutes. Chris Mullin was quietly efficient throughout the game, hitting 5-of-6 shots for 12 points and adding four rebounds, two assists, two steals, two blocked shots, and a few deflections as well.

The Pacers also stepped up defensively, forcing the Cavs into 39 percent shooting and 22 turnovers. Shawn Kemp, who had scored 25, 27 and 31 points in the first three games of the series, settled for 21 on 6-of-16 shooting as the Pacers forced him farther from the basket and double-teamed him more effectively.

The Pacers led by 15 points in the final two minutes of the third period, but found themselves staring at a two-point lead after Kemp's layup with 2:15 left in the game. That's when Antonio Davis made what might have been the game's biggest play, rebounding Mark Jackson's missed turnaround jumper and drawing a foul from Cedric Henderson.

"They put a little guy on me (Henderson) and once they did that I knew I had an opportunity to go in there and get it," said Davis.

Davis hit both foul shots, opening a 77-73 lead with 1:50 left. The Pacers allowed the Cavs just one point on their final four possessions. They clinched the game when Anderson missed a baseline jumper and McKey and Jackson combined to tip the rebound over Kemp to Miller, who hit two foul shots with 18.8 seconds left.

"Look at the stat sheet tonight and it won't be pretty," Jalen Rose said. "But we weren't trying to look cute. That's why we've all got bald heads."

Larry Bird signals one shot during the closing moments of the third quarter of the Pacers' 106-77 victory over the Cleveland Cavaliers in game 1 of their first-round series at Market Square Arena. (Paul Sancya)

Victory is sweet

But with one series in the book, there is still work to do

May 1, 1998

BY BILL BENNER

ONE SERIES DOWN, THREE TO GO.

Three victories down, 12 to go.

"You've got to remember the stakes, and the (championship) rings are the stakes," said Jalen Rose, who offered an immediate dose of perspective to the Indiana Pacers' elimination of the Cleveland Cavaliers from the NBA playoffs Thursday night in Gund Arena.

Which explains the Pacers' somewhat subdued reaction after the final seconds had disappeared and a hard-fought 80-74 victory—giving them a 3-1 first-round triumph—had gone in the books.

There wasn't the wild celebration that followed the first-round triumphs over Orlando in 1994 or Atlanta in 1995. That was another time, another team, seeing the bright lights for the first time.

Thursday night, the reaction was more of the realization that the first step—and the first opponent—was behind them, some well-earned rest and recuperation was ahead of them and there is still plenty of work to be done and basketball to be played before the back-slapping begins.

Nonetheless, the Pacers can take some sense of satisfaction from disposing of their young and dangerous first-round foes, and particularly in the manner with which they closed them out in Game 4 Thursday night.

Going in, they knew nothing would come easy against the Cavaliers and that the opening game blowout back at Market Square Arena was fool's gold.

Ultimate triumph in this series would ultimately require equal parts grit and guile, toughness and tenacity.

And so, after offering the Cavs a glimmer of hope in Game 3, it became necessary to close the door—now!— before Mike Fratello's precocious posse began to believe it could accomplish the nearly impossible and come back from a 2-0 deficit to win a best-of-five.

"You go to a Game 5 and anything is possible," said Reggie Miller. "Two years ago we had Atlanta in a Game 5 in our place and they came in and beat us...so."

So take care of business before business gets out of hand.

So the Pacers did, the hard way. In the manner of many of their road victories, they found the hows and the ways to overcome all the obstacles placed in their way.

They played big-time defense, limiting the Cavs to .393 shooting and forcing 22 turnovers. For the first time in the series, they outrebounded Cleveland. The Indiana bench rose to the moment and went beyond.

The Pacers had to overcome another significant free-throw disadvantage and a motherlode of foul trouble. They had to overcome 18,188 Gund Arena spectators who actually were more worried about the fate of the basketball team than they were of their beloved Cleveland Indians, playing at Jacobs Field next door.

The Pacers even had to overcome themselves, and an offense that sputtered and stagnated down the stretch.

But they got it done.

"Making plays, being tough, intense, just finding ways to win," said Mark Jackson, whose sprained ankle bothered him more than he would ever let on.

"We've done it all year long. This was the type of game we thought it would be and give (the Cavs) credit; they played their hearts out."

Yet it wasn't enough.

A 15-point lead melted away. The fouls piled up. The Pacers opened the fourth quarter with Mark West, Mark Pope, Jalen Rose, Travis Best and Chris Mullin on the floor.

Yet the Pacers would not blink.

"We tend to make things interesting," said Rik Smits. "Nothing comes easy. But we really never doubted ourselves. We felt we were the stronger team and fortunately, we were able to show it."

Over the long haul, this series will be good for the Pacers. It had been two years since they'd been in the playoffs, three since they've been to the second round. The Cavs were both a terrific warmup act and a great reminder of what it will take to move on.

"They're a very young, athletic, poised team," Miller said of the Cavs. "They're beyond their years."

The Pacers are in their primes. This is a team that can take out New York or Miami—if they don't kill each other first—and give Chicago a challenge.

"Time and again," said Antonio Davis, who offered a magnificent effort, "we've found ways to win. It's all about fighting for 48 minutes and giving yourself an opportunity."

The opportunity has been realized. The second awaits.

Remember the stakes, fellas. Remember the stakes.

Mark Jackson cheers on his teammates to help lift the Pacers over the Cleveland Cavaliers in their first-round playoff series. (Paul Sancya)

Pacers — Knicks
How they Match Up

Point Guard: A trouble spot for the Knicks. Charlie Ward (7.3 points, 5.7 assists) looks good at times but lacks experience and creativity, particularly in the halfcourt.
  Edge: Pacers

Small Forward: Chris Mills hasn't found his niche with the Knicks but is a solid shooter who can take his man inside. Chris Mullin remains a deadly 3-point threat and a potential explosive scorer.
  Edge: Pacers

Centers: If Patrick Ewing returns, his presence on defense would be of enormous benefit to the Knicks. If Ewing can't go, Charles Oakley slides into this role.
  Edge: Pacers

Coaching: Jeff Van Gundy is a battler who will either go to war for, or with, his players depending on the circumstance. Indiana's Larry Bird isn't as fiery but may be more competitive.
  Edge: Pacers

Shooting Guard: Though Allan Houston (18.4 points) lacks Reggie Miller's big-game personality, he has blossomed into the team's top offensive player in Patrick Ewing's absence.
  Edge: Pacers

Power Forward: His brawl with Mourning may have won the Miami series for the Knicks, but Larry Johnson's absence in the opener while he serves a two-game suspension could prove costly.
  Edge: Knicks

Bench: The Knicks bench, led by John Starks, is much deeper than usual. Indiana's second unit is more athletic and versatile, but not quite as physical.
  Edge: None

Intangibles: The Knicks would like nothing more than to avenge their '95 playoff loss while ruining Indiana's dream. If Ewing comes back, don't underestimate the emotional lift that would provide.
  Edge: Knicks

Prediction: This is a real test of the Pacers' growth level. If they stick to business, they should have little trouble with the Knicks.
  Pacers will win the series in six games.

Pacers take command with overtime victory

May 11, 1998

BY MARK MONTIETH

Some might call it luck. Some might consider it fate.

To the Indiana Pacers, it's what happens when you remain persistent and positive.

Down seven points to New York with 3 ½ minutes to go, the Pacers extracted a 118-107 overtime victory at Madison Square Garden on Sunday that added another dramatic episode to the memorable playoff history between these two teams.

Of more immediate importance was the dagger it drove into the heart of the Knicks, who were on the verge of evening the Eastern Conference semifinals at two games apiece. Instead, Indiana takes a 3-1 lead into Game 5 on Wednesday at Market Square Arena, with three chances to win one game and close out the best-of-seven series.

"They have to win three in a row, and I don't know if they can do that," Pacers guard Mark Jackson said. "But they're a veteran team, and we know it's not going to be easy."

Nothing ever is when these two teams get together. Sunday's victory, however, stretched the limits of the Pacers' knack for coming back. Trailing 100-93 after Patrick Ewing hit a baseline jumper with 3:46 remaining in regulation, they held the Knicks without a field goal until 1:23 remained in overtime. By then, it was much too late.

"It says a lot about this basketball team—the character, the will, the desire, the determination," Jackson said. "We have a unique group in here that does not quit and believes in one another, and we have a coach who believes in us and isn't yelling and screaming all the time. A lot of teams would have folded today."

Reggie Miller returned to his Knick-knocking ways with 38 points in 48 minutes, including a 3-pointer off a broken play that forced overtime with 5.9 seconds remaining. Rik Smits overcame a three-point first half with

23—14 in the fourth quarter, including 12 in a row when he personally kept the Pacers in the game. Chris Mullin added 18 points and five steals. And Jackson, booed loudly by his former home fans in Saturday's Pacers loss, had the last word with 16 points, 15 assists, six rebounds and two turnovers.

They all gave some of the credit to their coach, Larry Bird, whose calm sideline demeanor has helped pull them through many jams this season. Even when his team was down seven in the fourth quarter, had hit just five of its first 14 shots in the period and couldn't seem to keep the Knicks from getting easy baskets, Bird offered hope in the huddles.

"He continues to say, 'We're going to win, we're going to win, we're going to win,' no matter what," Antonio Davis said. "He asks for input from the assistant coaches and the players, and he doesn't panic."

Everyone pitched in for the Pacers in the final few minutes of regulation, including Lady Luck. Two Smits field goals, two blocked shots by Antonio Davis and two free throws by Davis led the Pacers to within one. Miller missed a 3-pointer and John Starks' hit two foul shots with 19.3 seconds left to give the Knicks a 102-99 lead, but the Pacers kept coming.

During a timeout, assistant coach Rick Carlisle diagrammed a 3-pointer for Miller, but the players were reminded a quick two-point field goal would suffice. Miller, double-teamed coming off a pick, was left with no choice but to feed Smits in the post.

Smits faked Ewing and got to the basket for a layup, but was hit in the face and missed. Ewing, unable to control the rebound, tipped the ball out with the hope a teammate would grab it. But Mullin—who was backpedaling downcourt for defense—was able to slap it to Jackson with his right hand.

Jackson passed up an open 3-pointer and fed Miller on the left wing. The Knicks fans behind Miller gasped as he let go the shot, and for good reason. He swished it, tying the game.

New York had a chance to win in regula-

tion, but Allan Houston rolled a driving one-hander from 5 feet off the front of the rim.

Indiana dominated the overtime, scoring 10 consecutive points before the shell-shocked Knicks could respond.

"A lot of times, as hard as you work and with all the scouting, it still comes down to the bounce of the ball," Mullin said. "It's hard to accept, but it's true."

It's particularly hard to accept for the Knicks and their fans, who saw Miller score eight points in 8.9 seconds two years ago and score 25 in the fourth quarter three years go in Pacers playoff victories.

"This is why I'm a Bulls fan," one fan was heard to say as he made his way toward the exit. "It's so frustrating. I mean it is so-o-o-o frustrating." ■

Reggie Miller makes "The Shot" to help lift the Pacers to an overtime victory against the Knicks in Game 4 of the playoff series. (Paul Sancya)

Mark Jackson does his signature "jiggle" while bringing the ball up court against the Knicks in the Eastern Conference semifinal series. (Paul Sancya)

Jackson makes playoff history with triple-double

May 13, 1998

BY BILL BENNER

A triple-double in the game for Mark Jackson. A quadruple-single in the series for the Indiana Pacers.

Absolute pandemonium for 16,767 spectators in Market Square Arena, including one particular New York filmmaker who managed to become shorter as the outcome became apparent.

And now the next challenge, if not, indeed, the ultimate challenge: the Chicago Bulls.

First, however, there was the business at hand Wednesday night, and you knew the New York Knicks, fighting for their playoff lives, would be a handful.

So in perhaps the biggest home-court victory in their National Basketball Association history, the Pacers put the Knicks in their rear-view mirrors with a 99-88 victory and a 4-games-to-1 triumph in the best-of-seven Eastern Conference semifinals.

All that means is that the Pacers' playoff work is halfway done.

Next up, in the conference finals beginning Sunday at the United Center, are the reigning world champion Bulls, who eliminated Charlotte later Wednesday night.

"We're on center stage now," said Reggie Miller.

"Chicago's obviously the best team in the world, and to beat them four games will be tough," said Larry Bird, who reluctantly accepted his coach of the year award in pregame ceremonies.

"But I've got a group of guys who believe in themselves and they're going to battle. And that's all I can ask—to go out and play as hard as they possibly can, and you never know what's going to happen."

The Pacers played as hard as they could Wednesday night. They had to. The Knicks are a tough, pride-filled bunch, and taking them out proved to be as difficult as Miami's Alonzo Mourning shaking Knicks coach Jeff Van Gundy from his leg.

But finally—with the kind of defense that's been there all season and the kind of rebounding that hasn't, and with Jackson, Miller and Rik Smits supplying the offense—the Pacers pulled away.

Larry Bird shouts instructions from the sidelines during action with the New York Knicks. (Paul Sancya)

Throughout, Jackson stood tall and taller as filmmaker/Knicks fan Spike Lee, sitting in fourth-row seats, got small and smaller.

Jackson, the New York native and former Knick who was booed lustily last weekend in Madison Square Garden, had the ultimate payback.

On the heels of Sunday's 16 points and 15 assists in Game 4, Jackson came back with 22 points, 14 rebounds and 13 assists. It was the first triple-double in Pacers playoff history.

Bird called Jackson's play "spectacular" and then paid him the supreme compliment.

"He reminds me of myself," said Bird. "He doesn't have foot speed, but he competes and he competes hard."

"Mark Jackson was fantastic," said Miller, who wasn't too shabby himself. "He played the game of his life, a game for the ages."

Yet Jackson said he took no satisfaction from wasting the team that gave up on him in 1992.

"The ultimate is to beat whoever you face," said Jackson. "It just so happened to be the New York Knicks. But it meant just as much beating Cleveland in the first round."

PLENTY OF HELP

As brilliant as Jackson was, this was not a solo slaying of the Knicks. Miller had 24 points, four assists and two blocked shots. Smits, 10 of 15 from the floor, added 22. Antonio Davis came off the bench for 12 points, six

rebounds and three blocked shots.

The Pacers out-rebounded the Knicks by 12. Their defense had two stretches in the third and fourth quarters. And they hit their free throws, going 29 for 34 at the line.

More than anything—both in Game 5 and throughout the series—the Pacers were the team with the inner confidence, with the composure, with the sense that somehow, they would prevail.

Filmmaker Spike Lee cheers on his favorite team, the New York Knicks. (Paul Sancya)

"We understand the job at hand," said Jackson. "We don't get rattled, we make plays and we get the job done. That's how this team was built."

And that's how this team has been led by Larry Bird.

Said Van Gundy, "Frankly, we got beat by the better team in this series."

The New York media are likely to make Patrick Ewing the Game 5 scapegoat. Certainly, the Knicks center's 4-for-13 shooting and his three turnovers were a factor.

But from this perspective, it looked like Ewing came back from his wrist injury and played on adrenaline for two games. Then, in Game 4, he hit the wall. That he played at all is a tribute to his heart.

More likely suspects were forward Charles Oakley, who had a terrible night; point guards Charlie Ward and Chris Childs, both used by Jackson; and the punkish John Starks, who offered up a 5-for-16 clunker in the biggest game of New York's season.

SAVE THE CELEBRATIONS

When it was over, the Pacers took this one in stride. There was no celebration.

"There was no reason to jump, rant, rave, high-five and hug," said Jackson, who even kept his "jiggle" on hold. "The ultimate goal is to win the whole thing, and if and when we do that, you'll see 12 to 15 guys and a couple of coaches acting the fool.

"But until then, it's unnecessary because we haven't accomplished what we wanted."

On an evening to remember, the point guard had made his final point. ■

Rooting for the reserves, Reggie Miller and Rik Smits are first off the bench to cheer on their teammates during the Game 1 win over the New York Knicks at Market Square Arena. (Matt Kryger)

Pacers — Bulls
How They Match Up

Point guard: Chicago's Ron Harper has the size and strength to defend Mark Jackson in the post and the quickness to prevent penetration. At 6-6, he's also more effective at double-teaming inside, leaving Jackson alone on the perimeter. Even with all that, the Pacers averaged 97.3 points against the Bulls and Jackson had 35 assists.
Edge: Pacers

Shooting guard: Michael Jordan is going to get his, no matter what. He averaged 28.8 points against the Pacers. He's also one of the best defenders ever at his position. But he hates to play against Reggie Miller, whose perpetual motion and strategic use of screens can wear a defender out. Miller averaged 23 points and shot 50 percent against the Bulls.
Edge: Bulls

Small forward: Scottie Pippen is possibly the second-best all-around player in the game and still is in his prime. Chris Mullin is in the final phase of his career and should be hamstrung by Pippen's quickness. Nonetheless, Mullin has shown a knack for putting together bursts of offense and his quick hands can bother Pippen.
Edge: Bulls

Power forward: There is some curiosity over whose head Dennis Rodman will attempt to climb inside. His guerrilla tactics generally don't work with Dale Davis, who has the ability to control his anger—to a point. Rodman still is a superior rebounder and post defender. Those also happen to be Davis' strengths, but Rodman is better at both.
Edge: Bulls

Center: Rik Smits has never been totally comfortable playing against Luc Longley, who has comparable height (7-2) and superior bulk (292). In two games against Longley this season, Smits shot 12-of-26 and totaled 27 points. Longley is coming off a troubling knee injury, and his ability to play heavy minutes against a premier player will be tested.
Edge: Pacers

Bench: Indiana's second unit has alternated between brilliant and invisible, and must find a level of consistency to fully exploit what should be a decided advantage.
Edge: Pacers

Coaching: Larry Bird is the NBA Coach of the Year, which kind of irritates him because most guys who win that trophy don't win the championship. One exception is Phil Jackson, the master motivator, who won the award in 1996. While Bird is treading new ground as a coach, Jackson has been there before, many times.
Edge: Bulls

Intangibles: The Pacers are one of the few teams not intimidated by the Bulls. Still, these are the Bulls, on the possible farewell tour for Jordan, Pippen and Jackson. There has been no greater force in the NBA in recent years than this team's will to win.
Edge: Bulls

Analysis: The Pacers went to the conference finals once in Jordan's absence, and once when he was not yet back in rhythm from his baseball sabbatical, and thus get their first crack at Chicago. The Bulls might be more vulnerable than usual but they aren't exactly obsolete.
Prediction: Bulls in six.

Boston Fans Rooting for Old Hero Bird

With Celtics sidelined for this year's playoffs, Pacers coach is town's go-to guy once again.

May 17, 1998

BY JOHN R. O'NEILL

Phil Castinetti, a Boston Celtics fan for 35 years, is rooting for another team these days.

He still loves his Celtics, but he also has a place in his heart for Larry Bird. Bird played for the Celtics from 1979 to 1992 and helped the team win three National Basketball Association championships. Now he's the rookie head coach of the Indiana Pacers, who are in the Eastern Conference finals. And since the Celtics didn't even make the playoffs, Castinetti is among the many Boston fans who have adopted the Pacers.

"If we're not in it, we've got to root for Larry, that's for sure," said Castinetti, who owns a sports memorabilia shop near Boston.

"I've never seen people love anybody like they loved him," he said.

"I was out last night at a bar and everybody had the Pacers game on, screaming for Larry," he added. "It was like the Celtics were playing again."

The conference finals start today; the Pacers face Michael Jordan and the rest of the Chicago Bulls, who are seeking their sixth championship in eight seasons.

"I hate Michael Jordan," Castinetti said. "I'm with Larry all the way."

So are a lot of people, said Ted Sarandis, host of a nightly talk show on WEEI-AM, an all-sports radio station in Boston that carries the Celtics games.

"Fans will forever have a tremendously passionate feeling toward Larry," he said. Bird, after all, was the last athlete to lead a local team to a world title.

"I think people follow the Pacers—I really do," he said. "It will really, really intensify with this next round of the playoffs."

When Sarandis stopped by two sports bars during one Pacers playoff game, Indiana was featured prominently on many of the bars' television screens.

At one of those bars, the Original Sports Saloon, a

The Pacers square off against the reigning World Champion Chicago Bulls in the Eastern Conference Finals. (Paul Sancya)

waitress offered a hurried endorsement of Bird before handing the phone off to customer William Saunders, a Celtics ball boy back in 1966.

He now works for a union of demolition workers—the same local that is tearing down Boston Garden, the team's old home, just a few feet away from the new Fleet Center arena.

Saunders isn't working on that job, but he did demolish a building used by team officials.

"I tore down Red Auerbach's office," he said, referring to the legendary Celtics head coach who now is the team's vice chairman.

Last week, when Bird was picked as the NBA's Coach of the Year, he won a trophy named after Auerbach that features a likeness of the former Celtics coach. Saunders thinks the honor was deserved.

"I think Larry Bird is an excellent coach," he said. "I'll certainly be following that team—so is all of Boston."

One easy convert was Boston resident Joseph Larry Bird, who said Celtics fans will be pulling for the Pacers.

"Sure they will—this is Boston, OK?"

Bird maintained he's a distant relative of Larry Joe Bird, the coach, but he added, "I've gotten to the point where I don't say my name, because people think I'm lying."

In the souvenir shop at the Fleet Center, one of the more popular items is a T-shirt with two images of Bird on the front—one as a Celtics player, the other as the Pacers' coach.

At $18, it's $2 more than most of the T-shirts in the store, but it's still a hot seller.

SOLD OUT BY HALFTIME

The shirt was introduced on the night the Pacers returned to Boston for the first time with Bird as head coach. The supply was sold out by halftime, said Ryan Anderson, a store supervisor.

"Bird's a very big seller here," he said, and Bird's coaching success is a frequent topic of conversation among shoppers.

"They like the fact that Larry Bird is doing well."

This season, the store has stocked more Pacers items, "which lately have been selling like crazy," Anderson said. "I think a big reason they made it to the playoffs is because of him."

Anderson will be pulling for the Pacers against the Bulls.

"That's why I'm happy they made it—so I have someone to root for," he said, predicting the Pacers will beat the Bulls.

"A lot of people don't think they can beat them. A lot of people think I'm crazy," he said. "You've just got to have faith, that's all." ■

Pacer guard Reggie Miller faced a barrage of microphones as he talked to reporters at Market Square Arena during the Pacers-Bulls series. (Mike Fender)

Bird, Pacers make no concessions, expect to put Bulls in hole early

May 17, 1998

BY BILL BENNER

Larry Bird's unorthodox coaching manner includes not borrowing from the book of Conventional Playoff Wisdom.

Which states, among other things, that the road team's goal is to gain a split of the first two games in a seven-game series.

Split, schmit, the Indiana Pacers coach said Saturday.

Bird is talking two wins in Chicago today and Tuesday in the NBA's Eastern Conference finals.

"We're one of the better road teams in the league," Bird said. "I'm so sick of guys (saying), 'Well, let's go get one.' That's not the way you do it. You go in there to win the first one, then get the second one.

"Then you've got them in a world of hurt."

Wait a minute, Larry. A world of hurt for the team that has inflicted more pain than any other in the '90s? A world of hurt for the five-time and defending NBA champion Chicago Bulls? And hurting them in the United Center, where the Bulls were 37-4 this season?

A world of hurt for Michael Jordan, the greatest ever? For Scottie Pippen and Dennis Rodman? For that triangle-and-two offense and the strangle-of-five defense?

Does Bird know what he's saying?

Sure he does. He believes.

"I never thought I was going to lose a game when I stepped on any court," Bird reiterated Saturday.

"My guys have a lot of talent, they're unselfish, they want to win. ...Now all they've got to do is believe in themselves, play with confidence and feel like they can compete with anyone in the league."

Does he think that belief can translate into performance against the Bulls?

"I don't think, I know," Bird replied. "If they stick together and handle the lows when they're low, keep their highs on an even keel, then they're fine.

"They're going to win it."

To Bird, that's not so much a prediction as the expectation.

To Chicagoans, that's probably just Bird talking the talk.

Probably, too, to the Bulls themselves, who nonetheless profess respect for the challenge the Pacers present.

Still, they've heard it all before, yadda, yadda, yadda from all those pretenders who've had their shots at the Bulls this decade. From Detroit, Cleveland, New York, Orlando, Miami—one by one they've come in with their mouths loaded and left with their hearts empty.

Now it's the Pacers' turn.

But more than talking the talk, they see it as believing the belief.

If, indeed, someone is going to dismantle the Bulls' dynasty before the house crumbles within, why not the Pacers? Why not a team with depth; with a good big man in Rik Smits; with a solid perimeter game from Reggie Miller and Chris Mullin; with toughness in the Davises, Antonio and Dale; and with the ability to play defense like, well, the Bulls?

Why not a team coached by Larry Bird?

Why not believe?

"I remember (former heavyweight boxing champion) Mike Tyson talking one day and he said he should have been beaten well before Buster Douglas beat him," Pacers point guard Mark Jackson recalled. "But the guys who stepped in the ring didn't believe they could beat him, so the battle was already won.

"That's the difference. You have to look (the Bulls) in the eye and compete and feel that you can win. We have a team that believes that and is capable of doing that."

Bird said he wants the Pacers to "keep attacking and attacking." He wants the team's only backward steps to be retreating down the floor for defense. When an open shot presents itself, he wants it taken.

"Don't go out there and watch them play; go out and play against 'em," said Antonio Davis. "As long as we keep that in mind—that we're there to beat them and not watch them—we'll be OK."

Added Jalen Rose: "If we go in tippy-toeing and timid, we're going to get blown away. You can't be intimidated or play not to lose, or you're already beat. We have to have the attitude that we're going to win, and that no matter what happens, we're not going to back down."

Again, the Bulls have been there, heard that.

"They have seen it all," Miller said. "But they haven't seen us in a seven-game series."

No, they haven't. Though the Pacers and Chicago have

developed a nice regular-season rivalry, this will be their first meeting in the playoffs. When Indiana crashed through to the conference finals in '94, Jordan was off playing minor league baseball. When the Pacers made it back to that stage the next year, Jordan had just returned and had not regained his enormous skills.

"I know what Michael's made of," said Bird. "He's going to compete, he's going to play hard, he's going to do whatever he can. That's what I'm telling my guys. Don't give up because he's not going to give up."

So here we go again. Another seven-game series. Another conference finals, the third in five years for the Pacers.

Only this time it's the Bulls and Jordan, the standards by which all of basketball measures itself.

"We're playing against the champs and the country will be watching," said Jackson. "This is what it's all about."

Larry Bird reacts to a Bulls run in the third quarter of game 1 of the Eastern Conference Finals. (Matt Kryger)

Injured Miller comes to rescue in the clutch

Strong fourth-quarter play from the second unit sparks comeback win and closes conference finals deficit to 2-1.

May 24, 1998

BY BILL BENNER

There was a taped pre-game pep talk from David Letterman for comic relief. There was an appearance by A.J. Foyt and his pole-sitting driver in today's Indy 500, Billy Boat, perhaps to signify it was time to for the Indiana Pacers to stand on the gas.

There was a Hoosiers film clip of the Hickory Huskers for inspiration. There was the sellout crowd of 16,576, who raised such an incredible ruckus it made Chicago's sterile United Center seem like a mausoleum by comparison.

And, of course, there was "Reggie...Reggie... Reggie" Miller, on one good leg, yet, busting out all over the Chicago Bulls.

But the Pacers played themselves away from a potential sweep and back into the Eastern Conference finals Saturday with a performance that went far beyond artificial stimuli and even that very real, very gutty performance from the spindly No. 31.

Indiana's 107-105 victory closed its deficit in the series to 2-1 and made Monday's Game 4 the next biggest game of the season. But without Saturday's triumph, even Miller acknowledged the obvious.

"If we had gone down love-3, you could have written us off," he said.

And yes, Reggie was sensational Saturday, and then some. Playing on a sprained right ankle injured midway through the third quarter and thereafter limping with every step—except for those when he would suddenly sprint into position to bury another jumper—Miller scored 11 points in a three-minute span late in the fourth quarter, closed with 28 overall and added another chapter to his book of playoff heroics.

And just when you thought he saved the good stuff only for the Knicks.

But to focus on Miller's effort would be like judging a pie by its crust, and ignoring the filling.

This was Dale Davis and Chris Mullin leveling Scottie Pippen with the kind of picks that should have been laid on him last Sunday.

This was Antonio Davis playing both the heated warrior in the lane and the cool cat at the free throw line.

This was Travis Best offering up the biggest (if still not the best, but he's gaining on it) 25 minutes of his career.

This was Jalen Rose, rising out of his playoff funk, dealing on the offensive end and even—stop the presses, we have a bulletin here—drawing an offensive foul from, yes, Michael Jordan.

It was Larry Bird, trashed in Chicago for his coaching ability, having the guts to go with his gut feeling and stay with a lineup that was working and ride with a player, Miller, who was obviously hobbled, even if the Bulls were somehow blind to that fact.

This was Mark Jackson, having done all he could to combat Pippen and run the offense, happily accepting a role on the sidelines.

"I've been around too long to be frustrated," said Jackson, who didn't play a minute of the fourth quarter. "We've got 12 guys on this basketball team and they can all get the job done."

Ten of them played Saturday. Nine—with the notable exception of Rik Smits, who disproved the "size matters" theory currently in vogue—brought their A games.

Overall, the Pacers dropped their turnovers to a tolerable 15, hit 53.7 percent from the field, finally played a good third quarter and got to the free throw line at a rate nearly comparable with the Bulls, remarkable when you consider Jordan was bailed out more Saturday than the race fans who will be filling our jails this weekend.

And while we're briefly on the subject of officiating, it was interesting to hear Pippen say afterward, "I got banged up pretty good."

What goes around comes around, Scottie.

Pippen also complained, "They didn't allow me to be aggressive."

No, what they didn't allow was for you to commit assault and battery on point guards. There's a difference.

This was, finally, the Pacers' quantity over the Bulls' quality.

What the Pacers lack in comparison to the skills of Jordan and Pippen, they can make up for in depth.

"Our bench won the game for us," said Jackson.

Reggie Miller gestures toward Michael Jordan while talking to an official in the second half of Game 3 in which the Pacers defeated the Bulls, 107-105. (Matt Kryger)

"Their bench killed us," said Pippen.

"Before the game, we wrote '12' on the board, and that meant we were going to need 12 guys if we were going to step up and win today," said Rose. "We know we have a first and second unit, but in that locker room, we're one team, and whoever's out on the floor, it's their job to make plays."

Rose and others have come and gone during the play-offs. The constant off that bench has been Antonio Davis, who had 10 points and 12 rebounds but, more importantly, set a tone of aggressiveness and force.

And as magnificent as Miller was, Antonio's two free throws with 22.5 seconds left—after the irrepressi-Bulls had suddenly closed within a point—were huge.

"I won't lie to you, I was a little nervous," said Antonio Davis. "But my team expects me to go up there and knock them down."

Make no mistake, however. The Bulls have been knocked back, but not down. This was just one win. Four remains the magic number.

"We've come too far, we've done too many things, we've expected too much of ourselves, we've reached too many goals to stop," said Davis. "We're going to go out fighting."

No, they still haven't slain the beast that is the Bulls. But Game 3 was at least a decent flesh wound. ■

Hobbling to victory

*Miller scores 28 with injured ankle to lead
Pacers to victory*

May 24, 1998

BY MARK MONTIETH

All season long, Reggie Miller has hit game-breaking shots.

Saturday, in the biggest game of the Indiana Pacers' season—for now—he added a dramatic element to a long-running theme.

Pain.

Playing with a sprained right ankle that required treatment in the locker room in the third quarter, Miller returned to score 13 points in the final 4:11 to lead Indiana to a 107-105 victory over Chicago at Market Square Arena. The longest nonovertime game of the season turned out to be worth the wait for the Pacers, who reduced the Bulls' lead in the Eastern Conference finals to 2-1.

Is this Miller Time or what? The Pacers play an even more momentous game against the Bulls on Monday at MSA and will do it with an injured leading scorer who thrives on showmanship.

"The plot thickens as the season goes on," Chris Mullin said. "Now we have a big, big game, and he's hobbled. It just gets better and better."

Miller scored 28 points, hitting 9-of-15 field-goal attempts, 4-of-7 3-pointers and all six free throws in the improbable win. It was a sudden and desperately needed turnabout for a player who hit just 9-of-27 shots in the first two games while he was healthy, and hit more than half his shots in just two of the previous 11 playoff games.

This was a go-figure game all the way around. Mark Jackson, so instrumental to the Pacers' success throughout the playoffs, was left on the bench in the fourth quarter in favor of backup point guard Travis Best. Rik Smits got off just six shots and scored 12 points in 28 minutes. The Pacers were outrebounded 40-29.

But a strong effort from the reserves, who outscored their Bulls counterparts 43-25, and an aggressive approach that dictated the tempo of the game was enough—thanks to Miller's finishing touch.

"That's Reggie Miller," said Antonio Davis, whose 10 points and 12 rebounds were his second double-double in three games against the Bulls. "That's the guy we count on to bail us out. I love the fact he's on my team. When the ball's in his hands, everybody feels comfortable.

"He kind of scared me a little bit. He was hopping around on one leg, but he has the heart the size of a lion's."

And a swollen foot to match. Miller suffered his injury when he landed on the outside of Michael Jordan's foot midway though the third quarter. He felt no pain at first but felt a twinge, then heard a pop, as he ran upcourt. He had the ankle retaped by trainer David Craig on the bench, then went to the locker room where assistant trainer Will Sevening performed a more restrictive taping.

Miller bounced on a minitrampoline in the locker room to test the ankle, then returned to the floor. He went back into the game with 9:54 left in the fourth quarter as the fans chanted his name but took awhile to warm to the task.

He didn't take a shot until just more than 6 minutes remained, missing a 3-pointer from the top of the key. Coach Larry Bird considered taking him out but decided to stick with him awhile longer. Finally, with the Pacer lead at 89-87, Miller hit a 3-pointer from the left baseline—replays showed his left foot might have been out of bounds—with 4:11 remaining.

Miller hit another 3-pointer at 3:19 to open a 95-89 lead, then added a 20-footer just ahead of the shot clock buzzer to extend the lead to eight. His 3-pointer with 1:34 remaining gave the Pacers a seemingly secure 101-93 lead, but the Bulls pulled within two points on Jordan's foul shot with 12.2 seconds remaining.

Miller, however, drew a hard foul from Ron Harper and hit both free throws with 10.6 seconds left to clinch Indiana's 12th consecutive homecourt victory.

Ironically, Miller was able to work free for open shots he didn't get while healthy in the first two games. Jordan guarded him most of the time while Harper, Miller's primary defender earlier in the series, watched from the bench. Miller guarded Scottie Pippen but found himself matched up with Jordan on a couple of occasions.

Fortunately for the Pacers, Jordan didn't challenge him. Miller left MSA with an electric stimulus attached to his ankle to limit the swelling. He'll receive treatment today and hope for the best on Monday.

(Paul Sancya)

Bird's calm demeanor sets playoff tone for the Pacers

May 27, 1998

BY BILL BENNER

Just when you think you've seen everything from Indiana Pacers coach Larry Bird, you see the most amazing thing of all.

Nothing.

Absolutely nothing.

At the moment of Monday's Game 4 when 16,000 Market Square Arena fans were going berserk, when Reggie Miller was spinning around so much you feared he might drill himself through the MSA hardwood and drop onto Market Street below, and when emotions were flowing with the force of a riptide, there was Bird.

Just... standing... there.

No reaction.

In fact, I want to see the tapes because I'm not sure he even blinked.

Miller had just hit his biggest big shot of the season. The Pacers were within seven-tenths of a second of winning their biggest big game of the season, at least until the next one comes along in tonight's Game 5 of the Eastern Conference finals at Chicago's United Center.

But to look at the expressionless Bird, you almost felt the need to grab his wrist and feel for a pulse.

Which is when it dawned upon me. All season long, the Pacers' rookie coach has been universally described as a non-control freak in a league filled with quite the opposite.

But the reality is this: Bird has ultimate control.

He has control over himself, and that has permeated throughout the team. The Pacers continue to be a reflection of their leader.

While everyone else at Market Square Arena was delirious with excitement after Reggie Miller hit the 96-94 game-winning shot, Coach Larry Bird remained expressionless during the final seconds of the Pacers' Game 4 victory over the Bulls. (Erin Painter)

And now Bird's control—which stems from his composure—is beginning to show its influence over the conference finals, especially in comparison to his Chicago Bulls counterpart, Phil Jackson.

Bird has countered Jackson's series-opening move of putting Scottie Pippen on point guard Mark Jackson by using Travis Best and Jalen Rose more, especially in the fourth quarter.

He's followed his instincts in sticking with the hot lineup or the hot player, having the guts to ignore the conventional wisdom that starters start and starters finish. He hasn't—like Jackson—fiddled with his starting lineup. Not in this series, not in the playoffs, not in the season, unless dictated by injury.

And his team has steadily reduced its turnovers this series: from 26 to 20 to 15 to 9, the surest sign of settling in and settling down.

The Pacers have been like Bird—unshakeable and unflappable.

Even with that, however, his stoic demeanor as Miller's shot sliced through the net at the end of Game 4 was extraordinary.

"Everybody was whooping and hollering but I knew there was still time on the clock, that there was still time to get a shot off," Bird said Tuesday. "Somebody's got to keep a level head. If a coach is jumping around, bad things can happen. I had to stay as calm as I possibly could to think about what we're going to do next."

Bird said he senses his team, especially in the playoffs, is taking its emotional cues from him.

"There's a lot of stress, a lot of pressure," he said. "I feel like they're watching every move I make. They know I've been there before, they know I've done it. They need somebody they can lean on. They don't need somebody who leads cheers for them and hollers when they make plays."

So when Reggie hits the big shot, Bird stays cool. When the Bulls take a lead, Bird stays calm.

"When we do make big plays, or if Chicago is making a run on us and we're down by 8 or 10, it's my calming influence that's going to bring them back and I understand that," Bird said. "I had coaches who got excited when the game wasn't over, and we ended up losing. I also had coaches who stayed calm throughout every situation and it really helped me as a player."

As a coach, Larry Bird can sometimes say it all by doing nothing. ■

Even the stoic demeanor of Pacer coach Larry Bird must occasionally give way. Here Bird pleads his case with the referee in the second half of Game 5 of the NBA Eastern Conference Finals. (Steve Healey)

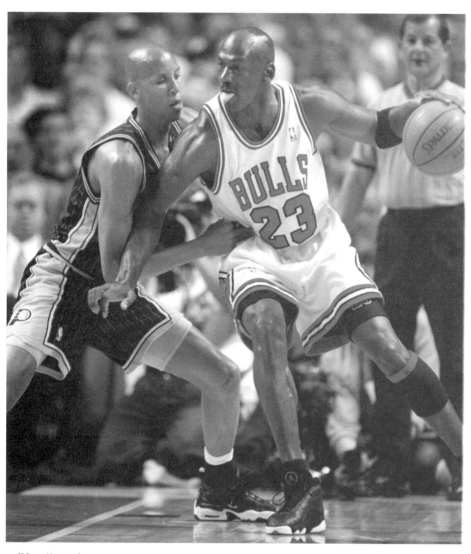

(Matt Kryger)

While facing the nearly impossible task of guarding Michael Jordan, the Pacers' Reggie Miller received the full support of his wife Marita.

(Matt Kryger)

Pacers fans celebrate and dance in front of Market Square Arena after the Pacers beat the Bulls 96-94 in Game 4, which tied the series, 2-2.

(Kelly Wilkinson)

(Kelly Wilkinson)

Pushed to the limit

Best comes through while Jordan
falls in the clutch

May 30, 1998

BY MARK MONTIETH

IN THE BASKETBALL-BASED MOVIE "He Got Game," Travis Best played a supporting role to the star player. But in the biggest game of the Indiana Pacers' season Friday, in a pair of real-life moments that contained more drama than anything Hollywood could drum up, the backup point guard stepped into a starring role.

He Had Game.

Best, once again playing the entire fourth quarter, scored four points in the final 33.3 seconds to lead a 92-89 victory over Chicago at Market Square Arena Friday night that forced an even bigger game. That will come Sunday in Chicago, where the Interstate-65 rivals will play a seventh and decisive game for the right to meet Utah for the league championship.

Rik Smits, hitting 11-of- 12 field goal attempts, led the Pacers with 25 points in 32 minutes. Dale Davis, playing his best game of the series, scored 19 points, grabbed eight rebounds and blocked three shots. Mark Jackson added 13 points in 27 minutes before giving way to Best. And the Pacer bench outscored Chicago's reserves, 25-8.

All that was barely enough to overcome Reggie Miller's eight-point effort on 2-of-13 shooting, the fact the Pacers missed 13 free throws in 35 attempts and the Bulls' 44-29 rebounding advantage.

Michael Jordan led Chicago with 35 points, but was unable to convert when it counted most for the Bulls. He also fouled Best, setting up the game-winning free throws.

Best, who played the final 15½ minutes of the game, scored six points in his 21-minute relief role, but made consecutive offensive plays that are the biggest of the best season in the Pacers' NBA history. With the score tied at 87, he took Bulls guard Steve Kerr one-on-one and banked in a running one-hander from 13 feet on the left side.

Jordan, drawing a foul from Antonio Davis with 19.7 seconds left, tied the game. But Best untied it. Without a timeout, Best took the ball upcourt and took matters into his own hands.

The play was designed for Miller, whose heroics had won Games 3 and 4 for the Pacers, but the Bulls shut off that option.

So Best went one-on-one against Jordan. Dribbling and juking from just left of the top of the key, he took off with a right-handed dribble into the lane and drew a foul from Jordan with 8.8 seconds left. A 90 percent foul shooter in the postseason (36 of 40), he hit both for all the points the Pacers would need.

"I just tried to get him leaning one way so I could spin back and go the other way," Best said. "I saw the shot clock running down. I just wanted to get in the middle and create something. I always feel confident, no matter who's guarding me, as long as there's space to create something."

Jordan had a chance to tie the game for Chicago, but lost his footing while driving the lane against Derrick McKey, who hit a free throw with 0.7 seconds left to complete the scoring.

Jackson had led the Pacers eliminations of Cleveland and New York in the earlier playoff rounds. Who would have thought Best—who has played the entire fourth quarter of all three Pacer victories against the Bulls—would take over in this series?

"It's somewhat of a shock, but at the same time I've always been ready for it," Best said. "That's all you can do when you come off the bench, be ready when you get your chance.

"It means the world. I've been playing here for three years, sitting on the bench. Just to be in these type of games late in the game means a lot. I definitely want to use the time wisely and make the most of it. I've always felt I was a fighter. I was just trying to make a difference."

The Pacers, who are undefeated in the playoffs at MSA, won't play here again this season unless they win Sunday in Chicago. If so, they'll be back on June 7, in Game 3 of the Finals.

But there is a lot of work to do first.

Jordan guarantees a Bulls victory.

"I don't make promises; I don't even make promises to my wife," Jordan said. "But we'll win Game 7."

Bulls now facing rare do-or-die situation

Chicago is moaning over referees' calls as they await first Game 7 at home since '92.

May 30, 1998

BY CONRAD BRUNNER

To hear the Chicago Bulls tell it, the Indiana Pacers have yet to win a game in the Eastern Conference finals.

Mark Jackson (13) and Rik Smits (45) corner Ron Harper (9) in Game 6 in Market Square Arena. (Rich Miller)

In their minds, they've won three, and had three taken away by the officials.

Perhaps the Bulls' overly defensive posture can be explained by the unfamiliarity of the challenge they face. The Pacers' 92-89 victory in Game 6 Friday night at Market Square Arena sends them to Game 7 for the first time—with Jordan—since 1992.

Though the Bulls return to friendly turf for the clincher Sunday at United Center, they are in unfamiliar territory.

"We haven't played one in six years, so what do you do?" said Michael Jordan. "You go out and play the game like there's no tomorrow, which is the way it basically is. Come 6:30 in Chicago, it's do-or-die. Somebody's going to be happy, somebody's going to be sad."

The only crying Friday night came from the Bulls, who had to get creative to find excuses, but they managed. They have, after all, had a lot of practice in this series.

Head coach Phil Jackson went so far as to claim an illegal defense against the Bulls with 1:27 remaining "changed the direction of the game," and that the officials "swallowed the whistle" on Chicago's final offensive play, when Michael Jordan tripped over Derrick McKey's stationary foot as he drove to the basket.

Jordan scored 35 points, moving within four of all-time postseason scoring leader Kareem Abdul-Jabbar (5,762), but was unable to beat McKey on the Bulls' most crucial offensive possessions.

With the game tied at 87-all, Jordan missed a jumper with 53 seconds left. Travis Best then drove for a one-handed bank shot to put the Pacers ahead with 33 seconds remaining.

On the ensuing possession, Jordan missed a pull-up jumper over McKey, but Luc Longley saved the rebound with 24 seconds remaining.

Instead of pulling it out for a final shot, either a two-pointer to send it into overtime or a 3-pointer to win, Jordan drove immediately back into the heart of the defense, drawing a foul on Antonio Davis with 19.7 seconds left.

He hit both free throws to tie the game—but left the determining possession in the Pacers' hands.

The Pacers tried to isolate Reggie Miller in the post,

but he couldn't get free, so Best drove to the hoop once more and was hacked by Jordan. He made both free throws for a 91-89 lead with 8.5 seconds remaining.

After calling a timeout to set up the final play—even though it was hardly a secret —the Bulls put it in Jordan's hands once again. As he started to drive from the left side of the key, he tripped and fell on the ball. McKey grabbed it and was fouled, making one of two free throws with four-tenths of a second left to seal the victory.

"People will think I tripped over my feet, but I'm not that clumsy," said Jordan. "Even if it was an inadvertent accident, that's a call that has to be made."

Jackson, who was fined $10,000 for complaining about the officiating after the Pacers won a pair of two-point games at home last weekend, was at it again.

"He got tripped," Jackson said. "What is there in basketball that's more evident than a guy getting tripped? Did he fall down on his own? Did anybody see him fall down on his own?"

Only about 16,566 in the arena, a few million television viewers, and the three men who counted most—those with the whistles.

The illegal defense Jackson so strongly objected to allowed the Pacers to tie the game at 87-all on a Reggie Miller free throw with 1:27 remaining.

After that, the Pacers scored on three of their final four possessions, while the Bulls failed on three of four.

"We've got Game 7, you've got to start focusing on that," said Jordan. "In situations where you're frustrated and angered, you've just got to laugh and let it go." ■

Larry Bird instructs Travis Best in the closing moments of Game 6 with Michael Jordan at the line. Best's two free throws in the final seconds of the game sealed the Pacers' 92-89 victory. (Rich Miller)

Pacers fans were dancing on Market Street after the Pacers' win over the Bulls in Game 6 at Market Square Arena. (Rich Miller)

Pacers fans who did not have tickets to Game 6 of the Eastern Conference Finals gathered on Market Street to watch the game on a giant screen TV. Indiana defeated Chicago, 92-89. (Erin Painter)

Game 7 just out of Pacers' reach

Offensive boards, FTs end Indy run

June 1, 1998

BY MARK MONTIETH

For want of a few offensive rebounds, the Indiana Pacers might be in the NBA Finals. But in the biggest game of their NBA history, they tripped over their Achilles' heel.

Outrebounded 22-4 on the offensive glass, the Pacers succumbed to Chicago 88-83 Sunday in the seventh game of the Eastern Conference finals. While the Bulls advance to the championship round against Utah, where they will try to win their third consecutive title, the Pacers must live with their third Game 7 loss in the conference finals in the past five seasons.

Chicago shot just 38 percent from the field, but gave itself a healthy margin of error by outscoring Indiana 24-3 on second-chance points.

"We got the effort tonight, but they were quicker to the ball," said Pacers coach Larry Bird, whose team ranked last in offensive rebounding during the regular season. "A couple of those offensive rebounds just ripped our heart out."

So did 14 missed free throws. A 76 percent shooting team during the regular season, the Pacers hit just 23-of-37 foul shots Sunday—leaving 14

points that could have come in handy in a five-point loss. Chicago was even worse, hitting 24-of-41 attempts, but made up for that deficiency with its work on the glass.

Michael Jordan, who guaranteed a Bulls victory after the Pacers won Game 6 on Friday, followed up his pledge with a performance that wasn't up to his playoff standards, but was good enough. He led all scorers with 28 points—becoming the NBA's all-time leading playoff scorer—despite hitting just 9-of-25 field goals and 10-of-15 free throws. He also had nine rebounds and eight assists and was instrumental in shutting out Reggie Miller in the fourth quarter.

Miller led the Pacers with 22 points, hitting 7-of-13 field goals and 4-of-7 3-pointers, but was scoreless in 10 fourth-quarter minutes. He got off just one field-goal attempt in the final period as Indiana had difficulty getting into its offense and usually went to Rik Smits when it did.

Smits scored 13 points, nine in the second half. He played just nine first-half minutes after picking up three quick fouls, and only 28 minutes overall.

"Early foul trouble just killed us," Bird said.

Despite the odds against beating the two-time de-

Dale Davis is fouled by Dennis Rodman in Game 7 at the United Center. (Matt Kryger)

Rik Smits cracks Scottie Pippen in the back of the head for his sixth foul in Game 7. (Rich Miller)

fending cham-
pions at the
United Center,
where they are
now 31-4 in
playoff games,
the Pacers
came prepared
to play. Liter-
ally. For the
first time all
season they
wore their uni-
forms to the
arena, so they
wouldn't have
to spend as
much time
preparing in
the locker
room before-
hand.

The mo-
mentum car-
ried over into
the game, as
they hit their

The Pacers' bench watches the final seconds of their 88-83 loss to the Chicago Bulls in Game 7 at the United Center. (Matt Kryger)

first eight shots and opened their largest lead of the series at 20-7. Mark Jackson hit 1-of-2 foul shots with
5:41 to provide the peak advantage, but that also marked
the start of their decline.

Chicago managed a 20-point turnaround before
halftime, taking a seven-point lead with less than a minute
to go. Miller's two 3-pointers in the final 40 seconds,
however, kept the Pacers within three at the break.

Toni Kukoc scored 14 of his 21 points in the third
quarter, hitting three of four 3-pointers, to keep the Bulls
in control. His 3-pointer with 2:42 left opened a 68-61
lead and Jordan added another point with a foul shot at
2:17. But Indiana scored the final four points of the period and the first seven points of the fourth quarter to
regain the lead.

Smits' second three-point play of the period gave
Indiana a 76-74 lead, then Antonio Davis added a free
throw with 6:55 left to open a three-point lead. At that
point one could almost hear the Bulls' dynasty crum-
bling around the edges.

Indiana nearly got a chance to add to its lead when
Derrick McKey stripped Jordan, and then Smits tied up
Jordan. Smits controlled the tip, but directed it at Scot-

tie Pippen. Jordan missed a jumper, but Pippen grabbed
the rebound and assisted Kerr on a 3-point basket that
tied the score with 6:12 left. The Bulls took the lead for
good when Pippen rebounded Luc Longley's miss and
wound up hitting an 18-footer with 4:45 remaining.

Indiana was still within two points after Antonio
Davis' rebound basket with 2:02 left, but Pippen scored
on a one-handed baseline runner that drew Davis' sixth
foul. Pippen missed the foul shot, but Jordan rebounded
to run more clock. Pippen—who hit just 6-of-18 field-
goal attempts but grabbed 12 rebounds—missed a 3-
pointer, but Indiana gave the ball back when Ron Harper
deflected Jackson's post feed to Smits.

Chicago got off two more shots, thanks to Harper's
offensive rebound, and McKey missed a rushed 3-pointer
on Indiana's final chance. Harper's free throw with 8.8
seconds remaining finished the scoring.

Ultimately, the series came down to location. The
home team won every game, and the Bulls had one more
of them because of its superior regular-season record.

"If they had homecourt advantage, it probably would
have been a different outcome," Pippen said. "But we'll
never know." ■

GAME 7

PACERS (83)

	Min	FG-A	FT-A	OR-T	A	F	T	Pts
Jackson	31	3-8	3-4	0-4	6	3	2	11
Miller	41	7-13	4-4	0-0	4	3	2	22
A.Davis	22	2-4	0-0	2-10	0	6	2	7
D. Davis	37	3-6	3-10	2-9	3	2	0	9
Smits	28	3-7	7-8	0-4	3	5	2	13
McKey	27	1-4	0-2	0-2	0	5	1	3
Rose	16	3-4	0-0	0-1	0	1	1	7
Best	17	2-5	0-2	0-1	1	4	1	4
Mullin	21	3-5	1-1	0-3	1	4	1	7
Totals		27-56	23-37	4-34	18	33	12	83

Three-point shooting: 6-16, (Miller 4-7, Jackson 2-4, Mullin 0-1, McKey 0-2, Best 0-2). Steals: 5 (Miller 2, D.Davis, Jackson, Best). Blocked shots: 2 (D.Davis 2). Team rebounds: 13.
Attendance: 23,844 (Sellout).

CHICAGO (88)

	Min	FG-A	FT-A	OR-T	A	F	T	Pts
Pippen	39	6-18	5-9	6-12	3	5	3	17
Kukoc	33	7-11	4-5	1-4	1	3	1	21
Longley	34	1-5	1-2	2-9	2	5	2	3
Harper	29	1-4	2-6	2-3	2	2	0	4
Jordan	42	9-25	10-15	5-9	8	3	2	28
Rodman	27	1-4	0-2	3-6	1	5	1	2
Burrell	5	1-1	0-0	0-0	0	2	0	2
Kerr	19	3-7	2-2	1-1	0	3	0	11
Buechler	11	0-1	0-0	1-5	1	2	0	0
Simpkins	1	0-0	0-0	1-1	0	0	0	0
Totals		29-76	24-41	22-50	18	30	9	88

Three-point shooting: 6-15, (Kukoc 3-4, Kerr 3-5, Rodman 0-1, Pippen 0-5). Steals: 7 (Pippen 2, Longley 2, Kukoc, Harper, Kerr). Blocked shots: 2 (Pippen, Rodman). Team rebounds: 10. Technical fouls: Harper.
Officials: Hugh Evans, Dick Bavetta, Jack Nies.

Larry Bird shows his dejection during the obligatory press conference following the Pacers' Game 7 loss to Chicago. (Rich Miller)

Pacers fans line the fence along the airport runway as the team returns from Chicago after their grueling seven-game series with the Bulls. (Damon Winter)

Pacers fans waited past midnight to welcome home players returning to the Indianapolis Airport after their Game 7 defeat in Chicago. (Damon Winter)

10

MAY 12, 1998

COACH OF THE YEAR

LARRY BIRD, LEGEND

May 13, 1998

EDITORIAL

Skeptics liked to smirk and snicker in May 1997 when general manager Donnie Walsh hired Larry Bird as head coach of the Indiana Pacers. Today, they are as silent as Spike Lee last Sunday night in New York.

What a difference a year makes. More to the point, what a difference the Bird makes. The Pacers' record of 58 regular season wins is the best in franchise history.

Professional sports has produced few coaches as deserving as Bird for selection as the National Basketball Association's Coach of the Year. The honor is all the sweeter for the spirit in which it was received—with a

Larry Bird is shown in the background of the Red Auerbach Trophy he received as the 1998 NBA Coach of the Year. (Paul Sancya)

genuine sense of down-home Hoosier humility.

"I have great people around me" said Bird, "It's as simple as that."

Bird's attempt to deflect the credit for his success to his players and to assistants Dick Harter and Rick Carlisle understates his superb leadership skills and his cutting-edge NBA strategy in cultivating coaching specialists and seasoned players with more than usual freedom to be their best.

"He's allowed us to be ourselves," said point guard Mark Jackson. "He's like that veteran teammate you look to when you're a younger player," said Chris Mullin, who played with Bird on the 1992 U.S. Olympic team.

Now 41, Bird has brought to coaching all those mental skills so critical to his success as a great player, chief among them intelligence and an absolute dedication to excellence.

His stoic game mask and his calm demeanor on the bench belie his demanding nature. But he has never asked his players to do any more than he himself has done as a player. Seldom has any athlete had a better role model than Bird, who has credited growing up poor in southern Indiana with learning early that "you have to work hard if you want to get something, and you had to work extra hard to get something extra."

That work ethic paid off handsomely for Bird. He hit the big time as college player of the year in 1979 when he led Indiana State to the championship game. The NBA's rookie of the year in 1980, he won three Most Valuable Player awards in as many NBA championships for the Boston Celtics.

If last year's skeptics doubted the potential for Bird as a coach, perhaps they knew too much NBA history. Few great NBA players have become great NBA coaches.

What they didn't know about was Bird, the legend. Larry Bird, the NBA's coach of the year, makes his own history. ■

Larry Bird admires the NBA Coach of the Year trophy he received in Market Square Arena on May 12, 1998. (Paul Sancya)

Players do the crowing on coach Bird's behalf

May 13, 1998

BY BILL BENNER

He said he was embarrassed. He said he hadn't paid any dues.

"I'm telling you, I'm not a great coach," the Indiana Pacers' Larry Bird said with characteristic humility.

The majority of media who cover the NBA disagreed. And on Tuesday, the official announcement of the obvious arrived.

French Lick's favorite son has yet another honor—NBA Coach of the Year—to add to his three world championships, his three Most Valuable Player awards and his Rookie of the Year award during his playing career with the Boston Celtics.

This would be, of course, the same Larry Bird about whom everyone was wondering a year ago when he was hired, "Can a great player coach?"

By guiding the Pacers from 39 victories to a club-record 58, by instilling in them the mental toughness to not lose more than one game in a row since December, by leading them to within one victory of the Eastern Conference semifinals—and no, we can't forget that Bird and his

bunch have unfinished work tonight with the New York Knicks—that question about Bird has been answered emphatically.

Bird became only the fourth rookie to be honored as Coach of the Year, joining St. Louis' Harry Gallatin (1963), Chicago's Johnny Kerr (1967) and Portland's Mike Schuler (1987).

Bird totaled 50 of 116 votes, more than the combined total of the next three finishers: Utah's Jerry Sloan (29), Cleveland's Mike Fratello (15) and Miami's Pat Riley (5).

Bird's success was built on the foundation of few rules, a strong work ethic, his own intuition, a basic approach, the skills of his assistants, Dick Harter and Rick Carlisle, and a calm, confident approach.

That helped resurrect the Pacers from the beaten-down team of Larry Brown's final season to one many believe can challenge the Chicago Bulls, provided they can eliminate the Knicks first. That opportunity comes in tonight's Game 5 at Market Square Arena.

On Tuesday, Bird said, again, that his success has more to do with others than with him.

"I have great people around me and everybody does their jobs," Bird said. "You hire people to do jobs and if

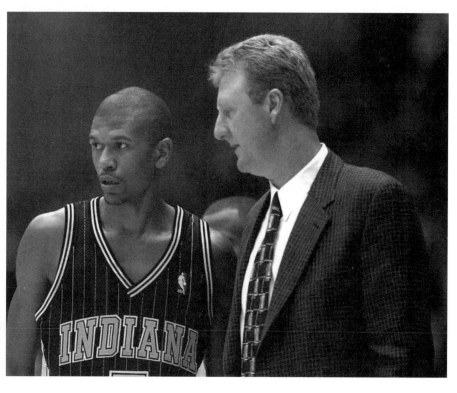

"He saw potential in me," said Jalen Rose about the NBA's Coach of the Year recipient. (Mike Fender)

they do them, you leave them alone and let them work."

Instilled with Bird's belief in them and their abilities, the Pacers responded.

"Any time you have a coach—or a boss in any work field—who believes in what you can do, as a team and as an individual, it enhances your level of play and it enhances your confidence level," said point guard Mark Jackson.

"We were a team that won 39 games last year. We were questioned individually and questioned collectively. It was the same coaching style that had gotten us to the Eastern Conference finals, but it had run its course.

"We needed something fresh and Bird came in and delivered just that. He stroked us, he criticized us, he did all the right things at the right time. But most of all, he believed in us."

Certainly, it helped that Bird inherited a veteran team, and he has stated often during the season that his style might not work with a younger group.

Then again, you see how a Jalen Rose—who was virtually abandoned by Brown last year—has flourished under Bird. You see rookie Mark Pope responding to his first playoff experience in the Knicks series Sunday with eight solid minutes, a rebound basket and a couple of solid picks that set up jump shots for teammates.

That's confidence. It's belief.

"He saw potential in me," Rose said. "He felt I was a resource that was fairly untapped. He thought I would be hungry and up to the task."

Bird treats his players like adults. There's no ranting, no raving and no sideline orchestration of every possession. If he's had something critical to say—as he did Sunday in New York, when he believed Jackson's "jiggle" came too prematurely in Saturday's Game 3—he's shared it privately and without rancor.

"I'm not going to be directing people all over the court on every play," Bird said. "I have a lot of confidence in my players. I expect Mark Jackson to run the ball club, I expect my players to play hard and I expect Reggie Miller to hit the shots at the end.

"It's that simple."

Bird thinks the Coach of the Year will be the coach with the ring at the end of the year.

"Right now everything looks rosy, but our goal is to win a championship," Bird said. "That's what it's all about. If we don't win a championship, I'll feel we failed this year, because I know we've got the talent to do it."

Although Bird didn't covet the coaching award, his players wanted it for him and stayed after practice to attend the news conference.

They applauded when Bird was handed the Red

Under Bird's leadership, the Pacers improved to a record-setting 58 victories in Bird's first season with the team. (Erin Painter)

Auerbach Trophy. Then Jackson, grinning, provided the first question.

"Now that this is out of the way, can I do my jiggle again?"

Bird laughed, leaned back and did a little shimmy of his own.

But he didn't reply. Take note, Mark. The coach of the year is still the coach of the day. ■

A champion in character

May 15, 1998

EDITORIAL

Let another praise you, and not your own mouth; someone else, and not your own lips.—Proverbs 27:2

Pacers Coach Larry Bird not only has excelled in coaching this year, winning the Coach of the Year honor, he also has excelled in deflecting praise from himself to the other people who have helped him and the Pacers become so successful.

Even as he was named Coach of the Year this week, he was attributing the well-deserved honor to his assistant coaches and players.

"I have great people around me, and everybody does their jobs," Bird said in response to becoming only the fourth rookie coach to win this honor. "You hire people to do jobs, and if they do them, you leave them alone and let them work."

His players are often his top fans and promoters, attributing their success to his coaching style. That includes respect for his players, rather than humiliating them for their errors.

Bird wants to win the NBA championship, which he suggests is the big test of any coaching honor.

But he already has won another kind of championship in setting a well-publicized example of giving credit to others.

11

OCTOBER 2, 1998

INTO THE HALL

HIS LEGEND GROWS

*Some see Bird's Hall of Fame nomination
as a formality*

February 3, 1998

BY MARK MONTIETH

Last week, Larry Bird earned the honor of coaching in the NBA All-Star game. Monday, he was selected the NBA's Coach of the Month for January.

Nice honors, those, but fleeting. Certainly nothing like the shot at immortality he also received on Monday, when he was announced as a nominee for the Naismith Memorial Basketball Hall of Fame.

Bird, an All-American at Indiana State and a 13-year NBA veteran with the Boston Celtics, topped himself by becoming one of eight players and three coaches nominated for the Hall of Fame.

"It's a great honor, but I don't think about that stuff too much," Bird said Monday from Sacramento, where the Pacers were preparing for tonight's game against the Kings. "It's been forever since I played.

"But I had a lot of great teammates and we had some success, so I guess that's why I got nominated."

Bird's players consider his election to the Hall a certainty.

"He should be in, no questions asked," Chris Mullin said. "That's an easy choice. To me they're like one in the same, Larry Bird and the Hall of Fame. They go together."

"It should be a no-brainer—a lock," Reggie Miller said. "He transcended the game and helped bring it where it is."

The nominees, selected by a screening committee, must receive at least 18 votes from the 24-member Honors Committee to gain election. Nominees for the women's, veterans and international categories will be announced later.

The voting will be announced June 29, and the induction ceremony will be conducted at the Hall's headquarters in Springfield, Massachusetts, in October. ∎

Larry Bird was all smiles after learning that he had been chosen for induction into the Naismith Basketball Hall of Fame. (Paul Sancya)

Larry Bird addresses a news conference at Market Square Arena after the announcement of his Hall of Fame selection. Bird was elected into the Hall of Fame with five others, including Marques Haynes of the Harlem Globetrotters, former coach Alex Hannum, early NBA big man Arnie Risen, Texas women's coach Jody Conradt, and ex-Yugoslavian coach Aleksandar Nikolic. (Paul Sancya)

Bird soars into Hall of Fame

Humble Pacers coach and former Boston Celtics' All-Star
blazes an unforgettable trail and leads by example
on his way to Hall of Fame.

June 30, 1998

BY CONRAD BRUNNER

They knew he was coming back. Their head coach had warned them to be prepared for the moment.

And still, the Indiana Pacers were powerless to stop the force known as Larry Bird.

They had never won a first-round playoff series but were poised on the brink, leading the storied Celtics by eight points in the the third quarter of Game 5 in Boston Garden in 1991.

Bird had left the game just before halftime after smacking his head on the floor while diving for a loose ball, and the early reports from the locker room weren't optimistic.

Just when the Pacers thought their moment had come, Bird wobbled out of the locker room, onto the court and his presence completely changed the game. Boston won 124-121.

It turned out to be the final magic moment of Bird's playoff career, but it also taught the young Pacers a lesson about greatness, and the qualities that would carry Bird into the Hall of Fame.

"I always put Magic, Larry and Michael on another level, I believe they really weren't born from this Earth," said Reggie Miller, one of two players (along with Rik Smits) still on the roster from that game.

> The NBA [Bird] entered was a league without a salary cap, that didn't even have its championship series telecast live, and on the verge of financial ruin. The league he retired from in 1992 was a thriving international conglomerate with revenues that approached $2 billion in 1997-98.

"It was one of those times when all the Gods kind of aligned together. We knew he was coming out, but to hear the crowd go crazy, it was unbelievable to actually be there.

"We had that game in tow. We were on our way, finally, to the second round—until he came back."

The coronation that was assumed the moment he retired in 1992 became official on Monday when Bird was elected, along with five others, to the Hall of Fame.

Also chosen were two other former players, Marques Haynes (of Harlem Globetrotters fame) and Arnie Risen (a star in the 1940s and '50s) and coaches Alex Hannum, Jody Conradt (University of Texas) and Aleksandar Nikolic (Yugoslavia).

Atlanta head coach Lenny Wilkens, enshrined as a player in 1992, will become the second person (following John Wooden) to be honored as both a player and a coach.

After guiding Indiana State to the NCAA championship game, where the Sycamores were beaten by Magic Johnson's Michigan State team, Bird had an immediate effect on the Celtics. A team that had won 29 games the year before he arrived won 61 in his rookie season; the first of his three championships came the following year.

But his greater legacy was his overall impact, in concert with Johnson, on a struggling league. The NBA he entered was a league without a salary cap, that didn't even have its championship series telecast live, and on the verge of financial ruin. The league he retired from in 1992 was a thriving international conglomerate with revenues that approached $2 billion in 1997-98.

"He rejuvenated (the league), or 'juvenated' it, whichever way you look at it," said Pacers president Donnie Walsh. "That decade that he came in with Magic Johnson turned the NBA into what it is today, which is not just a professional league but a league that has worldwide attention. He had a lot to do with that and we all owe him a debt of gratitude for that. This Hall of Fame (election) is one way of doing that."

Bird's only response to the election came in the form of a statement released through the team, in which he said he was "very honored to be part of the Hall of Fame."

"I would like to thank my teammates and coaches, from Springs Valley High School to Indiana State University and the Boston Celtics," Bird said. "I hope they all share in this because, like other awards I have received, this is as much a team accomplishment as an individual accomplishment."

The election caps another brilliant rookie season for Bird, who guided the Pacers to a best-ever 58-24 record during the regular season then to a thrilling seven-game series against the Chicago Bulls before falling in the Eastern Conference finals. He coached the East team in the NBA All-Star Game, another Indiana first, and was later named the NBA's Coach of the Year.

"Now," said Walsh, "he's working toward a second nomination as a coach."

To Bird, it's only so much hardware, and none of it substitutes for the ultimate goal: a championship ring.

"I don't think he's comfortable with all that," Walsh said of Bird's string of honors. "I don't think he did it for all that. Now that it comes, I don't think it holds the same importance. I'm sure he respects it and is happy to be in the Hall of Fame, but I don't think he played for those reasons.

"I know that he didn't get into the game for these kind of honors. Now that they're coming, he has a lot of respect for them. I don't think he needs all the attention that these honors bring to him, which is kind of refreshing, I think."

Larry Bird's Hall of Fame career with the Boston Celtics includes three World Championships, three MVP honors, 12 All-Star selections, and an impact on the game that went well beyond his accomplishments on the court. (Mike Fender)

A claim to fame

Bird joins basketball's all-time elite

October 3, 1998

BY MARK MONTIETH

Seven people were inducted into the Naismith Basketball Hall of Fame here Friday. Six of them rode in on a backseat.

Indiana Pacers coach Larry Bird dwarfed the enshrinement, conducted at the Springfield Civic Center before a sellout crowd of about 7,000 fans. His classmates—Jody Conradt, Alex Hannum, Marques Haynes, Aleksander Nikolic, Arnie Risen and Lenny Wilkens—were relegated to the role of virtual bench warmers.

"It's an honor for me to attend Larry's party," Wilkens joked when he was introduced at a news conference Friday morning.

Larry's party, indeed.

The crowd was splattered with fans dressed in Celtics garb, a rowdy and restless bunch who chanted, "Larry! Larry!" throughout the evening, sometimes while other inductees were speaking.

Bird received a three-minute standing ovation when he was first introduced at the start of the program, and another welcome that surpassed two minutes when he was introduced to speak, despite his persistent efforts to quiet them.

The ceremony, traditionally attended by about 1,500 people with connections to the Hall of Fame, was opened to the public for the first time.

About 5,500 fans—many of whom made the two-hour drive from Boston, where Bird played all 13 of his NBA seasons—purchased tickets at $25 and $50.

The ceremony also was moved from May to October, when it wouldn't be lost amid the NBA playoffs—and when Bird would be available to attend.

Media coverage also has focused on Bird. "It's Bird's show at induction" declared a Page One headline in the *Springfield Union News.* "Bird, 6 others go in tonight" another headline read.

A one-hour special of the ceremony will be televised on NBC today at 12:30 p.m., the first time it has received national television coverage. ESPN also will broadcast the proceedings to more than 100 countries via delayed feed for the first time.

Bird, who was saved for last in the ceremony, thanked the men who coached him throughout his career with Springs Valley High School, Indiana State and the Celtics. He also offered praise for former Celtics President Red Auerbach, who drafted Bird out of college, and Pacers President Donnie Walsh, for hiring him to coach.

"It was something I didn't think I ever wanted to do," said Bird, who won NBA Coach of the Year honors last season while leading the Pacers to 58 victories and the final game of the Eastern Conference finals. "But after talking to Donnie and promising him I'd win a championship, he took the bait and I'm in Indiana."

Bird also mentioned his deceased mother, Georgia.

Newly inducted Hall of Famer Larry Bird acknowledges the crowd's enthusiastic cheer of "Larry! Larry!" at the induction festivities. (Matthew Cavanaugh Photography)

"I wish my mother could be here, because I know she'd be very proud, looking down," he said. "A few years back she told me, 'For a blond-headed, snotty little kid, you did very well, Larry.'"

For Bird, the ceremony drew a formal close to his playing career, which began in the humblest of surroundings. Born in West Baden, Indiana, and raised in French Lick, Bird built his game on the hard asphalt of the outdoor courts in his isolated world, barely aware of the existence of professional basketball or a Hall of Fame.

Small-town life suited him just fine, however.

"It's all I knew," Bird said Friday morning. "We never had a family car where we could drive around and see other towns or other states. That's what I had, and I enjoyed it immensely. You knew everybody in school and everybody in town.

"How I ever came out of a small town like that and accomplished the things I did is beyond me, but growing up in a small town like that was good for me. It would have been nice to have more competition in the summer to improve my game, but hey, you go with what you have.

"The only thing I didn't have was a nice place to play. But we had a lot of outdoor courts with 10-foot baskets. One good thing about being from a small town, if somebody stole the nets you knew the next day who did it, and you could get them back."

Bird has never strayed far from his southern Indiana roots. The self-described "Hick from French Lick" became one of the most popular players in the game's history while leading the Celtics to three NBA titles, largely because of his blue-collar work ethic and candid nature. In a league increasingly self-conscious of image, he was a throwback to a less-uptight time.

Asked earlier in the week if he could explain his popularity, Bird smiled. "I worked hard, and I'm a (expletive)," he said. "I don't know. People knew I worked very hard, that I didn't have a lot of natural ability. I had to work for every thing I accomplished."

Bird makes no attempt to hide his common upbringing. Well-known for grammatical turnovers, he couldn't resist poking fun at himself Friday while meeting with the media.

Addressing Nikolic, a Yugoslavian who had given a brief introductory speech in halting, broken English a few minutes earlier, Bird said: "Aleksander, you don't have to apologize for not speaking English very well. I've been living in this country for 41 years, and I still have problems with it."

This sculpture of Larry Bird by Armand LaMontagne resides in the New England Sports Museum. (Chitose Suzuki Photography)

BIRD'S RETURN LIKELY,
BUT ROSE'S FUTURE UNCERTAIN

June 3, 1998

BY MARK MONTIETH

Larry Bird's status with the Indiana Pacers has been resolved.

Now Jalen Rose's is uncertain.

Bird, who was voted NBA Coach of the Year while guiding the Pacers to a 58-24 record this season, had created doubts about his plans for an encore because of comments he made as recently as the news conference following the team's loss to Chicago in Game 7 of the Eastern Conference finals.

He would return, Bird said, only after meeting with his players and asking them if they wanted him back.

They do, and said so at a team function Monday evening.

"We just let him know where we stand," said Mark Jackson, who brought up the issue at a private banquet at Sullivan's Steak House. "There's no sense to having a meeting. It's a no-brainer."

Bird, who has been unavailable for comment since Sunday's postgame session with the media, left Tuesday for the NBA's predraft camp in Chicago, so he's obviously thinking about next season. His contract calls for him to coach two more seasons, with a choice of continuing or moving into the front office after that.

Reggie Miller, who also has two years left on his contact, already has put in his request for Bird.

"I told him, as long as my contract is here, your contract is here," Miller said Tuesday after cleaning out his locker at Market Square Arena. "We're going to parallel. I told him, 'When I finish my contract, then you can go on home. Until then, you're going to be on the sidelines.'"

Whether or not Rose will join them has become slightly unclear. The contract Rose signed as a rookie, which has two years remaining on it, contained a clause that gave him the option of becoming a free agent this summer. However, that clause might have been voided by the collective bargaining agreement that was reached between the NBA and the Players' Association two summers ago.

Pacers president Donnie Walsh said this week he does not consider Rose a free agent. Rose's agent, Norm Nixon, believes Rose might be and hopes to negotiate a higher salary.

"I don't want to get into it too much," Nixon said from his Los Angeles office Tuesday. "It's a gray area that needs to be clarified."

Nixon said he plans to speak with Walsh next week, and "absolutely" wants Rose to continue playing for the Pacers.

"Jalen had a great year," Nixon said. "I'm anxious for him to go back to the Pacers. I'd like to see him play more, of course, but I'd like for him to stay in Indianapolis and he wants to stay."

Rose averaged 9.4 points while shooting 47.8 percent from the field in 20.8 minutes off the bench this past season. He averaged 8.1 points on 46 percent shooting during the playoffs. He led the reserves in scoring a team-high 39 times, and scored in double figures in the final nine games of the regular season.

Rose earned a reported $1.85 million last season, and is scheduled to make in the "ballpark" of $2.5 million next season, according to Nixon. Nixon would not say what he believes Rose should earn if the contract is renegotiated.

Chris Mullin and Travis Best leave Market Square Arena for the summer after a final team meeting. (Susan Plageman)

NOTES

The Pacers divided their playoff pool of $579,250 at a meeting Tuesday. After partial shares were awarded to support personnel, each player received approximately $40,000. The players also awarded a partial share to Ann Hart, wife of longtime equipment manager Bill Hart, who died during the season. ... None of the players are thought to need offseason surgery, although upcoming examinations might change that. Center Rik Smits will meet with therapist Dan Dyrek in Boston this summer for further treatment on his sore right foot. "It's feeling really good right now," Smits said. "It felt good in the Chicago series; the last time it bothered me was in the New York series. I'm confident with rest and treatment it should be back to 100 percent by the start of training camp."... Haywoode Workman will have his left knee, injured in the fourth game of the 1996-97 season, examined today. He believes his recovery is on schedule and plans to be at full strength by training camp. "If I need another surgery, I'm done," he said. ■

Going one-on-one with Larry Bird

*Following his successful debut, the Pacers coach talks about
the 1997-98 season and the one ahead*

June 10, 1998

BY MARK MONTIETH

Aside from the final few minutes of the final game, Larry Bird's first season as coach of the Indiana Pacers was a success.

A team that had won 39 games the previous season won 58 games and finished with the best winning percentage in franchise history. After a 2-5 start, they were a model of consistency, effort and harmony. And they took the two-time defending world champion Chicago Bulls to the seventh game of the Eastern Conference finals, where they held a three-point lead midway through the fourth quarter before succumbing.

Bird became the first coach in the Pacers' NBA history to work the All-Star Game, where he led the Eastern Conference to victory. He was later voted the league's Coach of the Year by the media.

Bird spoke Tuesday with *The Indianapolis Star* and *The Indianapolis News* about the season just passed and the one ahead.

Q. WHAT STANDS OUT IN YOUR MEMORY ABOUT GAME 7 IN CHICAGO?

A. I really felt the turning point of that game was when we didn't get the jump ball (between Rik Smits and Michael Jordan with 6:39 left and the Pacers leading 77-74). I should have called timeout. I really didn't like the way we were lining up and I felt if we called timeout we could have gotten them in a situation where we could have gotten a layup or drawn a foul. When you have a three- or four-point lead at a time like that, one possession can make the whole game. I'll take the blame for that.

Q. WHAT'S YOUR MESSAGE TO THE PLAYERS GOING INTO THE SUMMER?

A. We might have the lockout, so if these guys are serious about what we're going to do next year, they have to work out on their own. Just because there's a lockout don't mean they can sit around all summer and wait for it to get resolved. They have to prepare themselves for next year. I would expect them to come back in better shape than they did last year and once the season starts dedicate themselves to going all the way. If we can stay away from the injuries like we did this year, there's no doubt in my mind we can put ourselves in position to get there.

Q. WHAT CHANGES WILL YOU MAKE NEXT SEASON?

A. We're definitely going to make some changes on the offensive end. One thing we need to do is try to get the ball to certain players in different areas where they can maneuver better and have more freedom. Our defense will basically stay the same.

Q. IN WHAT WAYS DO YOU EXPECT TO BE A BETTER COACH NEXT SEASON?

A. I learned a lot this year. I know my players better now and how they react in big games. I know they believe me when I tell them some things, so I have to be more direct with them. I'm going to expect a lot more out of them. I'll try to get them to believe in themselves a little earlier (in the season) and to play with more confidence.

We want Mark Jackson to shoot the 3-pointer when he's open. We want Antonio Davis to drive to the basket more, or take the shot if he has it. Just minor things. I think Travis (Best) grew up in the playoffs. Opponents were a little scared of him because of his quickness. I look for bigger things out of Jalen (Rose), too. Everybody can improve.

Q. WILL YOU FEEL COMFORTABLE BRINGING THE SAME TEAM BACK, OR ARE THERE CHANGES YOU WANT TO MAKE BEFORE NEXT SEASON?

A. It's hard to tell right now. If I had to go with the same team, it would be fine with me. I'm sure there will be talk about trades. If I feel a trade can help our team, we have to try to make it better.

Q. REBOUNDING WAS THE ONLY STATISTICAL CATEGORY IN WHICH YOU DIDN'T OUTPERFORM YOUR OPPONENTS DURING THE SEASON, AND IT OBVIOUSLY COST YOU IN GAME 7 AGAINST THE BULLS. HOW DO YOU ADDRESS THAT?

A. We either get guys in here who want to rebound or we teach these guys to box out better. If guys won't rebound, that's a major problem. It's hard to win the whole thing if you can't rebound.

Q. DO YOU FORESEE CHANGES IN YOUR START-ING LINEUP NEXT SEA-SON?

A. This year we started the same guys all the time. Next year, I don't know, we might change some things. I don't know if (Chris) Mullin will start or Derrick (McKey) or Jalen or who-ever (at small forward). We have to look at all the op-tions. All the positions are open right now.

Q. WHAT ABOUT THE POWER FORWARD POSITION, WITH ANTONIO AND DALE DAVIS? DO YOU THROW THAT UP FOR GRABS?

A. It definitely will be open. No question. It worked well for us this year to have Tony come off the bench and re-place Rik early and then get Dale in the second quarter.

But if Tony is good enough to be a starter in this league and he wants to start, he should start. If he continues to play the way he's been playing, I at least look for him to get the most minutes.

Q. IS THE TEAM AS MENTALLY TOUGH AS YOU WANT IT TO BE?

A. They're getting there. They were pretty soft at the beginning of the year, but I could see as the season went on by the way they were winning the road games, especially down the stretch, they were becoming tougher. I saw a turning point when we went on the road (in April) and beat Atlanta, Boston and Chicago all in a row. They really started coming on then.

Q. WERE YOU HAPPY WITH THE LEADER-SHIP ON THE TEAM?

A. Yes, it was a lot better than I ever dreamed. I always heard we never really had a real leader on this team. I found out right away we had two guys (Reggie Miller and Mark Jackson) who are just excellent. You just can't have any better. I don't know if they stepped it up this year or what, but I was going in thinking we didn't have a true leader, but I found out we have two of the best I've ever seen.

Q. YOU WERE ASKED SEVERAL TIMES THIS YEAR IF COACHING WAS FUN, AND YOU ALWAYS SAID IT WAS "INTERESTING" AND "DIFFERENT." LOOKING BACK ON IT NOW, WAS IT ENJOYABLE?

A. It was a great learning experience for me to be on this end of it. I learned a lot this year. (Assistant coaches Rick Carlisle and Dick Harter) were both excellent to work with be-cause of the knowledge they had. I learned a lot from them. Plus, I learned about being the leader of a team. But it's never en-joyable until you win it all.

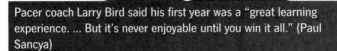

Pacer coach Larry Bird said his first year was a "great learning experience. ... But it's never enjoyable until you win it all." (Paul Sancya)

Q. DO YOU HAVE A PLAN FOR HOW LONG YOU WANT TO COACH?

A. I'll do it like this year. I'll go talk to the guys, and if they want me to come back I'll come back. If not I'll go do something else. I want the guys to be honest with me. Their careers are at stake here. If they want me to help lead them where they want to go it's fine. But I didn't get in this because I need the money or I want my name in the paper. I did it because I feel I can get these guys to win a championship.

Q. CAN YOU SEE YOURSELF DOING IT LONGER THAN A FEW YEARS?

A. I don't know about that. I see myself doing it next year and we'll go from there. I don't want to harp on it, but if these guys don't like what we're doing and they want somebody else leading them, fine.

Q. WHEN YOU TALK WITH THE PLAYERS, DO YOU GET LEVERAGE FROM THE FACT THEY WANT YOU BACK? DO YOU TELL THEM, 'OK, IF I'M COMING BACK, HERE'S WHAT I EXPECT FROM YOU?'

A. If they tell me they want me back, now they're in my hands. I expect them to do everything I tell them to do, even better than they did it this year.

Q. YOU SEEM TO HAVE ESTABLISHED A STRONG RELATIONSHIP WITH THE PLAYERS. HOW HAVE YOU DONE THAT?

A. Well, I treat 'em like men. I'm straightforward. I don't pull any punches. And I'll never lie to them.

If we go into a big game and some of them have never been there, I'll explain exactly what's going to happen and how the game's probably going to go. I stood up before Game 7 and told them it was probably going to be a two-possession game at the end, and whoever made the plays was going to win. It was going to be one loose ball or rebound that one of the teams didn't get that was going to determine the game. I knew that, and that's what happened.

So I know they believe in me and they know the coaches know how to prepare them. We got great effort all year in practice. We didn't have guys whining about not wanting to do this or that. We got great effort and got out of there. But I'm not going to be the guy who browbeats them every day and holds them in there to watch video all the time. I'm not going to stand up there 15 minutes and go over and over bad plays. I always like to watch a little positive (video) too. We had a plan and stuck with it.

Q. DO YOU FEEL LIKE YOU HAVE A NATURAL INSTINCT FOR COACHING?

A. I've always had a knack for getting people to do better than what they think they're capable of doing. I did that as a player. I've always had the ability to lead people. Not that I'm the great leader of this team—Mark and Reggie have a lot to do with it—but I'm able to communicate with these guys. Everyone thought that would be my downfall. But I always knew I could communicate in my own way and that they would understand what I was trying to do.

Q. ARE THERE FREE AGENTS YOU WANT TO TARGET AND MAKE A RUN AT THIS SUMMER?

A. You have to. Anybody out there who we feel can make our team better without distracting from the unit we have, sure, you have to look at them.

Q. ARE YOU CONCERNED ABOUT ALTERING YOUR TEAM CHEMISTRY BY BRINGING IN A PLAYER WHO MIGHT BE BETTER THAN WHAT YOU HAD, BUT DOESN'T FIT INTO THE GROUP AS WELL?

A. Yeah, but usually when you bring guys in and surround them with good people, they can change. I've been around that. We won't tolerate a player coming in here and disrupting things. We can't afford that. That's where Mark and Reggie come in. They do an excellent job of sitting people down and talking to them, and reporting back to me. There were many times this year where I brought Mark and Reggie in and said, 'You better get this boy under control or something's going to happen.' We'd talk about it for five minutes and they'd leave, then all of a sudden I'd bring the player in and talk to him and everything was fine.

Q. YOU'VE ONLY LIVED HERE A YEAR, BUT ARE YOU THINKING YOU MIGHT LIVE IN THIS AREA PERMANENTLY?

A. I never know from one year to the next, but I'll tell you, Indianapolis is a hell of a lot better than I thought it would be. The kids love it, my wife loves it. And I absolutely love the area where I live.

I used to come up here in the summers and stay with a friend for three or four days, but I never thought I would like it here. But I absolutely love it.

Pacers grab high school star

New Jersey prep standout Al Harrington chosen with 25th pick

June 25, 1998

BY MARK MONTIETH

Neither Indiana Pacers president Donnie Walsh nor coach Larry Bird care much for the idea of high school kids jumping straight to the NBA. But sometimes you have to forego ideals in the face of reality, and they couldn't resist the reality that presented itself on Wednesday night.

Al Harrington, a 6-9 forward from St. Patrick's High School in Elizabeth, N.J., became the first player selected by the Pacers directly out of high school, when they made him the 25th choice in the NBA draft. Harrington, who turned 18 on February 17, was the youngest player in the draft, and is the youngest player ever drafted by the Pacers.

The Pacers wound up choosing between two high school All-Americans. Their second choice was Rashard Lewis, a 6-10 forward from Houston.

"We really didn't think either one of these high school players would be available," Walsh said. "(Harrington) is more mature physically, and we thought he would fit with our team a little better. We think we have a veteran team that can allow this guy to grow the right way.

"It's a league of talent. We had an unusual opportunity to select talent that we didn't expect to be there. If he had gone to college for a couple of years, he could have been a lottery pick."

Harrington, who was projected to go between the 14th and 18th picks, was voted the National Player of the Year by *USA Today* and other publications. He averaged a school-record 15.7 rebounds for his high school team, along with 22.1 points, 3.4 assists and 2.1 blocks.

He considered attending Seton Hall or Georgia Tech, and had qualified academically. But he convinced his mother he was ready to play in the NBA, and backed up his claim in postseason All-Star games. He scored a

The Pacers' 1998 first-round draft pick, and number 25 overall, Al Harrington shares a laugh with Coach Larry Bird during a news conference introducing Harrington to the media at Market Square Arena. (Paul Sancya)

team-high 26 points and grabbed 9 rebounds in the Nike Hoops Summit game in San Antonio over Final Four weekend, had 17 points in the McDonald's All-American Game and 18 points in the Magic Johnson Classic.

"He showed a high skill level, and a lot of energy," said Billy Knight, the Pacers' vice-president of basketball operations, who was among the Pacer scouts to watch Harrington in person. "He exerted himself at both ends, he got out in the passing lanes, he tried to pressure people coming up the court, he'd get rebounds and take it the full length of the court, he pulled up for shots, he tried to finish strong ... he showed a mature game for an 18-year old player."

The Pacers invited Harrington in for an individual workout, but his agent declined because he didn't believe Harrington would be available for the 25th pick.

Bird's exposure to Harrington was limited to a few video tapes, but that was enough to convince him.

"I think these kids should stay in college," Bird said. "But he's very talented. In two or three years, he would have been in the top five of the draft.

"He's very confident. He's quick, and he can handle the ball. I doubt if he can shoot the 3-pointer right now, but he can shoot from 18 to 22 feet. He's a banger and he'll mix it up. The All-Star games I saw him play in, he'd get in there and never give up on a rebound. That's a good start."

Harrington, who watched the draft from a restaurant near his home with 55 or 60 friends, believes he can contribute next season.

"I hope after 20 games I can start getting 10 minutes a game and go from there," he said in a conference call after his selection.

Star of the future? There are high hopes for top draft pick, Al Harrington. (Paul Sancya)

Harrington was born during Bird's rookie season, but said he remembers Bird as a player and looks forward to playing for him.

"Sometimes people used to compare me to (Bird)," Harrington said. "I have a good work ethic and so did he. I'll come in and work hard and hope the best comes out of it. My heart is going to get me through." ■

Many wonderful moments created one lasting impression

June 4, 1998

BY BILL BENNER

Think back. Think back to a year ago, when we had no idea of what was to come.

The Indiana Pacers had failed to make the NBA playoffs for the first time in seven years.

Larry Brown, the architect of the Pacers' emergence among the league's elite, had departed. The players had tuned him out and the team tumbled into mediocrity.

In Brown's place came another Larry.

Last name Bird.

A genuine Indiana legend, yes. The unbelievable playing career at Indiana State and with the Boston Celtics, yes.

But could he coach? Wouldn't he be frustrated by players incapable of doing what he did? Was this a lark, just to get him off the golf course, or was he serious?

And what about those players? Reggie Miller's career seemed to have reached a plateau. Rik Smits' health was a major concern. Chris Mullin had not yet arrived. Derrick McKey was on the injured list. Mark Jackson was dependable, but limited. Travis Best was erratic. Jalen Rose was untapped. And many believed there was room for only one Davis on a roster that had two, Dale and Antonio.

Think back. Think back to six weeks ago.

It all had come together in a way only the most sunshine-seeking optimist could envision.

Larry Bird could, indeed, coach, and it started with his intuitive sense to hire the veteran Dick Harter and the up-and-coming Rick Carlisle as his assistants.

Donnie Walsh—the most underrated general manager in the NBA—brought Mullin into the mix, offering another perimeter force on the court and some solid leadership in the locker room.

And after a shaky 2-5 start, all the pieces fell into place. Smits stayed healthy for most of the year and became, for the first time, an All-Star. Miller was Lethal Weapon 31, hitting one game-breaking or game-winning shot after another. Jackson, the reins loosened by Bird, became an extension of the coach on the floor. The Davis boys were toughness in tandem. McKey came off the injured list and added another dimension to the bench. Rose flourished. Best developed. Fred Hoiberg, Mark Pope and Austin Croshere all had their moments.

Defense, thought to be a weakness going in, became a strength. Offensively, the Pacers were efficient: few turnovers and good percentages from the field and at the free throw line.

They won 58 games, an NBA franchise record. They developed a remarkable consistency, not losing more than two games in a row since early December.

Think back. Think back to Race Weekend, and think back to last Friday night. It was a week that will live forever in the city's sports history. Three times in seven days, the Indiana Pacers defeated the defending World Champion Chicago Bulls. Three times in seven days, the loudest fans in the NBA had turned Market Square Arena into a madhouse of emotion. Three times in seven days, spontaneous street parties erupted in the joyous aftermath.

Think about what we have here. Think about fortunate we are to have ownership like Herb and Mel Simon, who do nothing but sign the checks and stay in the background.

Think about a president/general manager like Walsh. What's one of the biggest complaints fans have these days about professional sports? It's the lack of loyalty among the players, the franchise and the fans. Yet, because of Walsh and his loyalty, the nucleus of the Pacers has been one with which the fans have been able to establish a bond.

Think about a coach like Bird: simple, straightforward, direct, composed. Think of the example he set for all the young coaches prone to thinking that the only way to motivation is somehow linked to voice volume. Coach of the Year? Maybe a coach for the ages.

Think about these players. Class, all the way. The essence of a team, the sum greater than all its parts. No bad actors and no criminals. No one whining about how hard it is to make ends meet on $3 million per year. No one trying to choke the coach. No one demanding the coach stays or he goes. No one blaming a bad shooting night on the traffic jams on the way to games.

Think about what we have here. It's something pretty special. Let the national media, the New York and Chicago types, make their wisecracks about the silos and tractors and hicks and Billy Bobs. Who cares?

We know what we have: terrific ownership, a solid front office, an Indiana legend as a coach, players who are both a pleasure to cover and a pleasure to watch, and fans who come to participate, not merely spectate.

And we haven't even mentioned that new fieldhouse rising out of the ground on South Pennsylvania.

True, an NBA championship still eludes the Indiana Pacers and, as Bird said all along, that is the only goal.

But this was a championship season in so many, many ways.

PACERS' 1997-1998 PRESEASON, REGULAR SEASON,
AND PLAYOFF RESULTS

		OCTOBER		
DATE	OPPONENT	BOX SCORE	W-L	HIGH PTS
		(PRESEASON)		
Fri 10	at Cleveland	L 98-105	0-1	Miller 15
Sat 11	Toronto	W 104-100	1-1	Hoiberg 21
Tue 14	Cleveland	L 90-93	1-2	Hoiberg 17
Fri 17	Utah	W 89-80	2-2	D. Davis 16
Sat 18	Utah	W 89-88	3-2	Miller 22
Tue 21	at Charlotte	W 95-83	4-2	Hoiberg 18
Fri 24	Sacramento	W 101-71	5-2	Hoiberg 20
Sat 25	Charlotte	W 88-81	6-2	Rose 16
		(REGULAR SEASON BEGINS)		
Fri 31	at New Jersey	L 95-97	0-1	Miller 35

		NOVEMBER		
DATE	OPPONENT	BOX SCORE	W-L	HIGH PTS
Sat 1	Golden State	W 96-83	1-1	Miller 33
Tue 4	at Cleveland	L 77-80	1-2	Miller 21
Wed 5	at Detroit	W 99-87	2-2	Smits 25
Fri 7	Seattle	L 93-99	2-3	Miller 22
Sat 8	at Charlotte	L 82-89	2-4	Miller 20
Wed 12	Atlanta	L 86-89	2-5	Miller 30
Fri 14	Miami	W 82-78	3-5	Miller 21
Sat 15	at Toronto	W 105-77	4-5	Mullin 20
Thu 20	at Milwaukee	W 109-83	5-5	Best 18
Sat 22	Charlotte	L 94-95	5-6	Miller 23
Thu 27	Vancouver	W 106-85	6-6	Mullin 27
Fri 28	Chicago	W 94-83	7-6	Miller 24
Sun 30	Philadelphia	W 101-89	8-6	Smits 25

		DECEMBER		
DATE	OPPONENT	BOX SCORE	W-L	HIGH PTS
Wed 3	at Minnesota	W 94-90	9-6	Miller 27
Fri 5	at Denver	W 96-85	10-6	Smits 24
Sun 7	at Phoenix	W 99-97	11-6	Miller 19

Mon 8	at Utah	L 97-106	11-7	A. Davis 19
Wed 10	at Portland	L 85-93	11-8	Miller 16
Fri 12	Miami	W 104-89	12-8	Smits 29
Sat 13	Washington	W 109-92	13-8	Smits 25
Mon 15	at Toronto	W 108-101	14-8	Miller 22
Wed 17	New York	W 87-80	15-8	Smits 18
Fri 19	Detroit	W 98-90	16-8	Smits 20
Sat 20	at Orlando	W 95-92	17-8	Mullin 18
Tue 23	at San Antonio	L 79-91	17-9	Miller 25
Fri 26	Orlando	W 107-81	18-9	Hoiberg 20
				Smits 20
Sun 28	at Miami	L 90-101	18-10	Miller 19
Tue 30	New Jersey	W 109-91	19-10	Miller 23
				Mullin 23

		JANUARY		
DATE	OPPONENT	BOX SCORE	W-L	HIGH PTS
Fri 2	at Washington	W 99-81	20-10	Smits 22
Sat 3	Toronto	W 89-77	21-10	Smits 24
Tue 6	Phoenix	L 80-81	21-11	Miller 15
Thu 8	at Houston	W 87-80	22-11	Rose 18
Sat 10	at Dallas	W 84-79	23-11	Miller 24
Wed 14	Detroit	W 100-93	24-11	Miller 25
Fri 16	Sacramento	W 117-92	25-11	Rose 23
Sun 18	at Boston	W 103-96	26-11	Smits 25
Wed 21	at New York	L 89-97	26-12	Miller 21
Fri 23	Utah	W 106-102	27-12	Smits 25
Sat 24	Boston	W 95-88	28-12	Miller 32
Tue 27	Washington	W 85-84	29-12	Miller 20
Wed 28	at Philadelphia	W 93-90	30-12	Best 17
Fri 30	Cleveland	W 89-83	31-12	Miller 24

		FEBRUARY		
DATE	OPPONENT	BOX SCORE	W-L	HIGH PTS
Sun 1	at L.A. Clippers	W 99-92	32-12	Smits 23
Tue 3	at Sacramento	W 115-93	33-12	Smits 18
Wed 4	at Seattle	L 97-104	33-13	Miller 25
Tue 10	Orlando	W 85-66	34-13	Miller 16
				Smits 16

DATE	OPPONENT	BOX SCORE	W-L	HIGH PTS
Wed 11	at Miami	W 110-101	35-13	Miller 30
Fri 13	Dallas	L 82-85	35-14	Smits 12
Sat 14	at Atlanta	W 96-92	36-14	Miller 31
Tue 17	at Chicago	L 97-105	36-15	Miller 34
Thu 19	Philadelphia	W 82-77	37-15	D. Davis 14
Fri 20	at Orlando	L 91-93	37-16	Smits 27
Sun 22	at Philadelphia	W 97-92	38-16	Miller 25
Wed 25	L.A. Lakers	L 89-96	38-17	Smits 19
Fri 27	Portland	W 124-59	39-17	Jackson 18

MARCH

DATE	OPPONENT	BOX SCORE	W-L	HIGH PTS
Sun 1	Denver	W 90-63	40-17	Smits 23
Tue 3	at Vancouver	W 111-103	41-17	Smits 26
Wed 4	at L.A. Lakers	L 95-104	41-18	Miller 24
Fri 6	at Golden State	W 101-87	42-18	Smits 21
Sun 8	Boston	W 104-100	43-18	Miller 25
Wed 11	at Detroit	L 91-122	43-19	D. Davis 15
Fri 13	Milwaukee	W 96-76	44-19	Smits 20
Sun 15	at New York	W 91-86	45-19	Jackson 28
Tue 17	Chicago	L 84-90	45-20	Mullin 18
Thu 19	at Washington	W 95-91	46-20	Miller 20
Fri 20	New Jersey	W 99-92	47-20	Miller 21
Sun 22	at Milwaukee	W 96-94	48-20	Miller 32
Wed 25	Houston	L 81-86	48-21	Miller 16 / Mullin 16
Fri 27	Charlotte	W 133-96	49-21	Miller 24 / Smits 24
Sun 29	San Antonio	L 55-74	49-22	Mullin 12
Tue 31	L.A. Clippers	W 128-106	50-22	Mullin 24

APRIL

DATE	OPPONENT	BOX SCORE	W-L	HIGH PTS
Thu 2	Minnesota	W 111-108	51-22	A. Davis 23
Fri 3	at Charlotte	L 89-96	51-23	Best 19 / Miller 19
Sun 5	Milwaukee	W 93-92	52-23	Miller 18
Tue 7	Cleveland	W 82-80	53-23	A. Davis 19
Thu 9	at Atlanta	W 105-102	54-23	A. Davis 19 / Miller 19 / Mullin 19
Sun 12	at Boston	W 93-87	55-23	A. Davis 28
Mon 13	at Chicago	W 114-105	56-23	Miller 22 / Rose 22
Wed 15	Atlanta	W 82-70	57-23	Miller 22
Fri 17	Toronto	W 107-98	58-23	D. Davis 20
Sat 18	at Cleveland	L 92-96	58-24	Rose 26

(PLAYOFFS BEGIN)

DATE	OPPONENT	BOX SCORE	W-L	HIGH PTS
Thu 23	Cleveland	W 106-77	1-0	Mullin 20
Sat 25	Cleveland	W 92-86	2-0	Miller 18
Mon 27	at Cleveland	L 77-86	2-1	Smits 26
Thu 30	at Cleveland	W 80-74	3-1	Miller 19

MAY

DATE	OPPONENT	BOX SCORE	W-L	HIGH PTS
Tue 5	New York	W 93-83	4-1	Best 18 / Rose 18
Thu 7	New York	W 85-77	5-1	Smits 22
Sat 9	at New York	L 76-83	5-2	Miller 23
Sun 10	at New York	W 118-107	6-2	Miller 38
Wed 13	New York	W 99-88	7-2	Miller 24
Sun 17	at Chicago	L 79-85	7-3	Miller 16
Tue 19	at Chicago	L 98-104	7-4	Miller 19
Sat 23	Chicago	W 107-105	8-4	Miller 28
Mon 25	Chicago	W 96-94	9-4	Smits 26
Wed 27	at Chicago	L 87-106	9-5	Best 14 / Miller 14
Fri 29	Chicago	W 92-89	10-5	Smits 25
Sun 31	at Chicago	L 83-88	10-6	Miller 22

1997-98 Season Player Averages

TEAM	G	MPG	FG%	3P%	FT%	REBOUNDS OFF	DFF	TOT	APG	PPG
Miller	81	34.5	.477	.429	.868	0.6	2.3	2.9	2.1.	19.5
Smits	73	28.6	.495	.000	.783	1.7	5.2	6.9	1.4	16.7
Mullin	82	26.5	.481	.440	.939	0.5	2.6	3.0	2.3	11.3
A. Davis	82	26.7	.481	.000	.696	2.3	4.5	6.8	0.7	9.6
Rose	82	20.8	.478	.342	.728	0.3	2.0	2.4	1.9	9.4
Jackson	82	29.4	.416	.314	.761	0.8	3.1	3.9	8.7	8.3
D. Davis	78	27.9	.548	—	.465	3.0	4.8	7.8	0.9	8.0
Best	82	18.9	.419	.300	.855	0.3	1.1	1.5	3.4	6.5
McKey	57	23.1	.459	.235	.714	1.3	2.4	3.7	1.5	6.3
Hoiberg	65	13.4	.383	.376	.855	0.2	1.7	1.9	0.7	4.0
Croshere	26	9.3	.372	.308	.571	0.4	1.3	1.7	0.3	2.9
West	15	7.0	.476	—	.500	0.4	0.6	1.0	0.1	1.5
Pope	28	6.9	.341	.333	.588	0.3	0.6	0.9	0.3	1.4
Bohannon	5	2.2	.000	—	—	0.4	0.8	1.2	0.2	0.0
Workman	0	—	—	—	—	—	—	—	—	—
Team Totals	82	241.8	.469	.390	.764	10.7	28.6	39.3	23.0	96.0
Opponents	82	241.8	.432	.316	.728	13.6	27.5	41.1	19.4	89.9

1997-98 Post-Season Player Averages

TEAM	G	MPG	FG%	3P%	FT%	REBOUNDS OFF	DFF	TOT	APG	PPG
Miller	16	39.3	.426	.400	904	0.3	1.4	1.8	2.0	19.9
Smits	16	29.8	.502	.000	.859	1.1	4.3	5.3	1.3	16.6
Jackson	16	30.9	.417	.378	.794	1.1	3.4	4.6	8.3	9.2
A. Davis	16	28.7	.462	—	.670	2.3	4.4	6.8	0.9	9.2
Mullin	16	25.8	.460	.385	.857	0.8	2.8	3.6	1.4	8.9
D. Davis	16	29.1	.651	—	.453	2.8	4.8	7.5	0.8	8.8
Rose	15	19.5	480	.375	.741	0.1	1.7	1.8	1.9	8.1
Best	16	17.5	.375	.278	.884	0.1	0.9	1.0	1.9	6.1
Hoiberg	2	10.0	.375	.500	1.000	0.5	1.5	2.0	0.5	4.5
McKey	15	18.9	.333	.300	.783	0.5	2.1	2.7	0.7	4.5
Pope	7	6.0	.667	.000	1.000	0.3	0.4	0.7	0.1	1.3
West	4	2.8	.500	—	.333	0.3	0.0	0.3	0.0	0.8
Bohannon	0	—	—	—	—	—	—	—	—	—
Croshere	0	—	—	—	—	—	—	—	—	—
Workman	0	—	—	—	—	—	—	—	—	—
Team Totals	16	241.6	.460	.375	.760	9.3	26.0	35.3	19.1	91.8
Opponents	16	241.6	.440	.352	.726	12.6	26.8	39.4	19.1	89.5